0 01 00 20167519

BSC

NO LONGER PROPERTY OF
SEATTLE PUBLIC LIBRARY

D0899352

BUSINESS/SCIENCE

Seattle Public Library

Please note the date this item is to be returned
and keep the date due card in the pocket.

Confucianism and Economic Development

An Oriental Alternative?

The Washington Institute for Values in Public Policy
The Washington Institute sponsors research that helps provide
the information and fresh insights necessary for formulating
policy in a democratic society. Founded in 1982, the Institute is
an independent, non-profit educational and research organization which examines current and upcoming issues with particular
attention to ethical implications.

ADDITIONAL TITLES

Vietnam: Strategy for a Stalemate
By F. Charles Parker (1989)

Stability and Strategic Defenses
Edited by Jack N. Barkenbus and Alvin M. Weinberg (1989)

*Soviet Nomenklatura: A Comprehensive Roster of Soviet Civilian
and Military Officials (Second edition, revised and updated)*
Compiled by Albert L. Weeks (1989)

*The Politics of Latin American Liberation Theology:
Challenges to U.S. Public Policy*
Edited by Richard L. Rubenstein and John K. Roth (1988)

Arms Control: The American Dilemma
Edited by William R. Kintner (1987)

*The East Wind Subsides: Chinese Foreign Policy
and the Origins of the Cultural Revolution*
By Andrew Hall Wedeman (1987)

Rebuilding A Nation: Philippine Challenges and American Policy
Edited by Carl H. Landé (1987)

Human Rights in East Asia
Edited by James C. Hsiung (1986)

Confucianism and Economic Development

An Oriental Alternative?

Edited by Hung-chao Tai

Published in the United States by The Washington Institute Press
Suite 300, 1015 18th Street, NW, Washington, D.C. 20036

© 1989 by The Washington Institute for Values in Public Policy

First Printing, April 1989
All rights reserved.

A Washington Institute Press book

Cover design by Paul Woodward

Cataloging-in-Publication Data

Confucianism and economic development.
    Includes index.
    1. East Asia—Economic policy. 2. Singapore—Economic
policy. 3. Confucianism—Economic aspects. I. Tai, Hung-chao,
1929– .
HC460.5.C66 1989   338.95   89-5483
ISBN 0-88702-048-8
ISBN 0-88702-049-6 (pbk.)

Table of Contents

Notes on the Contributors

HUNG-CHAO TAI, Ph.D., is director of the Asian studies program and professor of international political economy at the University of Detroit, where he was formerly chairman of the department of political science. He was a faculty research associate at the Center for International Affairs at Harvard University and has organized, under the sponsorship of the American Society of China Scholars, two seminars from which the present volume is derived. His publications include *Land Reform and Politics* (1974), *World Investment in Southeast Michigan and Detroit* (1984), and "Human Rights in Taiwan: Convergence of Two Political Cultures?" in James Hsiung, ed., *Human Rights in East Asia* (1985).

THOMAS J. BELLOWS, Ph.D., is professor of political science and director of the division of social and policy sciences at the University of Texas at San Antonio. He has authored or coauthored three books and more than 30 articles in professional journals.

HANG-SHENG CHENG, Ph.D., is vice president for international studies at the Federal Reserve Bank of San Francisco and was formerly an international economist with the United States Treasury. He was also formerly professor of economics at Iowa State University and has taught at the School of Business Adminstration at the University of California at Berkeley. He has authored three books and numerous articles in professional journals.

YOUNG-IOB CHUNG, Ph.D., is professor of economics and former head of the department of economics at Eastern Michigan University. He has authored several articles on the Korean economy in professional journals.

EDWARD F. HARTFIELD is commissioner, United States Federal Mediation and Conciliation Service, and executive director of the National Center for Dispute Resolution.

WEN-LANG LI, Ph.D., is professor of sociology at Ohio State University. He was a Fulbright Scholar in 1977 and is vice president of the American Association for Chinese Studies. He has authored or co-authored several books and many articles in professional journals.

KUO-HUI TAI, Ph.D., is professor of Oriental history at Rikkyo University in Japan. He has written widely on Japan, Taiwan, and China.

SIU-LUN WONG, Ph.D., is professor of sociology at the University of Hong Kong. He has authored numerous articles and book chapters on Hong Kong.

YI-TING WONG is chairman of the board, Taiwan Sugar Corporation, and is adjunct professor of political science at Chinese Culture University. He was a major architect of Taiwan's economic development from the 1950s through the 1970s. He has written widely on the economic development of Taiwan.

YUAN-LI WU, Ph.D., is senior consultant with the Hoover Institution on War, Revolution and Peace and is former professor of economics at the University of San Francisco. He served as deputy assistant secretary of the U.S. Department of Defense. He has authored many books and journal articles.

Preface

"Anything not amenable to statistical analysis is of no interest to me." This was how an economics professor at Kyoto University several years ago responded to my question concerning the relevance of culture to Japanese economic performance. As it turned out, his response was an indirect expression of his doubt on the contribution of culture to economic achievement. With rare exception, other economists I encountered in the United States and the Far East in connection with this present study also have doubt that the Oriental culture has a significant impact on East Asia's spectacular economic accomplishments. They attribute the prosperity of East Asian countries to the economic institutions and policies of these countries and to the favorable conditions of the world market.

Yet a minority of economists and many people in other professions—historians, sociologists, anthropologists, philosophers, political scientists, journalists, businessmen—have vigorously argued that East Asia's affluence is culturally based. Post-Confucianism, New Confucianism, or Neo-Confucianism have often been cited as the spiritual force that sustained the industrialism in Japan, South Korea, Taiwan, Hong Kong, and Singapore. In contrast, Asian countries outside the Confucian culture area or Asian countries having explicitly rejected Confucianism have witnessed an economic performance that is erratic at best and stagnant at worst.

To participate in this intellectual dialogue, a number of authors of the present volume started in the early 1980s to work on the project of Confucianism and economic development in East Asia. We believe that Confucianism does provide a common cultural basis for the five countries mentioned above. Moreover, the combination of Confucianism and industrialism cannot but create certain characteristics that distinguish the Oriental economies from their Western counterparts. We need to examine what these characteristics are, and policymakers and industrialists perhaps need to see how to make best use of these characteristics. However, we do not consider Confucianism the only determinant of high economic performance. Obviously, without foreign trade and foreign technology, none of the East Asian economies can be near where it is today.

The papers gathered in this volume are all solicited specifically for this project. The authors were invited to cover the five East Asian countries, to address a number of key issues, to present different disciplinary perspectives, and to assay the positive as well as negative economic effects of Confucianism. The manuscripts have been edited to achieve coherence in style and substance, for which I will assume responsibility. For the contributors' incisive analysis and their patience and understanding, I am eternally thankful.

I would like to acknowledge with deep gratitude the advice, assistance, and financial support given to this work during the various phases of its evolution: the American Society of China Scholars, the American Association for Chinese Studies, the Association of Chinese Social Scientists in North America, Cho-yun Hsu, Wonmo Dong, Fred. C. Hung, David W. Chang, Wen-hui Tsai, Hungdah Chiu, Susumu Saito, Robert Junn, Bertrand Mao, Gilbert Rozman, Marion J. Levy, Jr., Thomas B. Gold, Fei-lung Lei, George P. Chen, Shirley W. Y. Kuo, John Orr Dwyer, Donald R. Burkholder, Barbara Toth, Sheng-tsung Yang, Michael B. Tai and Shinmin Shyu.

INTRODUCTION

An Oriental Alternative?

Hung-chao Tai

Since 1965 Japan has piled up an ever larger trade surplus with the United States; in the 1980s, it also has become the fastest growing foreign investor in this country. A 1987 survey by the Japan External Trade Organization revealed that a total of 640 Japanese industrial plants with a workforce of some 160,000 people operated in the United States. Sony in California, Honda in Ohio, Mazda in Michigan, Kikkoman in Wisconsin—to just mention a few—have employed Japanese as managers and Americans as workers. Some operate on newly built sites; others reopened the closed-down factories previously owned by American companies. Many have produced high quality goods and rapidly expanded production. Honda even began in 1987 to export cars from this country to Japan.

Japanese manufacturing performance in the United States brings to the fore the relevance of culture to economy. For the markedly different cultures of Japan and the United States cannot but have decisively different economic impacts on these Japanese transplants. Beyond singing company songs, practicing group calisthenics, and abolishing executive perquisites, Japanese transplants have brought Japanese culture to bear on such key economic variables as work ethic and management-labor relations. Many American companies have been closely watching the Japanese managerial style; some have emulated it.

Now, where Japan has succeeded is being duplicated by other East Asian countries. South Korea, Taiwan, Hong Kong, and Singapore have amassed enormous trade surpluses (Taiwan's trade surplus with the United States is even larger than Japan's on a per capita basis), and some of them are beginning to advance on the path of international investment. All five of these East Asian countries have embraced Western capitalism. Tens of thousands of private corporations own and manage their economies; fully automated stock markets link them to the rest of the financial centers of the world; container ships and Boeing 747s deliver their mass-produced goods all over the globe; and office buildings and apartment complexes give their metropolises a skyscraper density comparable to that of New York, London, or Paris. Most of their people are dressed in Western suits; many of them speak English; a good portion of them travel, study, and do business abroad.

In their outward appearance these East Asian *nouveaux riches* are Westernized. Yet behind this facade the people of these countries pursue a way of life that remains essentially Oriental. They prefer to eat Oriental food, observe lunar-calendar-based national festivities, place the family in the center of their social and economic relationships, practice ancestor worship, emphasize frugality in life, maintain a strong devotion to education, and accept Confucianism as the essence of their common culture.

This combination of Western capitalism with Oriental culture has exerted a significant and pervasive impact on the economy of these countries. In many critical areas—the organizational characteristics of the enterprise, the relationship between management and labor, the disposition of surplus income, the value attached to human relations—East Asian economics are profoundly different from their Western counterparts. Indeed, one can raise the question: Aren't there enough similarities among these five East Asian economies and dissimilarities between them and the Western economies to warrant a hypothesis that the East and the West have followed two different models of economic development? This book proposes and discusses such a hypothesis.

Purpose and Assumptions

The editor of this volume, under the sponsorship of the American Society of China Scholars (a group of Chinese-Americans specialized in social sciences and humanities), organized two panel sessions in 1983 and 1984 to consider this issue. The papers presented at these sessions—with subsequent revision, reorganization, and addition—became the substance of the present volume.

The purpose of this study, it should be emphasized, *is not to examine whether cultural factors alone determine economic*

*growth; rather, it is to see how culture gives the East Asian
economic system its specific characteristics and how it differs from
its Western counterpart.*

The contributors come with a variety of backgrounds. Most are
academicians; some are economic policymakers. Their fields of
specialty include economics, history, political science, and sociology. They examine both the positive and negative economic effects
of oriental culture. Though their opinions are divergent, the
authors proceed with three common assumptions. First, they
recognize that Confucianism has undergone transformations both
in China and in other East Asian societies and even may have lost
its institutional and symbolic presence in some of these societies.
But they consider Confucian values to have become indelibly
marked upon the ethos of all these societies. And, as Confucianism
remains as the dominant feature of Chinese culture throughout
the ages, the authors use the term Confucianism loosely, treating
it as synonymous with Chinese culture.

Second, almost all the authors have cited and responded to
Max Weber's view that Confucianism retarded the rise of
capitalism in China; most have identified parallels and contrasts
between the Protestant ethic and the Confucian ethics. Indeed,
the authors have paid so much attention to Weber that they may
as well use *Confucianism v. Weberism* as a subtitle of this volume.

Third, among the many elements of the Confucian culture
regarded as having important economic consequences, the
authors consider the devotion to education and the emphasis on
savings as the most important.

The Major Issues

The authors have raised a number of key issues, over which
they have provided various interpretations.

If East Asian and Western countries are following different
models of economic development, what are their respective characteristics?

Why is it that Confucianism historically retarded the rise of
industrialism in China and now facilitates economic modernization in East Asia? What are the causes of the historical
underdevelopment of China?

Why did Ch'ing China and Meiji Japan start their modernization programs at the same time but achieve so dramatically

different results? Has Confucianism undergone certain significant changes in Japan to facilitate industrialization there?

In Taiwan—the only East Asian country where Confucianism is officially worshipped—what would be the most conspicuous manifestations of the Confucian culture in the realm of economic development?

Is it possible that certain elements of a common culture have different effects on the economic performance of different countries? Perhaps an elitist bureaucracy diverted economic resources and human talent from capitalistic undertakings in historical China and Korea; yet an efficient, duty-bound mandarinite can bridge tradition and modernization in today's Singapore. Heavy social consumptive spending may have slowed capital formation, as one author laments in the case of traditional Korea; yet such spending may well be a profitable investment in social cohesion, which has given the East Asian economies a competitive advantage in the world market.

What are the effects of a strong family structure on business enterprise? Does familism sustain a business firm in its pioneering stage but retard it later? Can a business firm acquire and maintain a family spirit without family members managing it?

What is the net impact of Confucianism on economic modernization when the positive and negative effects of Confucianism are balanced against one another?

When dealing with these and other issues, the authors have employed different methodologies and perspectives. They maintain no uniform positions; they reach no common conclusions. But the recent development experiences in Asia suggest to them that countries capable of uniting tradition with modernity achieve economic progress, while those that do not remain in poverty. Hence, they regard culture as having a plastic quality, its essential characteristics being constant over the long run but adaptable to new circumstances. They consider as their task to identify the positive and negative effects of Confucianism so that East Asian countries can reshape their culture and economy to benefit from the former and to avoid the latter.

The Expectations

This volume consists of three components. The first includes a chapter on an Oriental alternative model of economic development and a chapter on comparative statistical analysis of the economic performance of five East Asian countries and other economic regions of the world. The second component consists of three papers. They respectively examine why capitalism failed to rise in historical China, what kind of transformation of Confucianism has taken place in modern Japan, and why China and Japan have achieved different results in economic modernization. The third component comprises five papers that assess the economic significance of Confucian values in Taiwan, South Korea, Hong Kong, and Singapore.

This volume marches into a territory not yet fully explored; in fact, there is hardly any book written exclusively on the subject. In trying to delineate the specific characteristics of the Oriental economies as contrasted with those of their Western counterparts, this work hopes to foster among its readers a continuing dialogue on the subject. It may help identify items appropriate for future research. For instance, an international survey of East Asian countries and some Western countries on the differences of people's attitude toward education, family role in the economy, savings, and managerial-labor relations can significantly advance the knowledge on the impact of culture on economy. Such a survey may also help ascertain the extent to which the comparative advantage of East Asia in world trade is culturally related.

ONE

The Oriental Alternative:
An Hypothesis on Culture and Economy

Hung-chao Tai

To explain the rapid economic growth of five East Asian countries—Japan, South Korea, Taiwan, Hong Kong, and Singapore—observers often point to their many similarities. They refer to these countries' common physical attributes, historical circumstances, strategies of development, and cultural heritage. These similarities are well-known, and the economic significance of the physical attributes, historical circumstances, and developmental strategies of these countries has been extensively analyzed.[1]

What is less scrutinized is the impact of cultural heritage on economic performance. This subject concerns the question, in the words of Eliezer B. Ayal, "why some societies do, and others do not, behave in ways that bring about sustained economic progress. For this we need to go beyond the boundaries of economics" and delve into the realm of social values and institutions.[2] Variation in national economic behavior needs to be explained in terms of cultural factors.

In a major work on modern economic growth two decades ago, Simon Kuznets asked: "Are the economic principles taught in the West really susceptible of general application? Or are they culture-bound and relevant mainly to [Western] industrial capitalist countries?"[3] The post-World War II economic performance of the East Asian countries, as seen in the next chapter, suggests that Kuznets' questions need to be taken seriously.

The cultural setting of Japan, South Korea, Taiwan, Hong Kong, and Singapore has been to a considerable extent shaped by Chinese experiences, which have been, in turn, heavily influenced by Confucianism. Of these five countries, three—Taiwan, Hong Kong, and Singapore—have an overwhelming majority of ethnic Chinese in their population. South Korea remained until late last century under Chinese tutelage, and many South Koreans today consider Chinese traditions to have an even stronger influence in their country than in China itself. Japan has long been a recipient of Chinese cultural flow, from the Sixth Century to the end of the Tokugawa rule in 1867.[4] All these countries are within the Chinese/Confucian cultural order.[5]

This chapter presents a hypothesis on the relationship of culture and economy in the five East Asian countries. Their cultural setting, it is suggested, has created what may be called an Oriental or affective model of economic development, which emphasizes human emotional bonds, group orientation, and harmony. It stands as an alternative to the more established Western model of development. The latter may be called a rational model, which stresses efficiency, individualism, and dynamism. This chapter will proceed to elaborate on these concepts; it will then analyze the impact of culture on economic performance in the East Asian countries; and it will conclude with a brief assessment of the significance of the affective model in the context of world economic development.

It should be noted that the author does not espouse the idea of cultural determinism in economic development. Cultural factors are necessary, but not sufficient, conditions for the shaping of a nation's economic future. Thus, the analytical focus here is confined to how culture influences economic performance, not whether culture is the exclusive influential factor. Given the limitation of space and the preliminary nature of this research, the following analysis will pay more attention to East Asian than to Western countries. For the same reason, no comprehensive, systematic comparison of the culture and economy of the five countries will be attempted.

The Two Models

The Weber Thesis. An inquiry into the relationship of culture and economy in East Asia probably should start with the studies of Max Weber, who has done pioneering work on the subject. In his two classical studies relevant to the present inquiry, Weber traced the origin of capitalism to the Protestant religion and provided an incisive critique of Confucianism and its alleged role in retarding the industrialization of China.[6]

Weber attributed the rise of capitalism directly to the ethic of the Puritans in the Calvinist movement. The Puritans considered profit-making a religious duty and idleness a sin. Such an attitude, Weber observed, "is what is most characteristic of the social ethic of capitalistic culture, and is in a sense the fundamental basis of it." This social ethic was unique to the Puritans and was conspicuously lacking among people in historical "China, India, Babylon...and the Middle Ages."[7] To the Puritans, the pursuit of profit as a religious duty meant also that they had to practice an ascetic life. They had to work hard in order to maximize profit for honoring God, but they had to minimize its use for themselves. "You may labor to be rich for God, though not for the flesh and sin." Such an injunction was intended to warn against consumptive spending and to foster an "ascetic compulsion to save."[8]

The capitalist way of profit-making was a rational one; it involved efficient utilization of manpower and calculation of gains and losses. Modern capitalism, Weber emphasized, differed from all previous economic movements in three aspects: "the rational...organization of...free labour..., the separation of business from the household..., and...rational book-keeping."[9]

Turning his attention to traditional China, Weber cited two conditions as unfavorable to the rise of capitalism. First, the Chinese socio-political structure was a serious barrier. The cumbersome monetary system, the lack of local autonomy of cities, the persistence of the guilds, the lack of a formal and independent legal order, the conservative nature of the kinship system, and the stifling effects of the imperial bureaucracy—all these facets of traditional Chinese society prevented the emergence of an entrepreneurial class and contributed to economic stagnation.[10] The second condition had to do with the Chinese exaltation of the "cultured man" as the highest Confucian ideal. The Confucian gentleman valued harmony between nature and men and despised acquisitiveness in profit-making. As a scholar official or as a member of the gentry, the Confucian gentleman regarded landownership as a socially acceptable economic undertaking but disdained commercial pursuits. "Completely absent in Confucian ethic was any tension between nature and deity" or a demand from God for the people to work hard for profit-making.[11] Weber observed:

> The Chinese lacked the central, religiously determined, and rational method of life which came from within and which was characteristic of the classical Puritan. For the latter, economic success was not an ultimate goal...but a means [for serving God.... The Confucian] gentleman was "not a tool"; that is, in his adjustment to the world and his self-perfection he was an end unto himself, not a means for any functional end. This core of Confucian ethics rejected...training in economics for the pursuit of profit.... Confucian rationalism meant rational adjustment to the world; Puritan rationalism meant rational mastery of the world.[12]

The failure of capitalism to *rise* in China, Weber pointed out, did not mean an impossibility for China to *adopt* capitalism. Certain aspects of Chinese culture—such as early abolition of feudalism, freedom of migration, free choice of occupations, and a high value on education—were, in fact, favorable to the development of capitalism. "The Chinese," Weber suggested, "in all probability would be quite capable...of assimilating capitalism which has technically and economically been fully developed in the modern culture area."[13]

The Weber-Parsons Paradigm. Weber's theoretical formulations on culture and economy have become the foundation of a contemporary sociological school to explain the process of modernization. It was Talcott Parsons who elaborated on the Weberian concepts and developed a comprehensive theory to describe and evaluate the cultural and economic accomplishments of nations.[14] He developed a scheme of "pattern variables" consisting of five dichotomous concepts: "affectivity vs. affective neutrality," "self-orientation vs. collectivity-orientation," "universalism vs. particularism," "achievement vs. ascription," and "specificity vs. diffuseness."[15] "The modern type of 'industrial' occupational structure," Parsons has observed, is characterized by a "system of universalistic-specific-affectively neutral-achievement-oriented roles."[16] In contrast, the traditional Chinese social structure possessed a combination of opposite characteristics, which "blocked the development of anything like 'capitalism'.... [For] capitalism would have destroyed the Confucian synthesis by shifting the balance of internal power to a group which could not be integrated into the 'humanistic universalism' of the diffuse politico-cultural type which was distinctive of Chinese 'literati.' "[17]

Placing Weber's critique of Confucianism into his scheme of pattern variables, Parsons further observed:

> [One] of the fundamentals of our modern Western social order is its ethical 'universalism.' To a very high degree...our highest ethical duties apply 'impersonally' to all men, or to large categories of them irrespective of any specific personal relation involved....
>
> In this respect the Puritan ethic represents an intensification of the general Christian tendency. It has an extremely powerful animus against nepotism and favoritism. To this the Confucian ethic stands in sharp contrast. Its ethical sanction was given to an individual's *personal* relations to particular persons— and with any strong ethical emphasis *only* to these. The whole Chinese social structure accepted and sanctioned by the Confucian ethics was predominantly 'particularistic' structure of relationships.[18]

The Rational Model. The Weber-Parsons paradigm has gained wide acceptance among scholars of social change, and many specialists on Oriental societies have adopted it as a conceptual framework for their studies.[19] All of them accept the notion that the central, distinctive feature of modern cultural and economic change throughout the world is a trend toward increasing rationality, which Western historical experiences have demonstrated. In other words, the West's rational model of cultural and economic change is of universal applicability.

The rational model possesses three characteristics. First, rationality is aimed at achieving *efficiency,* which refers to the relation between effort and result, input and output, or investment and profit. Efficiency is achieved with a small commitment of the former and a great gain of the latter. In the realm of modern economics, efficiency requires mechanization and automation of the productive process and systematization of the managerial structure. Centralization, specialization, standardization are emphasized; quantitative analysis is vigorously pursued so that, in

Weber's words, "Everything is done in terms of balances....Before every individual decision a calculation [is made] to ascertain its probable profitableness, and at the end a final balance to ascertain how much profit has been made."[20]

Second, rationality is facilitated by *individualism*. A concept firmly rooted in Christianity, individualism refers to the notion that each person should have a maximal opportunity "to make decisions affecting his future and the future of others with whom he interacts."[21] This is so because, as Christians see it, each individual is endowed with a capacity for "rational pursuit of self-interest," and, as the Puritans would say, each individual is mandated to use his labor in the service of God.[22] Under such circumstances, individuals will become industrious and creative, developing an "achievement" type personality consistent with the requirement of industrialization. With industrialization, individuals will have further opportunity for "self oriented" pursuits. Thus, in Western experiences, individualism and industrialism are mutually reinforcing.[23]

Third, the Western model is impregnated with *dynamism*. The Westerner is commanded by religion to make over the world. Driven by an inner force to serve God, armed with science, motivated by self-interest, he is trying ceaselessly to conquer nature and to compete with fellow human beings in the achievement of a chosen goal. The pervasive and persistent contests between human will and the physical world give the Westerner a sense of control of the natural environment. The competition among individuals for intellectual and social achievements results in great strides in science, arts, economics, and other human pursuits.

To preserve the dynamic quality of Western culture and to maintain orderly human contests, a set of impersonal, universalistic rules has to be adopted. It assures all individuals fair treatment and equal opportunity in all their pursuits; it prevents human contests from degenerating into chaos. The rule of law is thus critically important to the functioning of a dynamic Western culture, and progress through competition remains a high social purpose to which the rule of law is dedicated.

The Oriental Critique. For two centuries the commanding lead of the West in the world economy has been widely assumed as unshakable, and for at least half a century the West's model of economic and social change has also been assumed universally valid. The economic experiences of the East Asian countries since the 1950s have led many people to raise questions about both assumptions.

Roy Hofheinz, Jr. and Kent E. Calder, for example, have warned that East Asia has now posed an unprecedented economic challenge to the United States and West Europe; yet Americans and Europeans remain remarkably unaware of it.[24] Others have pointed to the Confucian culture underlying the challenge. Herman Kahn, who was perhaps the first Western scholar to propound on this point, has written: "*Under current conditions* the neo-Confucian cultures have many strengths and relatively few weaknesses. Japan, South Korea, Taiwan, Hong Kong, Singapore, and the ethnic Chinese minorities in Malaysia and Thailand seem more adept at industrialization than the West.... The Confucian ethic...will result in all the neo-Confucian societies having at least potentially higher growth rates than other cultures."[25]

Similarly, the editors of *The Economist* have observed:

> For the 200 years since the onset of the industrial revolution, the west has dominated the world. Today that dominance is threatened, not just by the Russians, who are any way heirs, at least in part, to the western tradition; nor by the Arabs whose stranglehold will relax as the sands run dry; but more fundamentally by the East Asian heirs to Confucianism, who have so far provided the only real economic...challenges to the Euro-American culture.[26]

Many other people—including journalists, businessmen, politicians, and scholars—also have recognized the significant contribution of the Oriental culture to the rapid economic progress of Asian nations.[27]

As to the question of universal validity of the West's rational model, social scientists and historians have expressed reservations. In his monumental study on the economic development of Asia, Gunnar Myrdal pointed out that in the field of economics, "Western theoretical approaches have assumed the role of master models." He considered this "as a biased approach.... [For] the very concepts used in their construction aspire to a universal applicability that they do not in fact possess."[28] In a more frontal critique of this bias, Edward W. Said noted that Western scholarship on the Orient was often based on erroneous assumptions: The "European" is often considered "rational, virtuous, mature, 'normal,'" and the Oriental is regarded as "irrational..., aberrant, undeveloped, inferior."[29] Sharing Said's criticism, H.D. Harootunian commented: The West

> apprehends. Orientals. as objects who have failed to conform to Western expectations of what is human and rational. Marx and Weber—and before them all, Hegel—were particularly interested in demonstrating a peculiar development in the West, stemming from an ontological view of what was truly human (in contrast to nature), which could not be found, for example, in Asia.... It was in this sense that all three believed that Asia did not have any history; this conceit is still at the center of all those histories inspired by the idea of modernization.[30]

Focusing on China and Japan, other scholars have taken exception specifically to some of the Weber-Parsons conceptual formulations. For instance, Yü Ying-shih, Tu Wei-ming, and Thomas A. Metzger all challenged the Weberian idea that Confucianists lacked the equivalent of a religiously endowed "tension" to remold the world. Yü and Tu observed that it was the very distinctive and unique characteristic of the Confucianists (*shih*) to take on as their duty the improvement of humanity. Metzger suggested that since the Sung times, Chinese Confucianists have believed strongly in the use of an inner "transformative force" to create a world in their image. Similarly, many of today's Chinese intellectual and political leaders are intensely dedicated to the achievement of national independence and economic modernization as their life-long missions.[31] As to another tenet of the Weber-Parsons thesis, the close relationship of capitalism and individualism, Peter Berger registered his dissent. It is not true, Berger noted, that only individualism can breed capitalism. East Asia, especially Japan, has created a non-individualistic capitalism, which is shaped by a culture indigenous to the region.[32]

The case of Japan deserves special attention. That country has undergone economic modernization for the longest time in Asia; yet it remains fundamentally different from the West. As Hung-chao Tai has written:

> The Western model [of modernization] presumes that economic progress requires the reduction of traditional

institutions and values. The Japanese model reveals that economic growth can rest on a social structure and a value system that retain a substantial portion of the traditional—even feudalistic—elements. In the West, primary social institutions such as the family and the church are clearly separated from the secondary institutions such as the company, the union, and the professional associations. In Japan, the organizational and operational characteristics of the company, the union, and the professional associations are heavily influenced by those of the family, religions, the guild system, and the *samurai* class. The Western concept of modernity stresses individual freedom, specialization of tasks, and high social mobility. The Japanese notion of modernity emphasizes the subordination of the individual to group, the development of multiple skills by workers, and stable careerism for company employees.[33]

For precisely the reasons noted in Said's *Orientalism*, Richard H. Minear has pointed out, the West has failed to recognize the significance of the differences between the West and Japan.[34] Western theoretical formulations just cannot adequately explain the economic and social changes of modern Japan. Indeed, in the opinion of Nathan Glazer, when one attempts to use Parsons' pattern variables to explain these changes, the pattern variables become "part of the problem rather than part of the solution."[35] The Japanese, James C. Abegglen has suggested, must be regarded as having followed a third pattern of development—different from both the Western and Communist patterns.[36]

The Affective Model. The pattern of Japan's development, like that of all other East Asian countries, is characterized by the affective model. This model is shaped by the Confucian view that in an East Asian society all people maintain a sort of a familistic relationship with each other. This view, in turn, was shaped by the historical experiences of the Chinese people. Having lived in the same area for thousands of years, and leading a life without much geographical mobility, the Chinese have long believed that all of them were generally related to each other by blood. Thus, the Chinese call each other *t'ung-pao*, offsprings of common parentage; acquaintances address each other by family titles. The term "nation" in Chinese is *kuo-chia*, literally state family. In Max

Weber's terms, China is a "familistic state": the family is a miniature state; the state, an enlarged family.

It was Confucius who developed a code of ethics that governed the interpersonal relationships of the familistic state. In *The Doctrine of the Mean*, he identified "five sets of relationships: [those] between the sovereign and the ministers, between father and son, between husband and wife, between elder and younger brothers, and between friends."[37] In another work, Confucius listed the ethical properties of these relationships: "Father, kindness; son, filial piety; elder brother, goodness; younger brother, respect; husband, righteousness; wife, compliance; the sovereign, benevolence; the ministers, loyalty."[38] For two millennia, this ethical code was as faithfully and universally followed by the people in the Chinese culture area as the Bible was by the Christians.

Precisely as Weber and Parsons have observed, the Chinese ethical precepts were personalistic and particularistic. Each precept applied only to a specific individual in relation to another specific individual. The Chinese insisted on treating human beings in the context of these ethical relations, not to consider themselves as subject to a one-and-same set of social norms.[39] The Confucian code just could not have the impersonal and universalistic quality of the Protestant ethic.

The affective model puts a premium on *the emotional human bonds* in all undertakings of individuals. The Chinese consider rationality, efficiency, and profit-making as essential to economic success, but they do not attempt to achieve economic success at the expense of what they call human relations *(jên-shih kuan-hsi)* or human feelings *(jên-ch'ing)*.

To the Chinese, a fundamental pattern of human feelings uniting them is known as *jên*. Translated as benevolence or humanity, *jên* possesses a characteristic common to all Confucian ethical precepts. It means, at once, magnanimity, love, sincerity, righteousness, and fellowship. To the Japanese, the dominant pattern of feelings binding them together is the concept of loyalty—a concept derived from the Confucian ethical code but reinforced by Japanese feudalism. As such, it is regarded as a characteristic "peculiar to Japanese Confucianism."[40] The Japanese see the relationship between individuals as one between the subordinate and the superordinate. The former shows a total dedication to the latter; the latter reciprocates to the former with *on* (blessing). As the Japanese sociologist Chie Nakane has put it, the Japanese live essentially in a "vertical society."[41]

The affective model values highly *group orientation.* In East Asian countries, especially China, the family is the basic social grouping uniting individuals. Family ties are permanent, and individuals owe their loyalty to the family throughout their lives. The family relationship is often extended to other groupings. In many Chinese societies, this extension is accomplished by bringing family members directly into other social groups. For instance, the business enterprises in Taiwan, Hong Kong, and Singapore are mostly family owned and family managed.

The extension of family relationship also can be done through other means, by claiming *t'ung tsung, t'ung hsiang,*[42] or *t'ung hsüeh* (literally, a common ancestry, a common neighborhood, or a same school).[43] That is, those who have a common ancestry (same family name), those who live in the same neighborhood, or those who went to the same school are likened to family members. These three relationships are socially important, as they often form bases on which other social relationships are built. In Chinese bureaucracy and business enterprises these relationships can significantly affect employees' career paths, frequently leading to the formation of factions.

To a considerable extent the Japanese follow these social practices as well. However, the Chinese and the Japanese differ in the degree of importance they attach to the family. The Chinese consider the family as the primary focus of their loyalty; the Japanese also show their loyalty to the family, but they can demonstrate a stronger loyalty toward larger groupings, especially the nation. Moreover, when extending the family relationship into business organizations, the Chinese tend to accord family-related members (by blood or marriage) a more favorable treatment than non-family-related members. In a business enterprise, this condition makes it difficult to grow in size and strength. The Japanese have solved this problem by the application of what Francis L.K. Hsu has called the *iemoto* principle; they can create large, strong economic and social organizations patterned after the family without always placing family-related individuals into a leadership position. Unrelated individuals, on the other hand, can be absorbed into these organizations and be treated as if they were family members. The Japanese family adoption practice and primogeniture system are said to facilitate this development.[44]

In Chinese and Japanese societies, individualism as practiced in the West is not generally accepted as a social value. In both societies, individuals seek identity not so much in terms of who they are as in terms of whom they are associated with. Once an individual's group identity is established, the individual will maintain such an identity both within the group and without. And all individuals are supposed to uphold the interest of the group—ranging from the family to the nation—above their own. Thus, the late President Chung-hee Park of South Korea said:

> Just as a home is a small collective body, so the state is a larger community....One who does not maintain a wholesome family order cannot be expected to show strong devotion to his state....A society that puts the national interest above the interests of the individual develops faster than one which does not.[45]

The East Asians would wholeheartedly approve of Park's idealization of the collective interest, even though they can be—in reality—as self-seeking as people anywhere else.

The affective model is aimed at achieving *harmony*. East Asians perceive harmony to have a twofold meaning. It means both "a union of human beings with the natural world" and the maintenance of congenial relations among individuals. The concept of union of human beings with the natural world is contrasted to the Western view toward man and the supernatural world. To the Western mind, "this world" and "the other world" are separate orders, and the Western man is mandated to master this world in accordance with the edict of the other world. To the Oriental mind, the supernatural world, this world, and human beings are but parts of a whole order. The Oriental man prefers to be more concerned with human affairs; he does not feel a "tension" to conquer the physical environment but has a mission to improve the social conditions he lives in. Parsons has perceptively observed this point: "In prudent care for the interests of this world and lack of interest in any other, perhaps no people has ever surpassed the Chinese."[46]

The Chinese and, to a lesser extent, the Japanese tend to interpret religion in terms of human experiences. When ancestral worship is practiced in a Chinese society, it is conducted as a religious rite; but it rests almost entirely on the Confucian concept of filial piety. It creates another world on the basis of the preferred pattern of human relations in this world. In Japan, Shintoism was once based on the notion that the Japanese race had a divine quality in it; religion was created to sanctify a people. In both China and Japan, Buddhism was also "secularized."

Called *ch'an* in China and *zen* in Japan, the secularized Buddhism proposed to achieve Buddha in one's own mind, meaning that spiritual salvation was achievable by self-cultivation of the individual. On this particular point, Buddhism, Confucianism, and Taoism are all compatible with each other. All of them accept self-cultivation as the path to the union of man and nature.

To maintain congenial relations among individuals, the affective model prefers to use ethical norms to harmonize human conduct. It seeks interpersonal accommodation and mutual adjustment through moral persuasion; it discourages individuals from self-seeking pursuits that may jeopardize group cohesion. It is in this sense that Confucianism is widely known for its downgrading of profit-making. In the Confucian classics there are numerous references exhorting individuals to seek virtue, not wealth.[47] What is often neglected by people who commented on this Confucian view is that Confucius did not despise profit per se, but only profit-making that upset human harmony. He was against greed, not profit properly made.[48] As Shibusawa Eiichi, an influential Japanese businessman and Confucianist in modern Japan, has explained:

> Morality and economy were meant to walk hand in hand. But as humanity has been prone to seek gain, often forgetting righteousness, the ancient sage [Confucius], anxious to remedy this abuse, zealously advocated morality on the one hand and, on the other, warned people of profit unlawfully obtained. Later scholars misunderstood [Confucius'] true idea.... They forgot that productivity is a way of practicing virtue.[49]

One can perhaps summarize the essential difference between the Oriental and Western models in a way parallel to some of Weber's remarks cited earlier: Oriental rationalism is tradition-centered but not religiously oriented; Western rationalism is religiously based but not tradition-centered. The former is as conservative as the latter is dynamic.

The Cultural Impact

Operating under the affective model, the East Asian countries have seen the impact of the Oriental culture manifest itself in several key areas of their economies. These include business organization, employee behavior, work ethic, and human resource development. In most of these areas, the impact of the affective and rational models is markedly different.

The Company as an Economic and Social Organization. To Western countries, the company is considered an economic enterprise, pure and simple. It aims at profit-making through efficient production of goods and services. In contrast, the Oriental company functions not only as an economic enterprise but also a social entity. It is an organization to produce goods and services, but it is also an institution reinforcing social values.

The Oriental company maintains a paternalistic relationship between the employers and the employees, and such a relationship is supposed to be long lasting and to show up both within the company and also outside of it. As Shui-shên Liu has explained:

> In regard to management and organization,....[the Chinese] pay more attention to human relations than to "things" [i.e., impersonal business practices]. [They] often change the organization to suit the needs of individuals. In the West, "things" are more important than human relations....In another aspect, the Chinese are concerned about the concept of family in business operations. Employers frequently bring the concept of clan to business organizations. The relation between the employer and the employees is likened to that between king and subject, or between father and son. Thus, once you become my employee, you are my subordinate not only inside the company but also outside of it. In the West, this superordinate-subordinate relationship is perhaps maintained only within the company.[50]

In all East Asian countries, employers and employees consider their primary responsibility to be the production of goods and services, but they are often involved in the *familial* activities of each other. Marriages, birthdays, and funerals that occur on either side of employers and employees are treated as important social events of both. These are *human centered* activities requiring the involvement of company personnel just as company's business demands the attention of all employees. Both employers and employees may, in fact, complain about the high costs—in terms of money and time—of these activities. Nevertheless, all of them regard participation in these activities as their duty and are continuously involved.

This pattern of behavior merely reflects the dual nature of the company. The company is not organized for making profit alone; it also exists for the sake of group cohesion. *Familial* activities may be considered wasteful purely from the point of view of production efficiency, but they are a vital part of the company's *social investment*. And it is this social investment that gives the Oriental workforce its special characteristics. It is a workforce characterized by *industriousness* and *compliancy* that provides East Asian countries with a significant advantage in competition with the West.

Oriental workers are willing to work hard, to labor for long hours and to receive a relatively low pay. They are willing to do so partly because the prevailing living standards are low and partly because the social atmosphere of the company provides sufficient inducement. They certainly work to make a living for themselves, but they also feel obligated to further the interest of the company to which they have a sense of belonging. Their working conditions are less favorable than those of their Western counterparts, but they do not feel as militant or alienated. In no small measure, the social investment of the Oriental company helps maintain workers' morale and reduce labor discontent.

In Chinese societies, the strong family orientation in business organizations, it should be noted, tends to have two negative consequences. Capital and leadership positions are held primarily by family-related members. As already mentioned, family domination makes it difficult for businesses to grow. In Taiwan, as much as 80 percent of enterprises are family-controlled, small scale businesses.[51] Such is also the case in Hong Kong and Singapore. Moreover, strong family influence in business operations leads to nepotism, which demoralizes talented non-family-related employees and creates company instability during leadership succession.

In Japan, the application of the *iemoto* principle enables the Japanese companies to absorb non-family talents and to grow in size. Japanese companies can be large and competently managed; yet they retain a "family" atmosphere. In South Korea, both the government and private businesses have sought to create large enterprises to enhance international competitiveness. By encouraging business mergers and by emphasizing competence as criteria for personnel recruitment, South Korea has considerably overcome the negative effects of family-oriented business organizations.[52] However, a pattern of paternalistic relationship between employers and employees persists in South Korea corporations just as it does in the corporations of other East Asian countries.

The Two Tract Control. In the West, employers and employees are joined together for the sole purpose of making pecuniary gains. Both employers and employees are assumed to be capable of making rational calculation of their respective interests and of their money-earning capabilities. Through the market and by competition, the price of labor is determined. Human services can be purchased and sold just as commodities. In such a situation, employers use monetary means to impose a single-tract control on employees' economic behavior. Recruitment, promotion, transfer, demotion, and lay-offs are associated with the provision or withdrawal of monetary rewards.

In contrast, the Oriental company influences employee behavior by economic *and* social means, through a two-tract control. The company uses monetary means to meet employees' economic expectations; it also sees employees as having social needs it can fulfill. To influence an employee's behavior through economic means, the Oriental company adopts a compensation package that is different from its Western counterpart. As in the case of the Western company, the Oriental company provides employees with wages according to workers' skills, which are assumed to be dependent on the length of service. However, the Oriental company provides employees with an additional pay—in the form of a bonus. The bonus pay has certain distinctive features. It derives from the profit of the company; hence, it is a built-in incentive for *all* employees to improve the profit position of the company. Moreover, when the bonus is paid, its size is large in proportion to wages. It can range from the equivalent of one to three months' pay of a Taiwanese worker to as much as half of the annual base wage of a Japanese employee.[53] And the bonus is normally paid in a lump sum rather than in installments.

The bonus system is, therefore, an important device to improve group performance. It fosters solidarity among employees and facilitates management-labor cooperation. It is with this system in mind that Tetuo Ohsone, a union leader at the Mazda Company of Japan, said: "Our basic philosophy is that the improvement of

living standards of union members is closely related to the
expansion of the company itself.... Pay levels are decided according to the ability of the company to pay. Unless the standing of
the company is improved it cannot pay more. That is why we
believe in cooperation between union and management."[54]

The social means with which the Oriental company controls its
employees can be intangible or concrete. The Oriental company
actively encourages its employees to share their feelings, emo-
tions, and concerns through the social activities mentioned earlier. It considers loyalty and dependability rather than creativity
and skills as the primary criteria by which employee performance
is evaluated. In Taiwan, as Robert H. Silin has discovered, "the
management of interpersonal relations is a focal concern" in
business organizations. Employees are evaluated in terms of how
they fulfill their "'human obligations,' *jên-ch'ing* or *jên-ch'ing wei*,
the social obligations of the individual toward a group of known
others, the norms of interpersonal relations."[55] Similarly, in
Japan, as William G. Ouchi has observed in his widely read book
Theory Z, many business enterprises are successful because they
are able to develop a feeling of "trust, subtlety, and intimacy"
among their employees. These enterprises reject the notion that
"personal feelings have no place at work."[56]

The Oriental company devotes a considerable amount of money
and time to employees' personal welfare. It subsidizes employees'
housing and other financial needs, sponsors recreational and
athletic activities, and gives out gifts on festive occasions. These
Oriental "fringe benefits," which are generally absent in the West,
bring many non-production-related activities of employees under
the direct influence of the company. As a result, the Oriental
company possesses a far greater capacity than does its Western
counterpart to influence employee behavior to achieve company
objectives.

Diligence, Frugality, and Savings. The East Asians are generally
known for having a diligent attitude toward work, following a
frugal life, and maintaining high savings. To a considerable
extent, these human traits can be explained by East Asians' views
toward the natural world and their concept of human life.

Without a religious compulsion to conquer the natural world,
the East Asians believe that they can make best use of what the
physical environment offers them by exerting their own labor.
This belief is based on an awareness that human labor is in a
relatively abundant supply and natural resources are perennially

scarce. Formerly, as they lived in a subsistence economy, they deemed diligence not only a desirable habit but an attitude essential to survival. Today, they emphasize thoroughness and persistence in their working habits, which, in turn, requires discipline and patience. They seek small, gradual, and continuous improvement rather than quick results, dramatic gain, and breakthroughs. They are good at refining—but not at creating—new goods and services.

With their concerns focused on "this world," the East Asians consider that life has its meaning in the continuity of the family—from ancestors, to the present generation, and to posterity. They must live frugally, for frugality is necessary to the survival of themselves as well as the future generations of their families. "Most Chinese work diligently and live frugally for the sake of their families," Mao-ch'un Yang has stated. "In order for their families to continue to exist, they must assure their family members the necessary means to live on.... For this reason, they are willing to forsake current spending for personal enjoyment. Such a behavior moves beyond the realm of economics and gets into that of ethics."[57] This statement applies to other East Asians as much as it does to the Chinese.

Diligence in work and frugality in life lead to an accumulation of savings. The amount of savings, of course, varies with the extent to which a family's income exceeds its essential needs. In times past, when the East Asians lived at a subsistence level, very little savings could be accumulated. With their economy growing in recent decades, their savings have increased dramatically. This is clearly seen in Table 5 of the next chapter. In terms of the savings ratio (domestic saving as a percentage of Gross Domestic Product), Japan had an extraordinarily high 33 percent in 1965. Twenty-one years later, in 1986, its savings ratio remained very high—at 32 percent. Taiwan is considered to have achieved economic "take-off" in the mid-1960s; its savings ratio in 1965—at 20 percent—was below that of Japan even though it was high by world standards; in 1986, after it had experienced years of fast economic growth, its savings ratio jumped to 38 percent, which was comparable to that of Japan. The other three East Asian countries, whose savings ratio in 1965 ranged from 8 to 29 percent, all achieved very high ratios by 1986. By that year, the East Asian countries as a group had a higher savings ratio than any other bloc of nations in the world.[58]

Large domestic savings help restrain inflation and reduce the cost of capital borrowing, leading to an increase in business investment. Table 5 of the next chapter also reveals this condition. The investment ratios (gross domestic investment as a percentage of Gross Domestic Product) of the five East Asian countries in 1965 and 1986 were very high; in the latter year, these countries as a group had the highest investment ratios in the world.

The diligent and frugal behavior of the East Asians enabled them to launch successfully a labor-intensive industry in the early stage of industrialization. Subsequently, with a large reservoir of savings, they were able to shift from a labor-intensive to a capital-intensive economy. The impact of social behavior on economic performance clearly is evident. A commentary by Robert N. Bellah on how the Confucian economic thinking influenced Tokugawa Japan is perfectly relevant to all East Asian countries today:

> The core of the Confucian economic policy designed to ensure political stability is contained in the following often quoted statement from the *Ta Hsüeh* [*The Great Learning*]: "There is a great course [*tao*] for the production of wealth. Let the producers be many and the consumers few. Let there be activity in the production and economy in the expenditure. Then wealth will be always sufficient." This then is the nubbin of Confucian economic policy, in its ideal expression: encourage production and discourage consumption.[59]

In modern times, all East Asian nations have followed this Confucian prescription—with a modification: *Encourage themselves to produce and encourage others to consume.* A "supply-side" economic policy is adopted for themselves, and a Keynesian policy for their international competitors.

Emphasis on the Development of Human Resources. Central to the Confucian thinking, as John K. Fairbank has pointed out, is the belief in the perfectibility and educability of human beings.[60] More than 2,500 years ago, Confucius espoused the idea of universal education when he became a teacher of a great multitude of students and made the often quoted statement: "In education there are no class distinctions."[61]

The Confucian emphasis on education became one of the most prominent features of Chinese culture. For nearly two thousand years, Chinese government used a system of civil service examinations to recruit men of learning as political leaders, and the society accorded intellectuals a very high social rank. As natural resources were scarce, aspiring individuals saw studying and learning as a major means for the few to rise above the many. As the popular saying went, "You can discover a pot of gold in books."

This Confucian tradition is today carried over to every East Asian society, considerably facilitating the process of economic modernization. It underscores one elemental economic truth. Human resource development is a slow, long-term, and costly process, but the benefit is great, cumulative, and nearly always outweighs the cost. Intelligent and skillful human beings can make the most productive use of indigenous or imported natural resources. The East Asians subscribe wholeheartedly to an observation of the British economist Alfred Marshall: "The most valuable of all capital is that invested in human beings."

Today all East Asian societies have rushed to invest heavily in human resources. Parents, teachers, and students treat education almost like a national religion, and government and society devote considerable resources to a frantic expansion of schools and classes.[62] The results are impressive. As Table 7 of the next chapter has indicated, the East Asian countries generally experienced in 1965–1985 a greater expansion of enrollment in secondary schools and in higher education than any other group of countries in the world. They have now rapidly approached the highest international record of school enrollments, which is maintained by Western countries. The East Asian nations have not just expanded their school population; they have vastly improved their students' scholastic achievement. Japan and Taiwan have seen their primary and high school students attain the best scores in science and mathematics in competitive international tests.[63]

Educational achievement obviously is vital to economic growth. Many observers consider this especially evident in the case of Japan. Edwin O. Reischauer, for example, has written, "Nothing, in fact, is more central in Japanese society or more basic to Japan's success than its educational system." Concurred Ezra F. Vogel: "If any factor explains Japanese success, it is the group-directed quest for knowledge." Likewise, John Whitney Hall believed that "any attempt to explain Japan's exceptional success in national development must give a high degree of credit to the educational system which took on its modern guise just a hundred years ago."[64]

Emphasis on education can have a positive impact on income distribution. As Montek S. Ahluwalia has explained, inequality in educational opportunities perpetuates inequality in "human capital," which in turn accentuates uneven distribution of income. On the other hand, "proponents of the human capital approach argue that education—of the right type—increases the quality of the labor input leading to higher labor productivity, which is then reflected in higher wage earnings."[65] Hence, diffusion of education opportunities correlates with equality of income. This is the case in all five East Asian countries as seen in the statistics on income distribution and on educational development of these countries in Tables 6 and 7 of the next chapter.

Significance of the Affective Model

To conclude this discussion, a brief assessment of the significance of the affective model in the context of world economic development appears useful. Under the rational model of the West, the quest for efficiency, the belief in individualism, and the power of social dynamism are the fundamental forces for scientific creativity and technological innovation. Historically, the West harnessed these forces to bring about the machine age and matched the machine with a religiously ordained human will to transform an agricultural society into an industrial one.

For ages, the Orient always focused attention on the affective relations of human beings, with an emphasis on emotional bonds, group cohesion, and harmony. Under the affective model, the Orient failed, as Weber has explained, to *create* industrialism. But it borrowed the machine from the West through technological transfer—quickly, and at surprisingly little cost. By mating the machine with a human-centered culture, the Orient achieved in the last three decades an almost unparalleled economic performance in the world. In this connection, one may agree with Roderick MacFarquhar when he said, "If western individualism was appropriate for the pioneering period of industrialisation, perhaps post-Confucian 'collectivism' is better suited to the age of mass industrialisation."[66]

For the first time since the Industrial Revolution, the world may see a meaningful alternative to the rational model of the West (if the Communist model of development is considered to have posed more of a political and military than an economic challenge). To the developing countries, this alternative appears especially attractive. For it shows that cultural collectivism, which is a central feature differentiating the Third World from the West, and high economic achievement are compatible. Moreover, the Oriental alternative reveals that the East Asian countries, by relying on their cultural strength rather than following a Socialist strategy, have been able to accomplish precisely what many Socialist developing countries have avowed but failed to achieve. That is, to transform their economy from one heavily dependent on the West into one rivaling it. Significantly, the East Asian countries achieved this result while maintaining equality of income distribution. As Roderick MacFarquhar has observed, "The most promising sign of the East Asian development model is that East Asia is the region with the least income discrepancy among all developing countries."[67]

Of course, many developing countries do not have a long, coherent cultural tradition as do the East Asian countries. Many, in fact, suffer from cultural cleavages and social schisms. Nevertheless, the Oriental alternative has its value in that it seeks economic growth by emphasizing the union of these divisions rather than an intensification of them, which a competitive, individualistic, rational model of development may bring about.

NOTES

1. The common physical attributes of East Asian countries consist of insular geography, high population density, and scarcity of natural resources. Access to the sea provides a convenient transportation linkage with world markets, the relative abundance of labor provides a labor-cost advantage with Western economies, and a necessity to obtain raw materials from overseas makes trade inevitable. All these conditions contribute to the creation of export-oriented economies.

   The historical circumstances benefiting these countries include heavy United States spending in the Far East during the Korean and Vietnamese Wars, the infusion of Western capital and technology through foreign aid and investment, and the emergence of a global market receptive to these countries' exports and—until very recently—tolerant of their restrictions on imports.

   The developmental strategies of these countries involve agricultural reforms supporting manufacturing industries (except for Hong Kong and Singapore) and a phased industrialization process that gradually shifts from labor-intensive industries (e.g., textiles) to capital intensive projects (e.g., automobiles and steel) and to high-tech, knowledge-intensive enterprises (e.g., electronics and computers).

   Two representative works discussing these economic conditions may be cited: Roy Hofheinz, Jr. and Kent E. Calder, *The Eastasia Edge* (New York: Basic Books, 1982), and Edward K.Y. Chen, *Hyper-Growth in Asian Economies: A Comparative Study of Hong Kong, Japan, Korea, Singapore and Taiwan* (London: The Macmillan Press, 1979).

   Both works contain extensive citations of relevant literature, in the bibliography or reference notes. Neither, however, emphasizes the importance of cultural influence on economic performance. The former work discusses briefly the social setting of the five East Asian countries and, additionally, the People's Republic of China and North Korea, but considers it a mistake to attribute any great significance to these countries' "spiritual" heritages (see pp. 21–22, 41–52). The latter concentrates on an economic analysis of the subject without a treatment of the cultural setting.

2. Eliezer B. Ayal, "Value Systems and Economic Development in Japan and Thailand," *The Journal of Social Issues* 19 (January 1963): 35.

3. Simon Kuznets, *Modern Economic Growth: Rates, Structure and Spread* (New Haven: Yale University Press, 1966), p. v.

4. See Michio Morishima, *Why Has Japan Succeeded? Western Technology and the Japanese Ethos* (London: Cambridge University Press, 1982), pp. 2–20; Edwin O. Reischauer, *Japan: The Story of a Nation* 3rd ed. (New York: Knopf, 1981), pp. 21ff., and Robert N. Bellah, *Tokugawa Religion: The Values of Pre-Industrial Japan* (New York: The Free Press, 1957), pp. 54–55.

5. The inclusion of Japan in this study has a particular advantage. While sharing with the other East Asian countries the Confucian tradition, Japan has a much longer experience with industrialization than its neighbors and rivals the most advanced Western economies. A study of the Japanese experiences may reveal the durability as well as the adaptability of the Confucian tradition in modern economic development.

   Because of its anti-Confucianist ideology and practices, the People's Republic of China is not included in the present study. The PRC has introduced economic reforms to deemphasize certain Marxist features (see, for example, "A Programme for Reform of Economic Structure," *Beijing Review*, October 29, 1984, pp. 4–5; "Deng: Reform is 'Second Revolution,' " ibid., April 8. 1985, p. 6; Jin Qi, "China's Reform Enters Its 10th Year," ibid., January 4–10, 1988, pp. 7, 9). The PRC also has taken steps to reassess Confucianism, indicating a willingness to recognize the positive aspects of the Confucian thought and practices (see Li Li, "Confucianism's Relevance to Contemporary China," *Beijing Review*, December 14–20, 1987, pp. 26–28; Leung Yuen-sang, "The Uncertain Phoenix: Confucianism and Its Modern Fate," in Joseph P.L. Jiang, ed. *Confucianism and Modernization* [Taipei: Freedom Council, 1987], pp. 257–58; and Nicholas D. Kristof, "In China, The Buck Starts Here," *The New York Times Magazine*, December 20, 1987, p. 63). How these changes affect the PRC's economic development must await analysis.

6. Max Weber, *The Protestant Ethic and the Spirit of Capitalism*, trans. from German by Talcott Parsons (London: G. Allen &

Unwin, 1930) and *The Religion of China: Confucianism and Taoism*, trans. from German by Hans H. Gerth (Glencoe, IL: Free Press, 1951).

7. *The Protestant Ethic*, p. 54.

8. Baxter's *Christian Directory in Protestant Ethic*, quoted in Reinhard Bendix, *Max Weber, An Intellectual Portrait* (Garden City, New York: Doubleday, 1962), p. 62; and Weber, *The Protestant Ethic*, p. 172.

9. Weber, ibid., pp. 21–22.

10. Weber, *The Religion of China*, Part I.

11. Ibid., pp. 159–61; 235–36.

12. Ibid., pp. 243–44, 246, 248.

13. Ibid., p. 248.

14. Parsons summarizes Weber's principal observations on the culture and economy of the East and West as follows: "1. By contrast with other civilizations, rational bureaucratic organization and closely related forms are major elements in the distinctive social structure of the modern West. 2. There is a congruence of the ethic of ascetic Protestantism with the bureaucratic rational bourgeois element of modern Western Capitalism and its *geist*. 3. There is a lack of congruence with the spirit of capitalism of the ethical implications of the major Asiatic religions. Insofar as they have had an influence on secular social life it *could not* have been in a rational bourgeois capitalistic direction...." Talcott Parsons, *The Structure of Social Action* (New York: The Free Press, 1937), p. 575 (original italics).

15. Talcott Parsons, *The Social System* (New York: The Free Press, 1951).

16. Ibid., p. 177.

17. Ibid., p. 179.

18. Parsons, *The Structure of Social Action*, pp. 550–51 (original italics).

19. See, for example, John K. Fairbank, Alexander Eckstein, and L.S. Yang, "Economic Change in Early Modern China: An Analytic Framework," *Economic Development and Cultural Change* 9 (October 1960): 1–26; John K. Fairbank, *The United States and China*, 3rd ed. (Cambridge: Harvard University Press, 1972), pp. 36–42, 66–71; Dwight H. Perkins, ed.,

China's Modern Economy in Historical Perspective (Stanford: Stanford University Press, 1975); Marion J. Levy, Jr., "Contrasting Factors in the Modernization of China and Japan," in Simon Kuznets, Wilbert E. Moore, and Joseph J. Spengler, eds., *Economic Growth: Brazil, India, Japan* (Durham, NC: Duke University Press, 1955), pp. 496–536; G. William Skinner, "Marketing and Social Structure in Rural China," *Journal of Asian Studies* 24 (1964–65), in three parts; Albert Feuerweker, *The Chinese Economy ca. 1870–1911* (Ann Arbor, MI: Michigan Papers in Chinese Studies, No. 5, 1969); and Bellah, *Tokugawa Religion.* Bellah's work on Japan involved an explicit, systematic application of Parson's pattern variables to the study of Japanese religions and economy.

20. Weber, *The Protestant Ethic,* p. 18.

21. Marion J. Levy, Jr., "Some Aspects of 'Individualism' and the Problem of Modernization in China and Japan," *Economic Development and Cultural Change* 10 (April 1962): 226.

22. Weber, *The Protestant Ethic,* p. 108; and Parsons, *The Structure of Social Action,* pp. 525–26.

23. See Parsons, *The Social System,* pp. 182–84; Levy, "Some Aspects of 'Individualism,' " pp. 225, 228–29.

24. Hofheinz and Calder, *The East Asia Edge,* pp. 3, 12.

25. Herman Kahn, *World Economic Development, 1979 and Beyond* (Boulder, CO: Westview Press, 1979), pp. 118, 122 (original italics). Kahn's use of the term neo-Confucian culture or neo-Confucianism has caused confusion. Neo-Confucianism has long been used by Sinologists to refer to the intellectual movement in the Sung and Ming dynasties in China. For this reason, other scholars have opted for such terms as post-Confucianism and new Confucianism to refer to the contemporary connotations of Confucianism.

26. Roderick MacFarquhar, "The Post-Confucian Challenge," *The Economist,* February 9, 1980, p. 67.

27. For instance, for journalists, see Steve Lohr, "4 'New Japans' Mounting Industrial Challenge," *The New York Times,* August 24, 1982, pp. 1, 35; and Arthur Jones, "Where Adam Smith Meets Confucius," *Forbes,* December 19, 1983, p. 113; for businessmen, see Clayton Yeutter (former president Chicago Mercantile Exchange; and former U.S. Special Trade Representative) and Eric W. Hayden (chief economist of Bank of

America's Asia division) in *The New York Times*, August 24, 1982, p. 35; for politicians, see Jim Wright (then-Majority Leader of the United States House of Representatives) in *World Journal* (a Chinese newspaper in New York), October 21, 1983, p. 1; and October 22, 1983, p. 1; President Ronald Reagan in ibid., October 21, 1983, p. 1; for Western scholars, see Peter Berger, "*I-ko Tung-ya fa-chan ti mo-hsing: chan-hou T'ai-wan ching-yen ti wen-hua yin-shu*" ("An East Asian Development Model: Cultural Factor in the Post-War Experiences of Taiwan"), *Chung-kuo lun-tan* (*China Forum*, published in Taiwan), no. 222 (December 25, 1984), pp. 19–23; for Chinese scholars, see Chin Yao-chi, "*Ju-chia lun-li yü ching-chi fa-chan: Wei-pei hsüeh-shuo ti ch'ung-t'an*" ("Confucian Ethics and Economic Development: A Reexamination of Weber's Theory"), in Li Yih-yüan, Yang Kuo-shu, and Wen Ch'ung-i, eds., *Hsien-tai-hua yü Chung-kuo-hua lun-chi* (*Modernization and Sinicization*) (Taipei: Kuei-kuan t'u-shu ku-fên yu-hsien kung-ssu, 1985), pp. 29–55; Yü Ying-shih, "Confucian Thought and Economic Development: Early Modern Chinese Religious Ethics and the Spirit of the Merchant Class," *The Chinese Intellectual* 2 (Winter 1985): 3–55; Harry Hsiao, "What Can Confucian Thought Contribute to Economic Development?" *The Chinese Intellectual* 2 (Summer 1986): 15–23; Sun Chung-hsing, "From the Protestant Ethic to the Confucian Ethic," *The Chinese Intellectual* 2 (Summer 1986): 46–57; and Yang Chün-shih, "The Confucian Ethic, Weberian Thesis and Ideology," *The Chinese Intellectual* 2 (Summer 1986): 58–65. The magazine *Chung-kuo lun-tan* has sponsored several symposia on this subject in which many Chinese and American scholars participated. See ibid., no. 169 (October 10, 1982), pp. 5–60; no. 189 (August 10, 1983), pp. 7–40; no. 199 (January 10, 1984), pp. 8–41; and no. 222 (December 25, 1984), pp. 14–39.

28. Gunnar Myrdal, *Asian Drama: An Inquiry into the Poverty of Nations*, vol. 1 (New York: Pantheon, 1968), p. 16.

29. Edward W. Said, *Orientalism* (New York: Pantheon, 1978), pp. 40, 300. Though Said dealt with only Western studies on the Middle East, his criticism of Western scholarship is considered equally applicable to Western studies on Asia as a whole. The editors of *The Journal of Asian Studies* have considered Said's work sufficiently provocative that they in-

vited four authors to hold a "Review Symposium" on his book. See ibid. 39 (May 1980): 481–517.

30. H.D. Harootunian, "Metzger's Predicament," *The Journal of Asian Studies* 39 (February 1980): 247.

31. See Yü, "Confucian Thought and Economic Development," 19–23; Tu Wei-ming "Modern Changes in the Confucian Tradition," *The Chinese Intellectual* 2 (Autumn 1985): 90–92; Thomas A. Metzger, *Escape from Predicament: Neo-Confucianism and China's Evolving Political Culture* (New York: Columbia University Press, 1977). In a Review Symposium on Metzger's work, *The Journal of Asian Studies* invited five authors to participate in the discussions. See ibid. 39 (February 1980): 237–90.

32. Berger, "*I-ko Tung-ya fa-chan ti mo-hsing.*" Cf. Guy Allito's view on this point, *World Journal,* October 3, 1986, p. 16.

33. Hung-chao Tai, "Human Factor and Japanese Economic Performance," Report to the Michigan Council for the Humanities (Detroit: The University of Detroit, 1984), pp. 7–8.

34. Richard H. Minear, "Orientalism and the Study of Japan," *The Journal of Asian Studies* 39 (May 1980): 507–17.

35. Nathan Glazer, "Social and Cultural Factors in Japanese Economic Growth," in Hugh Patrick and Henry Rosovsky, eds., *Asia's New Giant: How the Japanese Economy Works* (Washington, D.C.: The Brookings Institution, 1976), pp. 816–21.

36. James C. Abegglen, *The Japanese Factory: Aspects of Its Social Organization* (Glencoe, IL: Free Press, 1958), pp. 1–2.

37. Chapter 20. My translation.

38. *The Book of Rites,* quoted in Fu-ch'üan Chang, *Tzu-yu yü Jên-ch'üan (Freedom and Human Rights)* (Hong Kong: The Asia Press, 1955), p. 22, my translation. See also other Confucian classics *The Analects,* Book XII, chap. 11; and *The Great Learning,* chap. 3.

39. Cf. C.K. Yang, "Introduction" to Weber, *The Religion of China,* p. xxxi; cf. Parsons, *The Structure of Social Action,* pp. 525–26.

40. Morishima, *Why Has Japan "Succeeded?"* p. 6.

41. Chie Nakane, *Japanese Society* (Berkeley, CA: University of California Press, 1970).

42. The term *t'ung hsiang* means literally "same village or township" where individuals maintain their residences. As most people in traditional Chinese society seldom moved their residences, individuals living in the same locality maintained a strong bond with each other.

43. *T'ung tsung* is a direct family-based relationship. *T'ung hsiang* and *t'ung hsüeh* are vicarious family relationships; people who claim these relationships are *likened* to family members.

44. Francis L.K. Hsu, *Iemoto: The Heart of Japan* (Cambridge, MA: Schenkman Publishing Company, 1975), pp. 62–69, 220–21. See also Levy, "Some Contrasting Factors in the Modernization of China and Japan," pp. 516–20.

45. Quoted in MacFarquhar, "The Post-Confucian Challenge," p. 70. Park's statement is strongly reminiscent of a famous passage in a Confucian classic. See *The Great Learning*, para. 5.

46. Parsons, *The Structure of Social Action*, p. 546.

47. See, for instance, *The Great Learning*, Commentary, chap. x, paras. 6–10, 20–23; *The Analects*, Book XIII, chap. xii; and *The Works of Mencius*, Book I, part 1, chap. ii.

48. Weber recognized this point when he stated, "Confucius, too, might strive for wealth 'even as a servant, with whip in hand,' if only the success of the endeavor were fairly guaranteed. But the guarantee does not hold and this fact leads to the one really essential reservation concerning economic acquisitiveness: namely, the poise and harmony of the soul are shaken by the risks of acquisitiveness." *The Religion of China*, pp. 159–60.

49. Cited in Frank Gibney, *Miracle by Design: The Real Reasons behind Japan's Economic Success* (New York: New York Times Books, 1982), pp. 30–31.

50. Shui-shen Liu, "*Chung-hsi kuan-li li-nien ti i-tung pi-chiao fên-hsi* ("A Comparative Analysis of the Similarities and Differences in the Managerial Concepts of the East and the West"), *Chung-kuo lun-tan*, no. 189 (August 10, 1983), 20–21 (my translation).

51. Kuang-kuo Huang, "*Tui chia-tsu shih chi-yeh kuan-li ti fên-hsi*" ("A Comparative Analysis of the Managerial Style of Familistic Enterprises"), Chung-kuo lun-tan, no. 189 (August 10, 1983), pp. 15–16.

52. The variation in the impact of family orientation on the volume of sales of business enterprises in the five East Asian countries can be seen in a 1984 survey of the 1,025 world's largest private companies outside the United States and Communist countries. Conducted by *Business Week*, the survey listed the 100 largest Japanese companies, all of which had multibillion dollar sales in 1983. The comparable figures for other East Asian countries are: in Taiwan 3 out of 26 largest companies had multibillion dollar sales; in Hong Kong 3 out of 27; in Singapore, 1 out of 11; and in South Korea, 11 out of 18. See ibid., July 23, 1984, pp. 176–81.

53. See *World Journal*, February 5, 1984, p. 4; and *The New York Times*, March 30, 1983, p. 43. In contrast, the profit-sharing pay in the American auto industry, which, as a concept, is similar to the bonus pay in Oriental companies, is insignificantly small in size, amounting to less than 3 percent of the base wage of a worker under the 1981 and 1984 labor contracts. Tai, "Human Factor and Japanese Economic Performance," p. 119.

54. *The New York Times*, March 30, 1983, p. 43.

55. Robert H. Silin, *Leadership and Values: The Organization of Large-Scale Taiwanese Enterprises* (Cambridge: Harvard University Press, 1976), p. 43. See also I-hung Chou," *O-kuo ta-hsing chi-yeh chih k'ung-chih hsing-wei*" ("The Means of Control in the Large Enterprises of Our Country"), *Chung-kuo lun-tan*, no. 189 (August 10, 1983), pp. 37–38.

56. (New York: Avon Books, 1981), pp. ix, 8.

57. Mao-ch'un Yang, "*Chung-kuo ti chia-tsu tsu-i yü kuo-min hsing-kê*" ("Chinese Familism and National Character"), in Yih-yuan Li and Kuo-shu Yang, eds., *Symposium on the Character of the Chinese, An Interdisciplinary Approach* (Taipei: Academia Sinica, 1972), pp. 141–42 (my translation). See also Dwight H. Perkins, "Introduction: The Persistence of the Past," in Perkins, *China's Modern Economy in Historical Perspective*, pp. 14–15; and Yüan-li Wu, *Becoming an Industrialized Nation, ROC's Development on Taiwan* (New York: Praeger, 1985), p. 115.

58. There are other reasons for the high savings ratios in the East Asian countries. The lack of fully developed financial and credit services for a consumer-oriented economy, the inade-

quacy of a publicly financed social welfare system, and public policies encouraging savings in these countries are the most relevant. The impact of culture, however, remains significant.

59. Bellah, *Tokugawa Religion*, pp. 107–08.

60. Fairbank, *The United States and China*, pp. 52–53.

61. *The Analects*, XV; 38.

62. The case of Singapore may be noted especially. In 1982, to demonstrate its serious concern for moral education, the government started a program to incorporate Confucian teachings into school textbooks. In 1983 Prime Minister Lee Kuan Yew proposed a program for what some have called human engineering. The less-schooled people were to be discouraged to have more than one child; the university-educated were to be given monetary and educational incentives to have more children. *The New York Times*, May 20, 1982, p. 11; Barbara Crossette, "The Opulence of Singapore," *The New York Times Magazine*, December 16, 1984, p. 146; and *World Journal*, June 30, 1983, p. 14.

63. Two studies—Torstein Husen, ed., *International Study of Achievement in Mathematics: A Comparison of Twelve Countries*, vol. 2 (New York: John Wiley & sons, 1967); and L.C. Comber and John Keeves, *Science Education in Nineteen Countries* (New York: John Wiley & Sons, 1973)—showed that Japanese students of different age groups had higher achievement scores in mathematics and science than their Western peers. A study of 1,440 primary school students in Taiwan, Japan, and the United States by the Center for Human Growth and Development of the University of Michigan indicated that the Taiwanese and Japanese students had higher achievement scores in reading and in mathematics than their American counterparts. See *Detroit Free Press*, June 17, 1984, pp. 1A, 8A.

64. Edwin O. Reischauer, *The Japanese* (Cambridge: Harvard University Press, 1977), p. 167; Ezra F. Vogel, *Japan as Number One* (Cambridge: Harvard University Press), p. 27; and Ronald S. Anderson, *Education in Japan: A Century of Modern Development* (Washington: U.S. Government Printing Office, 1975), "preface" by John Whitney Hall, p. v.

65. Montek S. Ahluwalia, "The Scope for Policy Intervention," in Hollis Chenery, Montek S. Ahluwalia, C.L.G. Bell, John H.

Duloy, Richard Jolly, *Redistribution with Growth* (published for the World Bank; London: Oxford University Press, 1974), pp. 81–82. Cf. Chen, *Hyper-Growth in Asian Economies,* p. 153.

66. MacFarquhar, "The Post-Confucian Challenge," p. 71. Cf. Hsiao, "What Can Confucian Thought Contribute to Economic Development?" pp. 17 ff.

67. Roderick MacFarquhar, "Chêng-chih Kai-kê" ("Political Reform"), *The Chinese Intellectual* 1 (July 1985): 11.

TWO

Economic Performance in Five East Asian Countries:
A Comparative Analysis

Yuan-li Wu and Hung-chao Tai

The economic achievement of Japan, South Korea, Taiwan, Hong Kong, and Singapore following the Second World War must be considered one of the most striking events in the economic history of nations. Rising from the ruins of the war, Japan soon took the lead in economic growth and became the world's third richest nation within two decades. Then, South Korea, Taiwan, Hong Kong, and Singapore quickly followed suit, growing at a pace even faster than that of Japan. They became known as Asia's "Four New Japans," or "Four Tigers," or "Four Little Dragons."

To place these countries' achievement in a global perspective, this chapter will compare their economic record with that of the rest of the world and will assess the significance of their performance to the international community. Economic records of nations can be compared in terms of *rates* of growth of national wealth and improvements of the *quality* of the economy. Insofar as the East Asian economies are heavily foreign trade-oriented, changes in the volume and content of *trade* constitute another criterion. For these comparisons, relevant data on the five East Asian countries and on the world's various other economic groups and their respective representative countries are arranged into a series of tables. The classification of the world's economic groups used in this chapter is the same as that of the World Bank in its annual World Development Reports, 1984–1988: *low-income economies, lower middle-income economies, upper middle-income economies, high-income oil exporters, industrial market economies, and East Europe, non-market economies.* It should be mentioned that although these Tables contain data from the "high-income oil exporter" countries, such countries will not be part of the following analysis because their economic performance fluctuated wildly in the last two decades with the rise and fall of oil prices.

The Economic Record

Economic Growth. The economic growth of a nation can be measured by the rate of increase of its Gross Domestic Product adjusted for inflation (real GDP) and its per capita Gross National Product. As seen in Table 1, in 1965–1980, each of the five East Asian countries had a higher growth rate of real GDP than practically any other country in the world. In 1980–1986, all these countries continued to maintain their lead. In both time periods they grew twice or three times as fast as Western countries (industrial market economies). As is also evident in Table 1, the five East Asian countries maintained in 1965–1986 the highest growth rate of per capita GNP in the world, again twice or three times the rates of Western nations. In 1986 they all had a higher per capita income than any other country in Asia and, also, two-thirds of the nations of the world.[1]

Qualitative Improvement of the Economy. Concurrent with the East Asian countries' high growth rate was a very marked improvement in the quality of their economies. The quality of an economy can be seen in the sectoral distribution of its Gross Domestic Product. As an economy begins sustained growth, changes in the relative size of the three sectors occur—agriculture, industry, and services. In the initial stage of development, the agricultural sector decreases, the industrial sector increases, and the service sector remains relatively stable. When a country reaches a very high stage of development, the agricultural sector becomes the smallest of the three, the industrial sector—especially its manufacturing component—decreases, and the service sector becomes the largest.

These trends generally prevailed in the five East Asian countries. As seen in Table 2, in 1965–1986, the decline in the agricultural sector was most dramatic. If Hong Kong and Singapore are excluded from consideration because of the insignificant size of their agriculture, the other three East Asian countries saw the relative size of their agricultural sector drop by 67 percent in Japan, 68 percent in South Korea, and 74 percent in Taiwan. Such a large

TABLE 1:
Economic Growth

Countries[a]	Average annual growth rate of real GDP, %		GNP per capita	
			U.S. Dollars[b]	Average annual growth rate, %
	1965–80	1980–86	1986	1965–86
East Asia (5)				
Japan	6.3	3.7	12,840 (8)	4.3
South Korea	9.5	8.2	2,370 (33)	6.7
Taiwan	10.0	7.2	3,751 (28)	6.9
Hong Kong	8.5	6.0	6,910 (22)	6.2
Singapore	10.4	5.3	7,410 (20)	7.6
Low-income				
economies (37)	3.1	2.9	200	0.5
Tanzania	3.7	0.9	250	–0.3
Lower-middle				
income (34)	6.5	1.8	750	2.5
Thailand	7.4	4.8	810	4.0
Upper-middle				
income (23)	6.7	2.5	1,890	2.8
Argentina	3.4	–0.8	2,350	0.2
Yugoslavia	6.0	1.2	2,300	3.9
High-income				
oil exporters (4)	7.8	–3.3	6,740	1.8
Saudi Arabia	10.9	–3.4	6,950	4.0
Industrial market				
economies (19)	3.6	2.5	12,690	2.3
United States	2.8	3.1	17,480	1.6
East Europe,				
non-market (8)	–	–	–	–
Romania	8.6[c]	7.6[d]	2,560[e]	5.1[f]

Sources: The World Bank, *World Development Report 1984–1988* (New York: Oxford University Press, 1984–1988), Annex: World Development Indicators; Taiwan, *Taiwan Statistical Data Book 1987* (Taipei, Taiwan, 1987) and Republic of China, Directorate-General of Budget Accounting and Statistics, *Statistical Yearbook of the Republic of China, 1983* (Taipei, Taiwan).

[a]Under the classification of the World Bank's *World Development Report*, all five East Asian countries except Japan and Taiwan are in the "Upper-middle income" group. Japan is in the "Industrial market economies" group, and Taiwan is a country most of whose data are not reported by the bank. Figure in parentheses following each group refers to the number of countries in the group. "Low-income economies" exclude China and India.

From each group, a representative country is selected. Selection is based on (1) the country's per capita income being the same or closest to the average per capita income of the group to which it belongs, and (2) availability of data. However, the United States is selected not for these reasons but because it has the highest GNP in the world. Data on most of "East Europe, non-market economies" are not available; under the World Bank's *World Development Report 1984*, Romania appears to be the best performer in the group. Yugoslavia is included in the table because of its unique status. It is located in East Europe with a socialist regime but is listed in the "upper-middle income" group by the World Bank.

[b]Figure in parentheses following each of the East Asian countries refers to the rank of the country in terms of per capita income among the nations of the world, excluding most of Eastern European, non-market economies, whose data are unavailable.

[c]For period 1960–70. [d]For period 1970–82. [e]For 1982. [f]For period 1960–82.

Symbols: – : Not available.   blank : None.

TABLE 2:
Sectoral Distribution of Gross Domestic Product
(in percent)

	Agriculture		Industry		(Manufacturing)*		Services	
	1965	1986	1965	1986	1965	1986	1965	1986
East Asia (5)								
Japan	9	3	43	41	32	30	48	56
South Korea	38	12	25	42	18	30	37	45
Taiwan	21	7	33	53	20	39	40	40
Hong Kong	2	0	40	29	24	21	58	71
Singapore	3	1	24	38	15	27	73	62
Low-income								
economies (37)	43	38	18	20	10	11	41	41
Tanzania	46	59	14	10	8	6	40	31
Lower-middle								
income (34)	30	22	25	30	15	17	43	46
Thailand	35	17	23	30	14	21	42	53
Upper-middle								
income (23)	18	10	37	40	21	25	46	50
Argentina	17	13	42	44	33	31	42	44
Yugoslavia	23	12	42	42	–	–	35	46
High-income								
oil exporters (4)	5	–	65	–	5	–	30	–
Saudi Arabia	8	4	60	50	9	9	31	46
Industrial market								
economies (19)	5	3	40	35	29	–	54	61
United States	3	2	38	31	28	20	59	67
East Europe,								
non-market (8)	–	–	–	–	–	–	–	–
Romania**	–	18	–	57	–	–	–	25

Sources, notes, and symbols: see Table 1.
*Part of industry.   **All data for 1982.

decline was not seen anywhere else in the world. In the same period, services in the five East Asian countries steadily grew, becoming at the end the dominant sector for all five. Generally speaking, the industrial sector remained substantial in size throughout the period, though in Japan and Hong Kong the industrial sector and its manufacturing component showed a decline. In the early 1980s, all five countries rapidly approached the pattern of sectoral distribution of GDP in the industrial West.

Foreign Trade. The five East Asian countries registered at various times very high rates of growth in exports and imports. As seen in Table 3, in 1965–1980, the annual growth rates for

TABLE 3:
Merchandise Trade

Countries	Million dollars		Rank in the world	Average annual growth rate %			
	Export 1986	Import 1986		Export '65–80	'80–86	Import '65–80	'80–86
East Asia (5)							
Japan	210,757	127,553	3	11.5	6.4	8.7	3.5
South Korea	34,715	31,584	15	27.3	13.1	15.2	9.3
Taiwan	39.758	24,165	16	19.0	12.7	15.1	4.3
Hong Kong	35,440	35,366	13	9.5	10.7	8.3	7.9
Singapore	22,495	25,511	21	4.7	6.1	7.0	3.6
Low-income							
economies (37)	17,922	29,690		0.5	0.6	1.1	–0.1
Tanzania	343	1,050		–4.0	–9.8	1.6	–1.3
Lower-middle							
income (34)	84,172	98,942		6.7	2.4	6.1	–2.4
Thailand	8,794	9,178		8.5	9.2	4.1	2.0
Upper-middle							
income (23)	280,615	269,715		1.7	5.6	6.0	–0.1
Argentina	6,852	4,724		4.7	1.5	1.8	–13.8
Yugoslavia	10,353	11,753		5.6	1.5	6.6	–1.6
High-income							
oil exporters (4)	43,374	36,844		5.6	–12.5	19.5	–7.7
Saudi Arabia	20,085	19,112		8.8	–19.2	25.9	–7.7
Industrial market							
economies (19)	1,443,629	1,510,671		7.1	3.3	6.7	4.3
United States	217,307	387,081		6.9	–2.7	6.2	9.0
East Europe,							
non-market (8)	–	–		–	–	–	–
Romania	12,543	11,437		–	–	–	–

Sources, notes, and symbols: see Table 1.

exports (except Singapore) ranged from 9.5 percent in Hong Kong to 27.3 percent in South Korea, while the comparable rates for imports ranged from 7.0 percent in Singapore to 15.2 percent in South Korea. In 1980–1986, Japan saw a significant drop in its trade growth rates, but it still maintained a healthy 6.4 percent average increase. In the same period, South Korea, Taiwan, and Hong Kong maintained the world's highest growth record in exports and imports. Singapore had only moderate growth in foreign trade in 1965–1986, but its export growth rate for 1980–1986 was 6.1 percent—a high rate by world standards. In fact, in 1986 all five East Asian countries were among the world's 25 largest trading nations.

Along with qualitative improvements in their economies, the

TABLE 4:
Distribution of Merchandise Exports
(in percent)

	Primary commodities*		Textile & clothing		Machinery & transport equip.		Other manufactures	
	1965	1986	1965	1986	1965	1986	1965	1986
East Asia (5)								
Japan	9	2	17	3	31	64	43	31
South Korea	40	9	27	25	3	33	29	33
Taiwan	59	9	5	18	4	29	33	44
Hong Kong	13	8	43	35	6	21	37	36
Singapore**	65	33	6	5	11	38	18	25
Low-income								
economies (37)	91	68	5	17	0	2	7	10
Tanzania	87	83	0	–	0	3	13	14
Lower-middle								
income (34)	92	72	2	–	1	3	5	24
Thailand	95	58	0	15	0	9	4	18
Upper-middle								
income (23)	78	41	6	12	3	19	13	26
Argentina	94	77	0	2	1	6	5	14
Yugoslavia	44	19	8	9	24	34	21	38
High-income								
oil exporters (4)	99	89	–	–	1	3	1	8
Saudi Arabia	99	91	0	–	1	4	1	5
Industrial market								
economies (19)	31	20	6	4	32	42	31	33
United States	35	24	3	2	37	48	25	26
East Europe,								
non-market (8)†	51	–	3	–	34	–	21	–
Romania	–	–	–	–	–	–	–	–

Sources, notes, and symbols: see Table 1.
* Include fuel, mineral, agricultural, and fishery products.
**Singapore's primary commodities include a sizable amount of petroleum product as the country is one of the world's major oil refinery areas.
†Data for 1960.

East Asian countries also saw important changes in the composition of their merchandise exports. As evident in Table 4, exports of primary commodities experienced their sharpest relative decline in 1965–1986. In 1986, the proportion of primary commodities in total exports (except Singapore) was smaller than that of any other group of economies, including the industrial West. The exception—Singapore—is attributable to the large volume of petroleum trade generated by its refineries. In most of the East Asian countries there was also a decline in the export of labor-intensive products (represented by "textiles and clothing") and a concurrent rise in capital-intensive and technology-intensive products (represented by the "machinery & transport equipment" and "other manufactures" categories).

The Economic Significance

The five East Asian countries appear to have become the world's top economic performers in the post-World War II years. The quantitative and qualitative changes in their economies were impressive, indeed. Yet, the significance of their achievement is not limited to these; it can also be seen in terms of a number of other considerations.

Speed of Economic Changes. The first consideration concerns the speed at which these countries achieved their economic gains. Compared with Western nations, these countries reached their present level of development with unprecedented rapidity. Today, Japan's economy clearly ranks among the most advanced in the world. The other four countries have decisively moved into a high level of industrialization. According to a rough estimate by Herman Kahn, it took Western countries two hundred years since the mid-18th century to bring about a mass-consumption economy. It took Japan one hundred years following the Meiji Reform of 1868 to do the same, and for the other four East Asian countries the comparable figure appears to be about fifty years.[2]

Kahn's estimate is partially corroborated by Shirley W.Y. Kuo, Gustav Ranis, and John C.H. Fei in a mathematical calculation of the speed of industrialization of a number of Western European countries, the United States, Canada, the Soviet Union, Japan, and Taiwan. Using data from different time periods when these countries underwent rapid industrialization, these economists devised a graph to show "the indexes of industrial products (in real terms) in a semilogarithmic scale, so that the slope of each line shows the growth rate of that particular country. A steeper slope indicates a higher growth rate."[3] As seen in Figure 1, the rate of industrialization in Taiwan was faster than that of Japan, whose rate was faster than that of the Soviet Union, the United States, and other Western nations.[4] Though this figure does not include data on South Korea, Hong Kong, and Singapore, it would be equally applicable to these countries as they and Taiwan had comparable high economic growth rates during the same period of time, as indicated in Table 1.

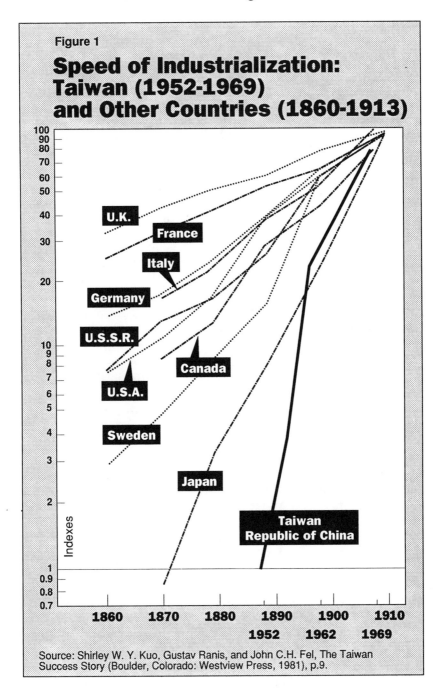

Figure 1

Speed of Industrialization: Taiwan (1952-1969) and Other Countries (1860-1913)

Source: Shirley W. Y. Kuo, Gustav Ranis, and John C.H. Fel, The Taiwan Success Story (Boulder, Colorado: Westview Press, 1981), p.9.

Thus, the five East Asian countries have become the world's fastest industrializing nations not only in contemporary time but also in the entire history of industrialization. One explanation for this extraordinary achievement is that as late-comers to industrialization, these countries were benefiting from the manufacturing and technological advances of the pioneering industrializing nations, which had taken a very long time to achieve. Undoubtedly this explanation is valid; yet it cannot explain why nearly every other developing country has not been able to do the same. "Of the 10 rapidly growing 'newly industrialising countries' pinpointed by the OECD [Organization for Economic Cooperation and Development]...," Roderick MacFarquhar has observed, "the only ones with non-European cultural origins are the post-Confucians: South Korea, Taiwan, Singapore and Hong Kong. These 58 [million] post-Confucians have a share of world exports of manufactures one-third larger than that of the 247 [million] Brazilians, Mexicans, Spaniards, Portuguese, Greeks and Yugoslavs who make up the rest of the OECD list."[5] Adding the Japanese to the side of the post-Confucians would make the performance of the two sides even more lopsided.

Changing Economic Relations with the West. There is a second reason why the economic performance of the East Asian countries is considered significant. Foreign trade has altered the economic relations of these countries with the West. The East Asian countries have generally traded more with the West than with any other group of nations.[6] Most of them have for some time obtained considerable trade surplus with the West, with Japan taking the lead since the mid-1960s. The East Asian countries have sold the West mostly manufactured goods and bought from it a considerable amount of raw materials and agricultural products. As a result, it is the West that has to take protective measures against the automobiles, steel, television sets, and textile products from the East Asian countries. This has created a pattern of trade between the two sides similar to the "economic colonialism" of the past; only this time the two sides have reversed their roles.[7]

The changing economic relations between the East Asian countries and the West also have an important political connotation. Marxists have traditionally held the view that capitalist countries used their superior economic strength and military power to exploit continuously and mercilessly the underdeveloped countries. Today, a variant of that view, known as the dependency theory, claims that the West has perpetuated its exploitation of these countries through a variety of sophisticated means, including foreign investment, foreign aid, and foreign trade.[8] The developing countries are said to be politically independent from the West but economically dependent on it.

The achievements of the East Asian countries have shown these Marxist views to be questionable. Though having long been the target area of Western investment, aid, and trade, all these countries have now achieved an economically advantageous position vis-à-vis the West. Though having in the past depended on the West for financing their early phase of industrialization, these countries have now amassed enormous domestic savings and have supplied their own capital for industrial expansion (see Table 5). These countries, in fact, have created for the West a dilemma. They supply the West with more and more goods it cannot reject because of its consumers' demand, but it cannot accept them without limitation because of its concern for trade deficit. *This is a dilemma neither the orthodox Marxists could anticipate nor the dependency theorists can explain.*

Impact on Income Distribution. The significance of the economic performance of the East Asian countries may be appraised in terms of another consideration: how economic growth affects the distribution of income. Simon Kuznets has done pioneering studies on the relationship of economic growth and income distribution of nations. His studies and a more recent work by the World Bank have found that "the *socialist* countries have the highest degree of overall equality in the distribution of income.... The *developed* countries are evenly distributed between the categories of low and moderate inequality.... Most of the *under-developed* countries show markedly greater relative inequality than the developed countries."[9] In short, income distribution is more equal in the socialist countries, relatively equal in Western countries, and unequal in the developing countries.

Kuznets and a number of other economists have also found that when nations begin to grow economically, their income distribution first becomes more unequal than before, but that with continued growth, their income distribution would become increasingly equal.[10] Plotting the relevant cross-national data on a chart, these economists created an inverted U-shaped curve to demonstrate this dynamic relationship between growth and equality, which has become known as the Kuznets effect or the Kuznets hypothesis.

The experiences of the East Asian countries conform to one of

TABLE 5:
Economic Conditions

	Gross Domestic investment as % of GDP		Gross Domestic savings as % of GDP	
	1965	1986	1965	1986
East Asia (5)				
Japan	32	28	33	32
South Korea	15	29	8	35
Taiwan	23	17	20	38
Hong Kong	36	23	29	27
Singapore	22	40	10	40
Low-income				
economies (37)	15	15	12	7
Tanzania	15	17	16	2
Lower-middle				
income (34)	17	19	16	17
Thailand	20	21	19	25
Upper-middle				
income (23)	23	24	23	26
Argentina	19	9	23	16
Yugoslavia	30	38	30	40
High-income				
oil exporters (4)	20	–	54	–
Saudi Arabia	14	27	48	18
Industrial market				
economies (19)	23	21	23	21
United States	20	18	21	15
East Europe,				
non-market (8)	–	–	–	–
Romania*	–	–	–	29

Sources, notes, and symbols: see Table 1.
*For 1982

these findings. Their sustained economic growth in the last two and a half decades did lead to major improvement in the equality of income distribution.[11] However, there are considerable differences from the other findings. Table 6 presents data on the percentage share of national income by quintile groups of different nations. For purposes of comparison, the table also provides the income equality ratios of nations, which are obtained by dividing the total income of the lowest 40 percent income households by that of the highest 40 percent.

As seen in this table, practically all the East Asian countries have achieved a greater equality of income distribution than all

TABLE 6:
Income Distribution*
(in percent)

Countries	Year	Percentage share of household income by percentile of households					Ratio of lowest 40% to highest 40%
		Lowest 20%	Second 20%	Third 20%	Fourth 20%	Highest 20%	
East Asia (5)							
Japan	1979	8.7	13.2	17.5	23.1	36.8	36.50
South Korea**	1982	6.8	12.0	16.2	22.0	43.0	28.90
Taiwan	1985	8.4	13.6	17.5	22.9	37.6	36.36
Hong Kong	1980	5.4	10.8	15.2	21.6	47.0	23.64
Singapore	–	–	–	–	–	–	–
Low-income economies (37)							
Tanzania†	1969	5.8	10.2	13.9	19.7	50.4	22.83
Lower-middle income (34)							
Thailand	1975/76	5.6	9.6	13.9	21.1	49.8	21.46
Upper-middle income (23)							
Argentina	1970	4.4	9.7	14.1	21.5	50.3	19.65
Yugoslavia	1978	6.6	12.1	18.7	23.9	38.7	29.85
Industrial market economies (19)							
United States	1980	5.3	11.9	17.9	25.0	39.9	26.50

Sources, notes, and symbols: see Table 1.

*Data of this table should be read with caution, as they belong to different years. Moreover, of the 129 countries listed in the World Bank's *World Development Report 1988*, only 46 have data on income distribution; these include none from the "high-income oil exporter" group or the "East-Europe, non-market" group.

**Source: *Korea's Economy* 3: 9 (October 1984): 2.

†Source: World Bank, *World Development Report 1984.*

other countries except Yugoslavia.[12] Three of them—Japan, South Korea, and Taiwan—have also attained equality ratios comparable to those of the high-income Western nations whose data are not shown in this table.[13] This is inconsistent with the findings of the above-mentioned economists. For these three countries—at least, South Korea and Taiwan—have not reached the same level of economic development as Western nations; hence, they should not have comparable equality ratios. What is more significant is the fact that Taiwan and Japan have the highest equality ratios among all the 46 countries of the world whose data are listed in the World Bank's *World Development Report 1988.*[14] They have a more equitable income distribution than even socialist Yugoslavia.

TABLE 7:
Social Indicators

	Life expectancy at birth (years)	Infant mortality rate, % (aged 0–10)		Daily calorie supply per capita
	1986	1965	1986	1985
East Asia (5)				
Japan	78	1.8	0.6	2,695
South Korea	69	6.3	2.5	2,806
Taiwan	74	–	–	2,874
Hong Kong	76	2.8	0.8	2,699
Singapore	73	2.6	0.9	2,696
Low-income economies (37)	52	15.0	10.6	2,100
Tanzania	53	13.8	10.8	2,316
Lower-middle income (34)	59	13.3	7.7	2,511
Thailand	64	8.8	4.1	2,399
Upper-middle income (23)	67	8.3	5.0	2,967
Argentina	70	5.8	3.3	3,216
Yugoslavia	71	7.2	2.7	3,499
High-income oil exporters (4)	64	13.8	6.2	3,213
Saudi Arabia	63	14.8	6.4	3,057
Industrial market economies (19)	76	2.4	0.9	3,357
United States	75	2.5	1.0	3,682
East Europe, non-market (8)	–	–	–	–
Romania	71	4.4	2.6	3,413

Sources, notes, and symbols: see Table 1.
*Additional source: Republic of China, Council for Economic Planning and Development, *Economic Development, Taiwan, Republic of China* (April 1987), p. 23.

The East Asian countries have another unusual experience: They have achieved, *simultaneously*, economic growth and equal income distribution. They did not suffer from the Kuznets effect.[15] Their experiences contain an important implication for the less developed countries. As the World Bank's *Redistribution with Growth* has pointed out, the long and widely accepted notion of incompatibility of growth and equality in the early stage of economic development has to be revised or discarded.[16] Many of

TABLE 7:
Social Indicators (Continued)

	Population per physician		Number in secondary school as % of age group		Number in higher education as % of age group	
	1965	1981	1965	1985	1965	1985
East Asia (5)						
Japan	970	740	82	96	13	30
South Korea	2,700	1,390	35	94	6	32
Taiwan	1,901	1,318	55	99	4	25
Hong Kong	2,460	1,290	29	69	5	13
Singapore	1,900	1,100	45	71	10	12
Low-income						
economies (37)	26,620	17,670	9	22	1	5
Tanzania	21,700	–	2	3	0	0
Lower-middle						
income (34)	17,340	7,880	16	42	4	13
Thailand	7,230	6,870	14	30	2	20
Upper-middle						
income (23)	2,310	1,380	29	57	7	16
Argentina	600	–	28	70	14	36
Yugoslavia	1,200	700	65	82	13	20
High-income						
oil exporters (4)	7,500	1,380	10	56	1	11
Saudi Arabia	9,400	1,800	4	42	1	11
Industrial market						
economies (19)	870	550	63	93	21	39
United States	670	500	–	99	40	57
East Europe,						
non-market (8)	–	–	–	–	–	–
Romania	760	700	39	75	10	11

today's poor countries, which once felt compelled to choose between growth and equality as their top development objective, may look to East Asia to find ways to achieve both.

Impact on Social Development. Fast growth combined with improved equality provides the East Asian countries with a social welfare that compares favorably with the world's best. As seen in Table 7, in reference to four of the six selected social indicators, the East Asian countries in general have approached the world's highest standard. In *life expectancy, infant mortality, calorie supply,* and *secondary school enrollment,* the East Asian countries are at the top. Only in the areas of *population per physician* and *enrollment in higher education* is the group (except Japan) below the world's best. However, even there they are quickly catching up.

From the perspective of modern economic history, the five East Asian countries have developed their economies with unprecedented speed. Their record indicates that they will continue to experience high growth in the future. Japan is already one of the world's most affluent nations. The other four East Asian countries are looking toward such a prospect within a couple of decades. The fact that all of them have moved far ahead of most other non-Western nations to achieve this distinction suggests a need for study of the common characteristics of their developmental experiences and of how these characteristics differ from those of other countries.

modern economic growth has been feeble. At a per capita national income of US $300 in 1986, it remains one of the poorest countries in the world. That modernization is the central rallying cry in China today bespeaks the lack of it.

The official explanation in China for the nation's relative economic underdevelopment is a series of policy errors, most notably the Great Leap Forward in 1958–60 and the Cultural Revolution of 1966–76. There is, undoubtedly, much truth to the explanation. However, a social scientist or historian may have to look beyond these incidents and to examine the social, economic, political, and cultural settings of the country to locate a more fundamental explanation. Unless the underlying forces are understood, the charting of a correct path for economic modernization cannot be really begun. The underlying forces are not created today and gone tomorrow. They are currents coming from deep in the nation's history, moving the minds and actions of today's Chinese and shaping the destiny of future generations. The greater our understanding of these forces, the less likely will past errors be repeated.

This brief review cannot possibly do justice to the literature it purports to survey. Rather than attempting comprehensiveness, the most significant and relevant explanations of China's underdevelopment will be highlighted from the viewpoint of one more interested in present-day conditions than the past.

Four Explanations

External Factors: Imperialism and Colonialism. When considering China's failure to achieve modern economic growth, it is tempting for the Chinese to blame the colonialism of foreign imperialist powers. I myself was brought up in an educational environment influenced by this thinking. Many in China today view foreign exploitation to be a principal cause of China's underdevelopment, and many outside of it may agree with this view. It appears to reflect the mentality of a proud people whose sense of dignity and self-respect was deeply hurt.

However, in attributing this feeling to xenophobia, one should not dismiss the explanation lightly. On the contrary, there appears to be circumstantial evidence that foreign colonialism probably did impede China's economic growth. It may be more than coincidence that the nations and territories neighboring

NOTES

1. See The World Bank, *World Development Report 1988* (New York: Oxford University Press, 1988), pp. 222–23 for complete data on per capita GNP of 129 nations.

2. Herman Kahn, *World Economic Development, 1979 and Beyond* (Boulder, CO: Westview Press, 1979), p. 333. Here, Kahn speaks of only Japan, South Korea, and Taiwan. However, he is presumed to refer to Hong Kong and Singapore as well. This is clearly seen elsewhere in his book, for instance, pp. 118, 124, and 380.

3. Shirley W.Y. Kuo, Gustav Ranis, and John C.H. Fei, *The Taiwan Success Story: Rapid Growth with Improved Distribution in the Republic of China, 1952-1979 (Boulder, CO: Westview Press, 1981)*, pp. 8–9.

4. Cf. E. Wayne Nafziger, *The Economics of Developing Countries* (Belmont, CA: Wadsworth Publishing Company, 1984), pp. 64–66. Nafziger's data are quite comparable to those of Kuo *et al.* except that data on Taiwan are not included.

5. Roderick MacFarquhar, "The post-Confucian Challenge," *The Economist*, February 9, 1980, p. 71.

6. This is especially evident in manufactured exports. In 1981, 47 percent of Japan's manufactured exports went to the West; the comparable figure for the other East Asian countries were 69 percent for Taiwan (referring to merchandise exports rather than manufactured exports), 77 percent for Hong Kong, and 49 percent for Singapore. Destination areas other than the West were East Europe, high-income oil exporter countries, and developing countries. See The World Bank, *World Development Report 1984*, p. 243; and *The New York Times*, December 9, 1982, p. 47.

7. See Steve Lohr, "4 'New Japans' Mounting Industrial Challenge," *The New York Times*, August 24, 1982, pp. 1, 35.

8. For the dependency theory, see Paul A. Baran, *The Political Economy of Growth* (New York: Monthly Review, 1957); Robert I. Rhodes, ed., *Imperialism and Underdevelopment: A Reader* (New York: Monthly Review, 1970); and Michael Smith, Richard Little, and Michael Shackleton, eds., *Perspectives on World Politics* (London: The Open University, 1981).

9. See Simon Kuznets, "Economic Growth and Income Ine-

quality," *American Economic Review* 45 (March 1955): 1–28; "Quantitative Aspects of the Economic Growth of Nations: VIII, Distribution of Income by Size," *Economic Development and Cultural Change* 11 (1963): 1–80; Hollis Chenery, Montek S. Ahluwalia, C.L.G. Bell, John H. Duloy, and Richard Jolly, *Redistribution with Growth* (published for the World Bank; London: Oxford University Press, 1974). The quotations are from the World Bank study, p. 7 (original italics).

10. See Kuznets, "Quantitative Aspects of the Economic Growth of Nations"; Irma Adelman and Cynthia Taft Morris, *Economic Growth and Social Equity in Developing Countries* (Stanford, CA: Stanford University Press, 1973); and Felix Paukert, "Income Distribution at Different Levels of Development: A Survey of Evidence," *International Labour Review* 108 (August and September 1973): 97–124.

11. See Edward K.Y. Chen, *Hyper-growth in Asian Economies: A Comparative Study of Hong Kong, Japan, Korea, Singapore and Taiwan* (London: The Macmillan Press Ltd., 1979), chapter 8, "Economic Growth and Income Distribution," pp. 152–76.

12. Comparable data on Singapore are not available. A number of studies on Singapore's Gini Coefficient of income distribution, which is one generally accepted standard for measuring income equality, indicate that Singapore moved toward increasing equality in the period 1966–1975, and that its Gini Coefficient in the early 1970s was roughly comparable to that of Japan and Hong Kong of the same time. See Chen, *Hyper-growth in Asian Economies*, pp. 156–64, 169–71.

13. For income distribution data of 17 Western nations, see the World Bank, *World Development Report 1988*, p. 273.

14. Ibid., pp. 272–73.

15. Kuo *et al.*, *The Taiwan Success Story*, p. 143; Chen, *Hyper-growth in Asian Economies*, p. 174; Yaun-li Wu, "Income Distribution in the Process of Economic Growth in Taiwan," in Yuan-li Wu and Kung-chia Yeh eds., *Growth, Distribution, and Social Changes: Essays on the Economy of the Republic of China*, University of Maryland, School of Law, Occasional Papers, no. 3 (1978), pp. 67–92; and cf. Chenery *et al.*, *Redistribution with Growth*, pp. 280–90.

16. Chenery, ibid., p. 7.

THREE

Historical Factors Affecting China's Economic Underdevelopment

Hang-sheng Cheng

The purpose of this chapter is to provide a brief review of the ongoing discussion on the historical background of China's relative lack of economic development. Simply put: Why has China lagged far behind other nations in Asia in achieving modern economic growth.

As defined by Simon Kuznets, "modern economic growth" is a sustained, rapid increase in a nation's per capita income, resulting from the application of science-based technology to production and distribution.[1] Kuznets shows that this growth process though centering on science and technology, requires thorough changes in a nation's social and economic structure as well as the prevailing philosophical outlook on life. Thus, for example Europe's historical context of modern economic growth, in the opinion of Kuznets, consists of secularism, egalitarianism, nationalism.

Modern economic growth originated in Europe around mid-18th century and has since spread to most of the world is well known in Asia, Japan was the first nation to adapt new world condition and rapidly developed into a mode dustrial state after the Meiji Restoration (1868). The rest region, other than China, was under colonial dominatic after 1945. It was only during the last two decades that economic growth took place in several states and territori fringe of China: South Korea, Taiwan, Hong Kong, gapore—all populated predominantly by the Chinese strongly influenced by the Chinese culture. Yet, in C

China did not attain modern economic growth until decades after their independence from colonial powers. Although China was not a foreign colony, from 1842 on the colonial powers through a series of wars did gain "spheres of influence" in China and impose "unequal treaties" on its people. Foreigners controlled China's customs as well as its railroad and telecommunication systems.

Like China, Japan at first also had to agree to a number of "unequal treaties." However, as it gathered strength, it succeeded in revising its treaty with Britain in 1874, and by 1901 all the obnoxious clauses suggestive of political inferiority were wiped out.[2]

A rich body of literature on China's rural economy of the 1930s produced by such leading Western-trained anthropologists, sociologists, and economists as Chen Han-seng, H.D. Fong, Fei Hsiao-tung, Franklin Ho, and members of the Institute of Pacific Relations have cited numerous references to the deleterious effect of imperialism on China.[3] These scholars have advanced the thesis that Western industry, technology, and commerce entering China under the protection of the unequal treaties destroyed the economic and social fabric of China's countryside and impeded industrial growth in China's cities.

The thesis has not stood up well, however, under the light of modern scholarship. Among others, Chi-ming Hou, Robert Dernberger, and Feng-hwa Ma have come up with convincing evidence that foreign trade and foreign investment were no hindrance to China's economic growth, but on the contrary served to stimulate and foster the industrialization that did take place in China in the late 19th century and early 20th century.

A few citations suffice to illustrate the point. Hou and others found that the growth of China's traditional handicraft industry was helped by expanding export demand and did not suffer from import competition. The traditional handicraft industry employed labor-intensive technology to produce goods not in *direct* competition with imports, which were produced with capital-intensive technology.[4] In his detailed study of the growth of China's cotton-textile industry, Kang Chao shows that China's handicraft textile industry relied on abundant rural surplus labor to hold its share of the national market during the 1930s until the outbreak of the Sino-Japanese War in 1937. The industry was not destroyed until the government's forced-industrialization policy cut off the supply of raw materials to the traditional sector after 1949.[5]

Dernberger estimates that between 1871 and 1936 China had a cumulative trade deficit of US $4.5 billion, which was financed through foreign direct investment and foreign borrowings as well as remittances from overseas Chinese. China could have used these external financial resources for industrial growth, but instead spent it mostly on consumer goods. In contrast, producer goods accounted for only 6 percent of total imports in 1880, 5 percent in 1900, 8 percent in 1913, and 17 percent in 1928.[6] Moreover, even this small amount of producer-goods imports was largely destined for use by foreign companies in China, which were insulated from the traditional economy (there was minimal technological transfer to domestic businesses).[7] Thus, foreign trade failed to provide China with the stimulus for industrialization in the 1880–1930 period, not because of any intrinsic impotence of foreign trade itself, but because of China's own failure to take advantage of the potential gains from foreign trade and to import foreign technology for boosting its industrial growth.

Modern international-trade theory does not deny that imports can injure competing domestic industries. Rather, it contends that injuries occur in industries where there is relatively inefficient use of a nation's resources. It suggests that the proper policy response is to welcome the acid test of import competition and to assist reallocation of domestic resources to more efficient industries when injury occurs. If wage rates or exchange rates are flexible, free trade benefits a nation in the long run, and protectionism hurts it. Chao maintains that China's handicraft-textile industry was able to compete against imports because, given the abundant rural surplus labor, the implicit household wage rate was highly flexible. In that case, no injury occurred.[8]

But, then, there is also the point about the indemnity payments. It is argued that China had to pay large sums of indemnity as a result of defeat in wars with foreign imperial powers, that the collection of indemnity funds strained government finance, and that their transfer abroad drained China's resources.

Two examples will suffice to illustrate the point. At the end of the war with Japan in 1895, China agreed to pay a total of 250 million taels of silver as indemnity for the return of the Liaotung Peninsula and other items. The sum was paid in four years from 1895 to 1898. The indemnity arising from the Boxer Revolution in 1900 amounted to 982 million taels (US $729 million), including principal (450 million taels) and interest, which China had to pay the 14 involved foreign powers over a 39-year period from 1902 to 1940.[9] Unquestionably, these were very heavy burdens on China's government finance. The normal annual revenue of the imperial government during that period was no more than 90 million taels. The government in Peking had to call on the provinces to remit no less than 21 million taels a year over and above their usual annual remittance of around 90 million, from 1902 to 1910, in order to meet the indemnity payments.[10] To a government that had already been hard strapped for funds, it must have been a severe strain indeed.

However, one must not be too hasty in equating these required indemnities with the actual payment, nor in equating strains on government finance with any resource drain from the nation. First, the indemnity payments to Japan were initially financed in part by the 48 million pounds sterling foreign loans the government contracted between 1895 and 1898. Second, about one-half of the total Boxer Rebellion indemnities were either remitted or cancelled, beginning with unilateral action by the United States in 1908 and the other nations after the First World War.[11] Thirdly, and perhaps most importantly, as stated earlier, China ran a perennial trade deficit from 1877 to 1937, which was financed by external sources.[12] That is to say, the indemnity payments notwithstanding, there was a steady net flow of foreign resources *to* China. One might rightfully argue that the net inflow would have been larger but for the indemnity payments. However, that is a rather thin reed to lean on for asserting that the indemnity payments were a serious drain of resources *from* China, constituting a significant impediment to the nation's modern economic growth around the turn of the century.

Personal and Social Philosophy. If foreign influences could not have been a principal deterrent to China's modern economic growth, one must then look inside China for possible factors, including the cultural and psychological make-up of the people.

Sociologists under the influence of Max Weber have found inspiration from his masterpiece, *The Protestant Ethic and the Spirit of Capitalism*, which advanced the theory that the rise of Protestantism was the dominant factor in the molding of the capitalist mind and thus of capitalism itself.[13] In his book *The Religion of China*, Weber compared the philosophical outlook on life and on the world in Chinese Confucianism with that in Western Protestantism.[14] He noted that "to a striking degree they [the Chinese] lacked rational matter-of-factness, impersonal rationalism, and the nature of an abstract, impersonal purposive association."[15]

Going further, Robert Bellah explains Japan's successful modernization and China's lack of it in terms of the difference in the two peoples' social philosophies: "China was characterized by the primacy of integrative value, whereas Japan was characterized by the primacy of political or goal-attainment value."[16] In other words, the Chinese are said to be more interested than the Japanese in the preservation of harmonious social relations, less in the seeking of power or wealth; or, to put it another way, the Chinese mentality is considered more accommodative, and the Japanese more aggressive.

In a similar vein but along a different line, Marion Levy has contrasted the Japanese and Chinese social philosophy and social structure.[17] He states that although the family is important in both societies, in feudal Japan a person's loyalty to his overlord took clear precedence over his loyalty to his family, whereas in China nothing was—and still is—more important than one's own family. Thus, once the emperor decided upon modernization, it was much easier to carry out in nationalistic Japan than in family-centered China.

These sociological explanations provide an interesting comparison of the national character of the Chinese, the Westerners, and the Japanese. However, generalizations based on philosophy or ideology are perilous. Although Confucian philosophy has had a strong hold on the Chinese mentality, the Chinese are also remarkably pragmatic. The philosophers and the scribes could be as lofty and abstract as they like; however, when it comes to practical daily living, there are few people more down-to-earth than the Chinese. Moreover, the assertion that the Chinese traditional mentality was inimical to the development of science and technology flies in the face of the fact that, with the same mentality, China from the tenth to the fourteenth century developed a systematic experimental investigation of nature and created the world's earliest mechanized industry, according to Mark Elvin.[18] Examples were abundant in such diverse fields as mathematics, astronomy, medicine, metallurgy, and military technology. Finally, strong family ties do not appear to have been a significant barrier to modern economic growth in Taiwan, Hong Kong, or Singapore; nor have they held back the economic success of the overseas Chinese in Southeast Asia.

Although not much credence can be accorded to this sociological approach to explaining China's economic underdevelopment, the conclusion that emerges from its assessment has noteworthy implications in China's present-day policy.

From the beginning of the 20th century, there has been in China an ongoing debate on the role of social ethics in China's modernization, traditionalists on the one hand and anti-traditionalists on the other. The former have maintained that modernization requires adoption of Western science and technology, but needs not be at the expense of China's traditional ethics and social philosophy. They see no necessary conflict between China's traditional values and the requisites of modernization. Japan is often cited as an example of a nation that has succeeded in achieving modernization while retaining its traditional values.

The anti-traditionalists, on the other hand, regard the traditional values and ethics as vestiges of a feudal past, which must be completely eradicated in order for China to modernize both economically and socially. In the early part of this century, the anti-traditionalists brought forth the May 4th Movement of 1919 and have since continued to be the prime moving force behind China's social and economic transformation. One branch of the movement is the so-called "complete-Westernization school." It advocates replacing Confucianism with science and democracy. The other branch has been the Marxist school, which advocates socialism and totalitarianism in place of Confucianism. The latter school has won out in China since the mid-20th century.

The Marxists carried out their beliefs with impressive vigor. In the name of modernization they systematically repudiated and destroyed traditional values and their outward symbols, including temples and churches, family shrines and burial grounds, family ties, fraternal organizations, and even personal friendship itself—denouncing the last-mentioned as "bourgeois sentimentalism." The movement climaxed in the Cultural Revolution of 1966–76. Since then, the tide has turned. Although traditional Confucianism, whatever that terms means, is still out, there has been less aversion, and even active encouragement, toward the nation's cultural heritage, including social ethics, as indicated by a national campaign to bring back civility and courtesy in daily life.

It would be naive to regard this change in the official attitude as a vindication of the traditionalist position in this historical debate. As so starkly presented here, the two sides represent polar views. In between, there are many ways of regarding the value of

China's traditional ethics in its modernization drive. One can afford to be eclectic and refuse to be a "true believer" of either extremist position. In any case, what is pertinent is that there appears to be no reason for believing that the Chinese mentality is fundamentally antithetic to modern economic growth. Perhaps China can achieve modern economic growth and preserve the best of its traditional values too.

The "High-Level Equilibrium Trap" Thesis. An influential school of China scholars subscribes to the "high-level equilibrium trap" hypothesis, which is essentially an application of Theodore Schultz's theory of agricultural growth.[19] Schultz maintains that agriculture is subject to sharply diminishing returns to all inputs, such that long-run agricultural growth depends on a steady supply of technological advances. Taking off from Schultz, Mark Elvin postulates that China was able to achieve spectacular economic growth during the T'ang and Sung Dynasties (619–906 and 960–1279, respectively) as a result of the great southward population migration under the steady pressure of the northern nomads. Flourishing foreign trade provided another stimulus. Prosperity continued through the Yüan Dynasty (1279–1367).

One manifestation of this sustained economic growth was the development of large cities and a sophisticated civilization of great complexity and specialization. The capital of the Southern Sung Dynasty, Hang-chou, was reported to be a city of more than one million residents in 1270.[20] After examining detailed accounts by a number of contemporary observers, Jacques Gernet concludes that at the end of the 13th century, "in the spheres of social life, art, amusements, institutions, and technology, China was incontestably the most advanced country of the time."[21]

From the 14th century to the beginning of the 16th century, economic growth slackened, as the last frontier disappeared and foreign trade became increasingly strangulated by government restrictions. However, according to Elvin, vigorous economic growth resumed from the 16th to the 18th centuries, as a result of an expanding market economy, manifested by increasing commercialization of agriculture, greater mobility of labor, and enlarged markets for the products of handicraft industries.[22] Recent scholarship has found evidence of impressive technological progress during that period, including the use of small explosives in coal mining, development of waterpowered bellows for iron smelting, and new implements for yarn spinning and cloth weaving.[23] Nevertheless, even though the economy functioned efficiently in disseminating new products and new technology, it remained basically a rural economy, employing small-scale, labor-intensive methods of production. In any case, stagnation is said to have set in by the middle of the Ch'ing Dynasty (1644–1911), supposedly as technology advances dwindled and the predominantly agricultural economy reached the "equilibrium trap."

The hypothesis may be an interesting and plausible description of the economic growth process in China from the 7th to the 18th centuries. However, a fundamental weakness of the theory is that technology is assumed to be given. Hence, it throws no light on why technological advances slowed down, and why China was unable to absorb new Western technology in the 19th century.

The Bureaucratic State. This leads us to the next proposed explanation, which states that the growing calcification of the authoritarian, hierarchical, bureaucratic state gradually stifled incentives for technological advances and made it impossible for China to adapt to the demands of a modern industrial society. In essence, it postulates that a necessary condition for an economy to generate or absorb technological advances is a social and economic order that provides sufficient incentives for producers to invent or adopt new technologies. It is alleged that the condition did exist in medieval China, but over time disappeared as the bureaucratic state increasingly dominated China's economic life.

The basic thesis is provided by Etienne Balazs and extended by Victor D. Lippit.[24] The extended version recognizes that China has had an authoritarian, bureaucratic state dating back at least to the Ch'in Dynasty (221–206 B.C.). Nevertheless, as late as the T'ang and Sung Dynasties from the 7th to the 13th century, there existed a prosperous and bourgeois merchant and craftsman class in the cities and well-to-do farming landlords in the countryside.[25] In addition, the bureaucratic state was administered in such a way that it facilitated commerce and encouraged the growth of agriculture and handicraft industries. Because many landowners were farmers themselves, surpluses were constantly reinvested in land improvement and adoption of new technology. The craftsmen and the merchants prospered in an environment of political stability and economic freedom. Although the emperor's authority was supreme, the society was basically pluralistic. Social success and prosperity could be attained by pursuing a variety of economic activities.

Over time, conditions changed. It is not clear from the literature what brought about the change. The pluralistic society gave way to a bureaucratic state, in which the governing class—the gentry—gained dominance over all economic activities. Dominance meant neither ownership nor active management, but an absolute authority that placed all classes of the population and all aspects of life under the whims of the governing gentry.

Unlike the feudal lords in medieval Europe, whose titles and authorities were hereditary, the gentry in China were selected through the imperial-examination process, which tested the candidates' mastery of Chinese classics as embodied in the *Four Books*. Up the hierarchy the candidates would try to move, as they passed the examinations from the local to the provincial level, to the national capital, and finally before the emperor himself. Once certified as a member of the gentry—that is, having passed the examination at the local level—one was to enjoy for life privileges denied the commoners, including exemption from draft services of all sorts. Those who passed the examination in the capital served as magistrates at the county level or worked in the various ministries in the capital. The examination system tested the candidates' familiarity and conformity with official doctrine; success in examination depended on the purity of one's thoughts in accordance with Confucian precepts. Innovation and originality had no place in the system. The bureaucrats, thus selected, wielded enormous power over all aspects of people's lives.

The state itself was ineffectual in carrying out normal state functions during the Ming Dynasty (1368–1644). A major reason was inept public finance. Aside from imperial taxes, which were collected in kind and shipped physically to the capital, local government expenditures were met by local collections at the county level. Most of China's 1,100 counties were financially self-sufficient. Where trans-county expenditures had to be financed, the disbursing agency would levy charges on the affected counties on the basis of ability to pay. Public finances were highly fragmented. According to Ray Huang, "the Ministry of Revenue ceased to be an operating agency; it had become a huge accounting office.... The [Ming] dynasty had permanently restricted its own ability to make fiscal adjustments.... When an economic activity produced a social consequence that the government could not handle, it had to be abandoned."[26]

Inept public finance resulted in low salaries for bureaucrats, which, when combined with enormous authority, made corruption almost inevitable. According to one account, "a minister, rank 2a, was entitled to an annual salary of 152 ounces of silver; in practice, he might receive cash gifts from provincial governors of ten times that amount on a single occasion."[27] The practice was repeated at all levels of the government down to the counties. Corruption permeated the entire body politic and weakened the social fabric. Apparently, the condition was not confined to the Ming period, but persisted into the Ch'ing Dynasty, and in the 19th century "reached unprecedented proportions, not to be exceeded until the first half of the 20th century."[28]

What life was like and how the society functioned under the authoritarian, corrupt, bureaucratic state in the 16th century are vividly depicted by Ray Huang.[29] He shows that the necessary social and economic order for generating or absorbing new technology had been thoroughly eroded. Examples to illustrate the point abound in his book. But, perhaps, one will suffice. This concerns a certain Yü Ta-yu, a contemporary of General Ch'i Chi-kuang, who is renowned for his victory against Japanese pirates plundering China's coasts in the 16th century. Yü proposed to the governor-general in the area to build larger ships with bigger guns to fight the pirates. According to Huang's commentary:

> Unknown to Yü himself, his suggestion involved more than modernizing weapon systems. In order to follow his advice the fiscal authorities in the provinces would have to be integrated, and centralized treasuries and large arsenals set up. Not only would additional personnel have to be recruited to manage these offices, but also their functions, more responsive to modern technology, would differ from all lines of duty hitherto known to the bureaucrats.... Thus, although he was unaware of it, *Yü had already touched on the dilemma that China had yet to face for many centuries to come. A large agrarian nation which had been settled with a common ideology in pursuit of uniformity and stability could find no easy way to avail itself of modern technology, which could never be employed to serve such a loose organization and preserve its status quo.*[30]

It is clear that Huang attributes China's inability to adopt modern technology to a loose organization that was bent on preserving its status quo. Huang has painted a vivid tableau of an inept bureaucratic state which had destroyed individual initiative and was itself unable to effect the necessary reforms for meeting the needs of modern technological advances.

It is almost uncanny how Huang's description of 16th century China also fits 19th century China, when the challenge of a superior Western technology appeared. Not surprisingly, China was unable to rise up to the challenge and achieve modern economic growth, as did its neighbor Japan.

Conclusion

In attempting to explain China's economic underdevelopment, I have emphasized the negative aspects of China's historical heritage, especially its bureaucratic state. However, taking all four proposed explanations into consideration, the assessment is not all negative. In fact, coupling the discussion of external factors with that of the equilibrium trap, one might conclude that the challenge of foreign modern technology should give China a big boost *provided* that the underlying conditions are favorable. My discussion of personal and social philosophy also indicates that there is little evidence for suggesting that the Chinese are culturally and philosophically unprepared for modern economic growth.

However, the bureaucratic state appears to have been a great hindrance to China's modern economic growth. If conditions already were deplorable in the 19th century, China sank even deeper into social chaos, economic disruptions, widespread corruption, and hyper-inflation toward the mid-20th century on the eve of the Communist Revolution. In the 1960s and 1970s, territories on the fringe of China—South Korea, Taiwan, Hong Kong, and Singapore, which were comparatively less constrained by the evils of the bureaucratic state—were able to open themselves to modern technology, make drastic adjustments in their social and economic structures, and achieve economic "take-off." Unfortunately, the same cannot be said of China itself during the last three decades. Although in recent years hopeful signs of change have appeared, whether or not China under the new leadership will be able to break away from the shackles of the bureaucratic state and achieve sustained modern economic growth remains to be seen.

NOTES

With the permission of the author and the editor, an earlier version of this paper was published in *Journal of Chinese Studies* 1 (June 1984): 221–33. The views expressed in this chapter are strictly the author's and do not necessarily reflect those of the Federal Reserve Bank of San Francisco.

1. Simon Kuznets, *Modern Economic Growth* (New Haven: Yale University Press, 1966), pp. 9–12.
2. *Encyclopedia Britannica* (1959), "Meiji Tenno."
3. Cited in Robert F. Dernberger, "The Role of the Foreigner in China's Economic Development, 1840–1949," in Dwight H. Perkins, *China's Modern Economy in Historical Perspective* (Stanford: Stanford University Press, 1975), p. 22.
4. Chi-ming Hou, *Foreign Investment and Economic Development in China, 1840–1937* (Cambridge: Harvard University Press, 1965), pp. 168–88.
5. Kang Chao, "The Growth of a Modern Cotton Textile Industry and the Competition with Handicrafts" in Perkins, *China's Modern Economy*, p. 201.
6. Dernberger, "The Role of the Foreigner," p. 35.
7. Dernberger errs in asserting that "in addition, a large share of the machinery and equipment imports was for the textile industry, and industry producing consumer goods, not materials for use in other industries." Dernberger, ibid. The alleged distinction between consumer-goods industry and capital-goods industry has little basis in economic theory.
8. Chao, "The Growth of a Modern Cotton Textile Industry."
9. Hou, *Foreign Investment in China*, pp. 24–25.
10. Ibid., pp. 42–43.
11. Ibid., pp. 25–26.
12. According to Hou, from 1864–1937, there were only six years, 1864 and 1872–76, when China did not have a trade deficit. Ibid., p. 206.
13. Max Weber, *The Protestant Ethic and the Spirit of Capitalism*, trans. from German by Talcott Parsons (London: Allen and Unwin, 1930).

14. Max Weber, *The Religion of China,* trans. from German by Hans H. Gerth (New York: The Free Press, 1968).

15. Ibid., p. 240.

16. Robert H. Bellah, *Takugawa Religion* (Boston: Beacon Press, 1970), cited in Wen-hui Tsai, *The Modernization of China: A Socio-Historical Interpretation* (Taipei: Institute of the Three Principles of the People, Academia Sinica, Monograph Series, no. 2, May 1982), p. 7.

17. Marion J. Levy, Jr., "Contrasting Factors in Modernization of Japan and China" in Simon Kuznets et al., eds., *Economic Growth: Brazil, India, Japan* (Durham: Duke University Press, 1955), cited in Tsai, *The Modernization of China,* pp. 9–10.

18. Mark Elvin, *The Pattern of the Chinese Past* (Stanford: Stanford University Press, 1973), cited in Victor D. Lippit, "The Development of Underdevelopment in China," *Modern China,* (July 1978), p. 255.

19. Theodore Schultz, *Transforming Traditional Agriculture* (New Haven: Yale University Press, 1964).

20. Lippit, "The Development of Underdevelopment in China," p. 253.

21. Jacques Gernet, *Daily Life in China on the Eve of the Mongol Invasion, 1250–1276* (Stanford: Stanford University Press, 1970), cited in Lippit, "The Development of Underdevelopment in China," p. 253.

22. Elvin, *The Pattern of the Chinese Past,* cited in Ramon Myers, "Society and Economy in Modern China: Some Historical Interpretations," *Studies in Modern History* (Taipei: Academia Sinica, Monograph Series, no. 11, July 1982), pp. 219–20.

23. Myers, ibid., pp. 210–11.

24. See Etienne Balazs, *Chinese Civilization and Bureaucracy (New Haven: Yale University Press, 1972); and Lippit, "The Development of Underdevelopment in China."*

25. Lippit, ibid., pp. 314–15.

26. Ray Huang, *1587, a Year of No Significance* (New Haven, 1981) p. 144; see also Ray Huang, *Taxation and Government Finance in Seventeenth Century Ming China* (London: Cambridge University Press, 1975).

27. Huang, *1587, a Year of No Significance,* p. 3.

28. Frederick E. Wakeman, Jr., "The Evolution of Local Control in Late Imperial China" in Wakeman, ed., *Conflict and Control in Late Imperial China* (Berkeley: University of California Press, 1975), cited in Lippit, "The Development of Underdevelopment in China," p. 317.

29. Huang, *1587, a Year of No Significance.*

30. Huang, ibid., p. 170 (italics added).

FOUR

Confucianism and Japanese Modernization:
A Study of Shibusawa Eiichi

Kuo-hui Tai

Introduction

As scholars in East Asia, Europe, and the United States are now reassessing the role of traditional Chinese culture and thought in the process of economic development, the issue of Confucianism and modernization has become once again an intriguing question to me. More than thirty years ago I first confronted the subject. In 1955, I was a graduate student at Tokyo University attending a class on Japanese economic history taught by Professor Tsuchiya Takao. An economist employing Marxist methodology in his studies, Tsuchiya was then discussing the life and career of a man who might be called the father of Japanese modern industries or the father of Japanese capitalism: Shibusawa Eiichi. As the editor of the collected works of Shibusawa, Tsuchiya introduced to his class a number of best sellers by the famed Japanese businessman, including *Seienhiyakuwa*. A compilation of Shibusawa's words and deeds, *Seienhiyakuwa* went to the eighth printing in 1912, the very first year it was published.

Tsuchiya then mentioned another, even more popular book by Shibusawa, *Rongo to Soroban*. First published in 1928, it is still widely read today, twice reprinted in 1985. Upon hearing the title of this book, which means *The Analects and Abacus*, I was astonished and puzzled. For *The Analects*, the most important book identified with Confucius, always was perceived by Confucianists as a body of moral norms diametrically opposed to the concept of profit-making, of which the abacus was seen in Far Eastern societies as both a symbol and an instrument. It was totally inconceivable to me how *The Analects* and *Abacus* could be linked together. That this book was highly recommended by a Marxist economic historian was all the more astonishing. Yet the book proved to be something refreshing and exciting, whetting my curiosity.

Prior to the Second World War, Tsuchiya was a major participant in an academic debate on the nature of Japanese capitalism. As a member of the *Rono-ha* (Agrarianism) School, he considered Japanese capitalism to possess a modern spirit of its own; he was opposed to the *Koza-ha* (Seminarian) School, which claimed Japanese capitalism to have a feudalistic character. After the war, Tsuchiya continued his decades-long study of Japanese economic history in the search for evidence to substantiate his theory.

Through subsequent contact with Professor Tsuchiya, I came to know his colleague, Professor Otsuka Hisao, who pioneered the so-called Otsukaism by attempting a synthesis of the thoughts of Karl Marx and Max Weber.[1] He accepted many Weberian concepts, but in examining Weber's criticism of Confucianism as inimical to modern capitalism, Professor Otsuka considered it necessary to reappraise both Weberism and Confucianism so as to establish a model of modernization uniquely appropriate to Asia.[2]

Professors Tsuchiya and Otsuka have changed my opinion on Confucianism: from rejecting it as irrelevant to economic development to accepting it as an important factor affecting modernization. But many questions remained. Why did Japan's modernization bear fruit after the Meiji Reform and why has China's industrialization lagged behind since? In what way did Japan instill Confucianism into Japanese business institutions and practices? Why have the Chinese often polarized their views on Confucianism— either complete rejection of it or total adulation?

To answer these questions obviously requires a thorough, critical examination of both Confucian thought and the process of modernization. Contemporary Chinese scholars such as Tu Wei-ming, Liu Shu-hsien, and Yü Ying-shih have addressed themselves to this task, and I shall attempt to make a limited contribution to this endeavor by finding out—through Shibusawa's studies—how Japan built Confucianism into that country's modern enterprises.

The Life of Shibusawa[3]

Shibusawa Eiichi was born in Saitama, Japan, in 1840 when the Opium War occurred in China. In that year, China—a nation long regarded by Japan as its largest, most powerful neighbor— was defeated by an island nation like Japan itself—England. The event shocked Japan, precipitating significant internal changes. At the same time, the social and economic conditions of a prototypical capitalism already existed in Japan.

The Shibusawa family was then operating what may be called an estate-based business composed of three components: farming, commerce, and finance. In farming, the family raised rice, wheat, and silk; in commerce, it manufactured and sold fabric dyes; in finance, it managed small local banks. The operations of this sort of agricultural-industrial-banking conglomerate deeply affected Shibusawa's life and thinking.

When Shibusawa was 14 years old (Japanese count themselves as one year old in the year of their birth), his father sent him away for the first time for a business trip to purchase raw materials for the dye industry. That was in 1853, the year in which Commodore Matthew Perry called on Japan. Under the intimidation of the guns of Perry's ships, Japan opened its door to the West. The following year Perry came again, concluding a treaty with Japan in Yokohama. The setting was thus cast for Shibusawa to emerge as one of Japan's most influential industrialists.

It should be noted that in the era of Japan's modern transformation, Shibusawa was well educated in traditional Chinese studies. First receiving the Han learning from his father, he enrolled at the age of seven in a private school to study the teachings of Confucius and Mencius.

In 1863, when he was 24, he participated in *Sonno Joi*—an organization seeking to restore political power from the ruling Tokugawa *shogun* (military governor of Japan) to the Japanese emperor. After a failed attempt to overthrow the Tokugawa Bakufu, he escaped to Kyoto, in which a residence of the Tokugawas was located (in the Hitotsubashi section). By an ironic twist of fate, the then head of the residence, Tokugawa Yoshinobu, on the recommendation of mutual friends, hired Shibusawa as manager of this household finance. Political failure led to an access to great power!

In the spring of 1866, Tokugawa Yoshinobu became the fifteenth *shogun*. This event placed Shibusawa in a dilemma. On the one hand, he was against the rule of *shogun* and was unwilling to be part of what he considered a soon-falling military government. On the other hand, he did not want to betray the friends who had recommended him to the Tokugawas. He tried in vain to persuade Yoshinobu not to become the *shogun*, but an event spared him of ensuing trouble. In 1867 he became an aide to Yoshinobu's brother, Akitake, who was then leading a mission to Paris to visit the World Fair. Shibusawa joined the mission and stepped into a capitalist Europe which, in his view, created "in less [than] one hundred years a new civilization exceeding all the human progress in the last several thousand years." This trip not only saved him from involvement in the political turmoil that precipitated the fall of the Tokugawa regime but also opened for him a great new vista—modern capitalism.

At the end of 1868, he came back from Europe to participate in the new government under the Meiji Reform. In the Ministry of Finance, he first helped institute reforms of the finance, banking, and monetary system. He became the head of the ministry's taxation division in 1872. Two years later, in 1874, because of policy differences within the government, he and Finance Minister Inoue Kaoru resigned from the government. In the same year, he joined the business world and created the first modern banking institution in Japan—Daiichi Kokuritsu Bank. (He had gained some experience with modern enterprise in 1872 when he helped the former *Shogun*, Yoshinobu, create Japan's first company under joint stock ownership, Soho Kaishio.)

Before he died in 1931, Shibusawa organized more than 500 business enterprises which dealt with banking, textiles, real estate, paper mills, shipbuilding, ocean freight, railroads, motor vehicles, beer, petrochemicals, hotels, and insurance. These covered practically every line of modern business. In addition, he participated in the establishment of Hitotsubashi University, an institution noted for turning out today's Japanese business elite.

Of his 92-year life, he devoted more than 70 years to business. Spanning the reigns of Tokugawa, Meiji, Taishō, and Hirohito, his career was in a sense the life history of modern Japanese economy. No wonder he became known as the father of Japanese capitalism. An analysis of his life will enable us to unlock some of the secrets of the Japanese economic miracle. Moreover, we will be able to see how he used *The Analects* to achieve success in business. He gave Confucianism a new meaning, making it a catalyst for the social and economic transformation in Japan.

Shibusawa's Works and Thoughts

Before we proceed to introduce Shibusawa's works, it is appropriate to reiterate three factors influencing his thinking. First, his life coincided with a great transformation of Japan. He witnessed the emergence of an economic and social foundation that supported capitalism. He saw his country forced to open its doors to the West but not subjected to colonial rule, as had happened to Japan's neighbor, China. And he participated fully in the Meiji Reform to bring capitalism to his nation. Second, his formal education was limited to that of a private school whose curriculum was centered around Confucianism. He never went to a modern school, nor studied abroad.

Third, his on-site observation of Europe whetted his appetite for European capitalism. Under the influence of these three factors, Shibusawa skillfully dovetailed Confucianism with modern business and integrated the essence of Eastern and Western civilization in order to advance Japanese industrialization.

Shibusawa devoted his whole life to this endeavor, first expressing his ideas about Confucianism in *Ama yo gatari* (a memoir) and the previously mentioned *Seienhiyakuwa*. Both were memoirs. Both remain popular in the Japanese business community even to this day. In these works, he discussed from the perspective of a business leader during the Meiji Reform his views on life, society, the nation, religion, youth, and enterprise. But it was in *The Analects and Abacus* and *Rango Kogi* (The Essence of the Analects) that he focused more narrowly on the relationship between Confucianism and modern enterprise.[4]

Like his other works, *The Analects and Abacus* is not an academic treatise but a collection of personal thoughts and speeches derived directly from his business experiences. Today, as we open the volume half a century after its first publication, we do not see a stale book but a work of fresh, lively, eloquent ideas—and full of inspiration. The book contains ten chapters, under the following headings: 1. Mottoes of life; 2. Goal setting and studies; 3. Common sense and customs; 4. Righteousness and prosperity; 5. Idealism and superstition; 6. Character and cultivation; 7. Abacus and power; 8. Enterprise and *bushido;* 9. Education and empathy; and 10. Success and failure and fate.

As can be seen from these topics, the book is as much concerned with philosophy and ethics as with profit-making. The central theme of the book, however, is to reconcile righteousness with profit. Shibusawa writes in the very beginning of his book:

> The origin of today's moral norms can be traced to the book that embodied Confucius's words and deeds as recorded by his disciples—the well-known *The Analects*. [On the surface,] this book has nothing to do with [profit-making as symbolized by the instrument] abacus. But I am fully convinced that abacus is wholly compatible with *The Analects*, whose true value can be realized through abacus. The relationship between *The Analects* and abacus is at once distant and close.... I believe that without a strong profit motivation, no improvement of the popular welfare is possible. Similarly, people seeking abstract theory will not be able to find truth. Today, our task is not only to curb the arbitrary power of government and the military forces but also to expand business. Without business expansion we can never achieve national prosperity. On the other hand, national prosperity will not last long if it is not based on the moral principles of benevolence and righteousness. Our urgent task today is to unite *The Analects* with abacus.[5]

Shibusawa thus charted a mission for the Japanese: to reinterpret Confucianism to meet the needs of the day. This stands in stark contrast with China, which has seen the emergence of a movement resisting Confucianism. In the Tokugawa and early Meiji times, the Japanese—like the Chinese—accepted the orthodox view of Confucianism, which belittled the social status of business.[6] But as soon as the Meiji government commenced its modernization program, the Japanese did not condemn Confucianism—as some Chinese did during the May Fourth Movement—but set out to make Confucianism serviceable to their new way of thinking. For that purpose, Shibusawa coined the term "shikon shosai," literally a union of *bushido* and commercial talent. *Bushido*—the moral code of the samurais—was the embodiment of the Japanese concept of Confucian ethics; commercial talent referred to modern managerial skill. Shibusawa observed:

> Sugawara Michizane has coined a very interesting term *Wakon kansai* [Japanese spirit, Chinese talent]. I

am advocating *shikon shosai* [scholarly spirit, commercial talent].... In order to gain social respect one must follow *bushido*, but if one goes into business by following *bushido* and possessing no commercial talent he will be certainly doomed to failure. To cultivate the scholarly spirit, one must not only read many books but also follow the moral precepts of *The Analects*. But then how does one develop the commercial talent? One can develop commercial talent by following *The Analects* too. For commercial undertaking without a moral basis borders on deceit, dilettantism; it is chicanery, sophistry, but not truly great commercial talent. A man who wishes to acquire true commercial talent must learn from *The Analects*.[7]

Looking at Shibusawa's career, one feels that Shibusawa himself exemplified *shikon shosai*. When he joined the Meiji government in the 1870s, the bureaucrats still adhered to a traditional interpretation of Confucianism, belittling business. With the Meiji Reform, the Japanese downgraded the samurais but did not elevate the status of business. Indeed, the reform initially brought about an uncertain future to Japan's emerging capitalism. Under the circumstances, Shibusawa thought it necessary to devote himself to the creation of a socially respected business class capable of rational management of large modern enterprises. It was at least partially for this reason he resigned from the government and began to pursue a business career. Thus, in *Shibusawa Eiichi den* (The Biography of Shibusawa Eiichi) Tsuchiya Takao observed,

[In 1871, as the head of the Commerce Division at the Ministry of Finance,] Shibusawa was in frequent contact with many businessmen in Tokyo and Osaka. The subservient attitude of businessmen was still a social custom not yet eliminated. They bowed their heads deep when facing government officials; they had neither learning nor influence; they had never thought about the need for business reform and business regulations. Japanese businessmen and the French businessmen Shibusawa had met in Europe lived in two entirely different worlds.

Under the circumstances, all that Shibusawa could do was to help the government formulate a new monetary law to stimulate business development. He considered Japanese businessmen of the day would never be able to make a contribution to industrialization. For this reason, he left the government and joined the business world so that he could devote himself to the cultivation and promotion of a new business class appropriate to industrial development.[8]

Thus, in promoting *The Analects* and abacus, Shibusawa hoped to reshape the Japanese businessman's personality. He wanted his new businessman to possess both a knowledge of economics and business ethics, so that he would feel equal to government officials.

Similarly, Chio Yukio of Tokyo Foreign Language University has commented: "At the risk of oversimplification, one can suggest that Shibusawa's thinking represented a critique of the feudalist thought under the *bakufu* and *han* system and an affirmation of the capitalist thinking in the Meiji period. In short, Shibusawa's thinking was the thinking of the Japanese capitalist class."[9] Chio also compared Shibusawa's and Max Weber's observations on Confucianism. He identified a number of Weber's reasons for considering Confucianism a hindrance to the rise of capitalism: Confucianism accepted without question traditional norms, authority, and social order; it rationalized the status quo; its objective was to perfect the character of the gentleman but not to improve the physical world; and it lacked an inner, voluntary transformative force to effect modernization. Confucianism did not possess the kind of critical spirit challenging the status quo that characterized the Protestant ethic. Thus, even though commerce and usury produced substantial capital in pre-modern China, the country lacked an inner driving force to sustain a revolutionary movement for the creation of a rational, modern capitalist system.

Chio then asked, if Weber's analysis was correct, "how then could the Confucian ethics as articulated by Shibusawa become the ethos of post-Meiji Japanese capitalism?" He gave two explanations.

First, Confucianism is a familistic moral code built on the axis of the superior-subordinate relationship of father and son. It commands individuals to engage in self-cultivation for the sake of accepting the authority of the superior. Thus, if Japan decided to accept the kind of Western European capitalist social order as a goal for the Japanese to "achieve or surpass," then the Confucian concept of self-cultivation would perform the same social function as did the Protestants' asceticism. Second, modern capitalism operates on the market-economy principle and determines the value of a product through competition. Shibusawa's idea of "union of righteousness and profit" was intended to use the Confucianist language to introduce the modern capitalist fair-exchange principle as new economic ethics. With this idea, Shibusawa would like to banish such unscrupulous business behaviors as bribery, abuse of power, speculation, and fraud. Of course, in a capitalist economy it is not possible to eliminate completely bribery, abuse of power, and speculation. However, the true source of wealth must be a competitive market that rationally determines the value of products. An unscrupulous grabbing of wealth can never be a fundamental principle for any rational economic system. Thus, "union of righteousness and profit" and *The Analects and Abacus* were the very concepts used by Shibusawa to formulate the new business ethics.[10]

Now let's return to the question of how Shibusawa united *The Analects* and abacus, how he brought his theory in line with the social and economic conditions of Meiji Japan. In the chapter on "Enterprise and *Bushido*." Shibusawa stated:

As the highest social norms of Japan, *bushido* had long been followed in the gentlemen's circles but was not applicable to those in the business world. In the past, merchants and artisans clearly misunderstood *bushido*, seeing righteousness, integrity, and magnanimity as incompatible with business transactions. They considered the *bushido* concept "bushi wa kuwanedo takayoji" [the samurai would rather starve than misbehave himself] as a bane to business. This may well be so under the circumstances of the time.

However, just as the samurais could not live without *bushido*, businessmen could not survive without a moral code of their own....

The notion that *bushido* and profit-making were incompatible was erroneous in the feudal times just as it is today. People now have seen the reason why benevolence and prosperity are not contradictory. Confucius said: "Riches and honors are what men desire. If they are not obtained in the right way, they should not be held. Poverty and lowliness are what people dislike. If they are brought to the people in the right way, they should not be avoided" [*The Analects*, Book IV, "Li Jen"]. This saying is consistent with the essential precepts of *bushido*—i.e., righteousness, integrity, and magnanimity. The Confucian idea that poverty and lowliness should never deter one from following the right way is quite similar to the *bushido* notion that the samurai should never run away from his enemy. Moreover, the Confucian idea that one cannot truly enjoy riches and honors if they are not obtained in the right way is exactly the same as the *bushido* exhortation that one should never take a penny in the wrong way. Of course, even the sage desires riches and honors and dislikes poverty and lowliness. However, the sage regards morality as of primary importance and the issue of wealth and poverty as of secondary importance. In the past, many businessmen practiced otherwise. They were mistaken.... *Bushido* and enterprise, I believe, must have and can have the same spirit.[11]

Shibusawa emphasized that the idea of uniting righteousness and profit was consistent with the original teaching of Confucius, but that many latter-day Confucian scholars mistakenly considered benevolence and wealth as contradictory.

In his preface to *The Works of Mencius*, the great Confucian scholar of Sung Dynasty, Chu Hsi, stated: "Obtaining business achievement through calculation is selfish; such an endeavor is a world apart from the way of the sages." This statement really belittles the idea of making profit through production.... Viewed in another way, this statement means that righteousness and morality are the exclusive characteristics of god-like sages, not at all applicable to businessmen. This cannot be the essence of the teachings of Confucius and Mencius.[12]

From Shibusawa's writings, one discovers that during the late Tokugawa Period and the Meiji Reform there were two transformations in the Confucian ideology. The first was to reinterpret the Confucianism-based *bushido* so as to make it a new national ethos to sustain the emerging Japanese capitalist system. Both the social and economic conditions within Japan and the international environment surrounding the country made this transformation possible.

The decision by Tokugawa Yoshinobu to restore political power to the Meiji emperor led the new government to abolish feudalism by replacing in 1871 the traditional *han* system with an administrative district system *(hai han chi ken)*. For the first time, Japan created a uniform political structure for the nation as a whole. The collapse of the *bukufu* and *han* feudal system, however, also can be attributed to the emergence of a nationwide market, rapid capital formation, the appearance of wage labor, the creation of communication networks, the spread of education, and the advancement of popular culture. All these conditions converged to form a "national power" that effectively resisted the pressure of Western imperialism and liberated Japan from the threat of colonialism.

Irobe Yoshiaki, former Chairman of Koyo Wa Bank and the Japanese business leader best known in post-World War II Japan for mastering Confucianism, has flatly stated:

> The moral code of traditional Japan—in both the Tokugawa and Meiji periods—did not come from Buddhism, nor from Christianity, but only from Confucianism. Japan's civic virtue as revealed in the "*Kyo iku chiyoku go*" ["Guides for Education"] clearly indicates the influence of Confucianism. The religious concept of divinity is non-existent in Confucianism, and since the Middle Ages, the Japanese sense of guilt had come about only as a reflection of Confucianism.... Confucianism became the foundation of Japanese social norms vitally affecting *bushido*. The schools in Edo

and Osaka and all the famous *han* schools in *daimyo* promoted the study of *The Analects*. Among the disciples of Confucianism were the young members of the samurai families who naturally had a respect for ancient Chinese moral precepts.[13]

As to the second transformation of Confucianism in Japan, one may discern it from Chio's writings:

Shibusawa's theory is designed to unite what had traditionally been considered opposite ends—morality and economics. To do this it is necessary to negate to a certain extent both of them; it would then be possible for a new, mutually adaptable content to appear. Shibusawa's conception of *The Analects* seeks in the contemporary times a transformation of the formalistic Confucianism as represented by the Chu Hsi School and a renaissance of the classical Confucianism. Shibusawa's thoughts about economic enterprise negated the idea that business was a purely profit-seeking proposition. He regarded commerce and industry as vital components of modern business.... He was not worshipping a dead Confucius, but was looking for a living Confucianism marching in the real world. Thus, the spirit of Confucius would be a spirit for objective inquiry that can bring about knowledge through a thorough study of the physical world.[14]

The Impact of Confucianism on Modern Chinese and Japanese History

Wakon Yousai (Japanese spirit, Western talent) was a Japanese slogan adopted during the Meiji Reform to promote Western learning. Some considered it to have derived from *Wakon Kansai* (Japanese spirit, Chinese talent), for pre-modern Japan had learned almost everything from China—from governmental system to culture and technology. Similarly, in its modern history, China had a comparable slogan—*Chung-hsüeh wei-t'i, Hsi-hsüeh wei yung* (applying Western technology within the structure of Chinese learning, or Chinese essence). On the surface, *Wakon Yousai* and *Chung-hsüeh wei-t'i, Hsi-hsüeh wei-yung* have similar connotations. In reality, they are very different, and their impact on the modern history of the two countries is quite opposite.

Chinese and Japanese Perceptions of Confucianism

Confucianism existed in China for more than two thousand years; its history in Japan was quite lengthy too. However, the social environments of China and Japan within which Confucianism functioned were vastly different, and this difference was made all the more prominent after the Meiji Reform.

The Analects can be considered an ethical code of semi-legalistic character; it can also be considered a prudent way to handle interpersonal relations. In the dynastic history of China, it seems, the people did not have a full trust of the government. For this reason, the rulers tended to use *The Analects* to maintain a loyalty-based political order. For the ordinary people, who could not gain access to power through the traditional civil service examination, they really had no sense of "loyalty" to the government. They tended to use the "filial piety" concept of Confucianism to maintain a clan-based, semi-religious order. The filial piety-based social order and the loyalty-based political order were not always mutually reinforcing as the rulers wished; on the contrary, they might at times contradict each other.

In my view, no matter how hard the governments in Chinese dynasties tried to use Confucianism as an instrument of governance, the people tended to ignore or dodge it. In their daily life, the people did not really emphasize Confucianism at the expense of Taoism—a thought system not favored by the rulers—but often mingled the two as a prudent guide to their life. On the other hand, there were always scholars in historical China who wanted to obtain power and wealth through Confucianism. To pursue their objectives, they sometimes distorted Confucianism, making it merely an instrument of governance. But in Japan, the people, especially since the Meiji Reform, have demonstrated strong loyalty to the imperial institution—so strong as to amaze foreigners; they have always displayed a trust in government.

The gentleman in China, as Confucius' *The Great Learning* has exhorted, should "cultivate himself, regulate his family, govern his state, and achieve peace in the world." However, the ordinary people could never realize these noble objectives; for them these exhortations became mere ritualistic slogans. In fact, they saw contradictions among them. But in Japan, because of the strong emphasis on the concept of loyalty, the people could accept the linkage between "personal cultivation and family regulation" and between "state governance and peaceful world." Post-Meiji Japan has accepted the notion of unification of personal and political objectives.

The filial piety concept in China was built along the father-son axis; the son's relationship with his father was predetermined and unchangeable. Under the circumstances, the social values upheld by the father's generation became absolute. The father could never do wrong; the son could never question the father's authority. Such an orientation restrained social innovation and constituted a barrier to progress. In Japan all individuals— regardless of their sex, family position, or official rank—always maintained an *inkyo* (retirement) system: the parental generation in *inkyo* passes the "key" or "authority" to the second generation. A system having been followed since the ancient time, *inkyo* allowed the assimilation of new ideas and new blood into the society.

Wakon Kansai *and* Wakon Yousai

Shibusawa advocated *The Analects* to emphasize righteous-ness; he advocated abacus to seek profit. Shibusawa's education was Confucianism-based Chinese learning; his career was im-mersed in Western-type business practices. Shibusawa's task, one can therefore suggest, involves a transformation of *Kankon* (Chinese spirit) into *Wakon* (Japanese spirit) and then a union of the latter with Western technology. Many Japanese who consider Shibusawa merely a representative of *Wakon Yousai* without noticing his contribution in the transformation of *Kankon* into *Wakon* miss a significant point.

Indeed, Sugawara Michizane (845–903) long ago proposed the concept of *Wakon Kansai* (Japanese spirit, Chinese talent). Only when Chinese learning lost its utility in modern times did the Japanese seek Western learning. This change occurred during the Meiji Period, when *Wakon Yousai* substituted for *Wakon Kansai* as the slogan of the day.[15] What deserves our attention is that the Japanese always insist on maintaining the Japanese spirit; they can revise, reinforce, or adapt it, but never are willing to abandon it completely in favor of total Westernization.

Shibusawa's effort to transform or reinterpret Confucianism has several manifestations.

First, in modern China many people tend to hold two extreme views of Confucianism. Some would like to see a total liquidation of Confucianism; others consider it a moral code good for all times. In a sense, both look at Confucianism as an instrument of governance, a means to rationalize the family-based bureaucratic system. What Shibusawa did was to step out of the sphere of politics, liberating Confucianism from its position as an instrument of governance and gave it a new, economic interpretation. He made *The Analects* the dialogue of the business class, the ethics of modern business.

Second, during Shibusawa's time, the mainstream Confucianism was dominated by the Chu Hsi School, which had rendered Confucianism into an ivory-tower learning for a small cluster of orthodox Confucian scholars. Shibusawa daringly challenged the orthodoxy, liberating *The Analects* from the constraints of the Chu Hsi School and giving it a new life. In other words, he removed Confucianism from its doctrinal, religious cast and returned it to its original form. The reinterpreted *Analects* became a practice-based learning; as such, it could apply to economics and become the guiding principle of modern business.

Third, Shibusawa used the Confucian notion of "deriving knowledge from studying the physical world" as a way of comprehending the meaning of life. Embracing the idea of "uniting knowledge with practice" as proposed by the great Confucian scholar Wang Yang-ming, Shibusawa launched *The Analects* on a path entirely different from the Neo-Confucianism of the Sung and Ming times, which Wang Yang-ming had challenged. In his *The Analects and Abacus*, Shibusawa attempted to use *The Analects* to interpret his personal experiences, his contacts with others, and his observations during his trip to the West. Relying on intuition as well as reasoning, he purged Confucianism of its conservative and formalistic features, creatively transforming it, improving it, and eventually reshaping it into the spirit of modern Japanese capitalism. In a sense, Shibusawa's writings can be considered his response to Max Weber's critique of Confucianism. Shibusawa used Wang Yang-ming's idea of "uniting knowledge with practice" to create *The Analects and Abacus*, and his reinterpreted Confucianism is different from the Confucianism as perceived by Weber. He has made a lively use of Confucianism, with which he bridged tradition and modernity.

Finally, a close reading of *The Analects and Abacus* would reveal that Shibusawa praised Confucianism but did not worship it blindly. He found that in its original content *The Analects* was very much concerned about interpersonal relations but not much about individuals themselves. He noticed that Confucian teachings touched more on the process of governance than on the position of the governed. Such teachings, in Shibusawa's view, deprived the masses of their sense of personal independence, making them subservient to the ruling class and tolerant of political authoritarianism. To remedy this shortcoming, Shibusawa devoted one section of his book *Seienhiyakuwa* (Section 72) to a discussion of the concept of self-governance.

Similarly, modern businessmen must possess, he believed, a self-reliant, self-sustaining spirit so that they can decisively, promptly, and effectively handle their business in a highly competitive environment. Here, Shibusawa raised a very important question—the autonomy of businessmen. When he resigned from the Ministry of Finance, he did so not only because of disputes within the Ministry but also because of his dissatisfaction with the subservient attitude of businessmen toward officials. He believed that if businessmen lacked a sense of independence, a will of their own, their business could not long endure and flourish. A nation could create economic institutions by imitation but could not develop a business spirit by import. The business spirit had to emanate from the nation's own cultural and social conditions. In Japan, the transformation of *Kankon* (Chinese spirit) into *Wakon* (Japanese spirit) and the acquisition of *Yousai* (Western learning) forged a powerful force pushing forward Japanese capitalism and modernization.

The Setback to Chinese Modernization Theory

In the late 19th century, when Japan used the *Wakon Yousai* slogan to launch its modernization movement, the Ch'ing China coined the *Chung-hsüeh wei-t'i, Hsi-hsüeh wei-yung* slogan (applying Western technology within the structure of Chinese learning). But the Chinese modernization movement soon suffered a great setback, the Chinese defeat in the Sino-Japanese War (1894–95). The "Chinese learning" of late Ch'ing, it must be emphasized, differs from the *Wakon* of early modern Japan. The "Chinese learning" was not a lively knowledge but a calcified Confucianism preserved for the sake of worshipping the dead Confucius. The Chinese reformers wanted to create a modernization theory by grafting Western learning onto an outmoded

Confucianism. Even such a listless theory was unacceptable to the conservative forces then entrenched in the court and in the provinces of China. These forces instituted token political reforms and made a half-hearted attempt at modernization; what they really wanted was to perpetuate the traditional political order and their power. The failure of the Ch'ing modernization movement led to the Hundred-Day Reform of 1898, whose intellectual leaders, K'ang Yu-wei and Liang Ch'i-ch'ao, suggested the Meiji Reform as a model for China.

However, the circumstances of late Ch'ing China and of late Tokugawa and early Meiji Japan were entirely different. The social and economic conditions in China were not conducive to transforming Confucian thought. Economic development was uneven in many parts of the country. But even where it was strong, the prerequisites for capitalism were lacking. Moreover, the economic backwardness of the country coupled with the centuries-old conservatism created a cleavage between the need for social and economic reform and the effort to preserve the political status quo. And fresh thoughts from abroad were incomprehensible to the ignorant Chinese population. These conditions were the quagmire stalling the Chinese modernization movement. Those in favor of reform and change could express their regret but little else.

The Opium War in the mid-19th century turned the ailing Manchu Dynasty into a terminal case, with the traditional social and political institutions suffering an irreversible decline. In the last-ditch effort to save the dynasty, Tseng Kuo-fan, Li Hung-chang, and Tso Tsung-t'ang defended the imperial institution by relying on modern weapons and economic assistance from the West to put down the spreading anti-government movements—the T'ai-p'ing Rebellion, the Nien Rebellion, the Moslem rebellion in China's Northwest, and the rebellion led by Tu Wen-hsiu in Yunnan. The suppressions by the Manchu government resulted in massive casualties among peasants and national minorities, eventually giving rise to the anti-monarchy, anti-feudalism movements in China. The dynasty was saved for a moment, but there was no genuine institutional reform nor development of human talents for modernization. Its fate was doomed.

The international environment of the late Ch'ing times was no more auspicious for modernization; indeed, Western imperialism was an outright obstruction. Foreign powers' excessive exploitation of China drained the country of the very resources it needed for successful modernization. The lack of progress led to a replacement of reform with revolution. The 1911 Revolution, the May Fourth Movement, and the Communist revolution of 1949 are all in a sense manifestations of China's repeated failures to find a peaceful process of modernization.

The abandonment of peaceful reform in favor of revolution only intensified Chinese radicalism, which was in no way interested in a transformation of Confucianism. Chinese radicals wanted to topple the Confucian School and reject Confucianism completely. On the other hand, there were forces defending Confucianism. The Kuomintang promoted Confucianism as a means to secure its power in the aftermath of the 1911 Revolution. Certain ultra-conservative scholars also formed the so-called "Chinese Orthodoxy" School to preserve traditional Chinese culture. Both the Kuomintang and the "Chinese Orthodoxy" School were dedicated to a textual examination not a reinterpretation of Confucianism.

The Chinese Communists have long opposed Confucianism; and their vehement attacks on it—from their base on the Chinese mainland—stand in stark contrast to the "New Confucianist School" that has developed in North America, Taiwan, and Hong Kong among scholars specializing in Chinese philosophy, history and thought. It is interesting to note that four of the chief representatives—Carsun Chang (founder of the Chinese Democratic Socialist Party), Mou Tsung-san, T'ang Chün-i, and Hsü Fu-kuan—were disciples of friends of Hsiung Shih-li (1885–1968) and Liang Sou-ming (1893–1988), two great Confucian scholars who stayed in China when the Communists took over.

The New Confucianists opposed the Chinese Communist anti-Rightist Campaign but they discerned in it certain problems of traditional Chinese culture. They issued a declaration on Chinese culture, urging others to revitalize Confucianism. The New Confucianism School differs from the Chinese Orthodoxy School; it does not advocate an unqualified preservation of traditional Chinese learning, as the latter school did, but tries to identify through a study of Chinese philosophy and history certain universally applicable concepts, an ethic of new Confucianism.

Now a second generation of New Confucianism scholars has emerged—represented by Harvard's Tu Wei-ming and Princeton's Yü Ying-shih. They lectured in China, Taiwan, Hong Kong, Singapore, and South Korea, attempting to reassess the value of

Chinese culture and to reinterpret Confucianism. It is noteworthy that both the first and second generation New Confucianists have specialized in Chinese thought and history; we are still waiting for an early appearance of scholars who analyze Confucianism from a perspective of sociology, economics, or social and economic history.

Conclusion

Having introduced Shibusawa's thinking, and having compared the different fate of Confucianism in modern Japan and China, I would conclude with two points of interest.

The first relates to the issue of economic growth in the so-called "Confucian cultural area." The economic achievements of Japan, South Korea, Taiwan, Hong Kong, and Singapore in the last twenty years make it necessary to revise Max Weber's theory. Many Western scholars have raised the question, as Nakajima Mineo has noted, whether "there is a [new] model of economic development in the Confucian cultural area."[16] Those who answer the question affirmatively, such as the new Confucianists, attempt to explain the economic performance of East Asia from structural and cultural perspectives.

Structurally, they believe that East Asia differs from the West in the area of political institutions. The governments in East Asia have established a rationalized bureaucracy dedicated to the promotion of industry and commerce. These governments have been engaged in a prudent administrative engineering. Culturally, the new Confucianists look upon East Asian countries as having embarked on the path of "Confucian capitalism"—a third phase of Confucianism, following the Confucianism of the Han Dynasty and the Sung/Ming dynasties. As such, it is a creative response or challenge to Western culture.

These explanations of the economic success of East Asia seem to be a rather simplistic *post facto* rationalization. The internal and external conditions surrounding economic development have been and remain vastly different. The five countries can be divided into three categories: (1) Japan, (2) Taiwan and South Korea, and (3) Hong Kong and Singapore. Japan is the only completely modernized country in East Asia—far more industrialized than any of the rest. Taiwan and South Korea obtained the pre-conditions for capitalism during the Japanese rule prior to the end of the Second World War; both countries subsequently have been under the influence of the United States, separating themselves from mainland China and North Korea, respectively. Hong Kong and Singapore are city states without any substantive agriculture; they derive their income from commerce, industry, and tourism. Hong Kong cannot survive without the market of the Chinese mainland; nor can Singapore without the market of Malaysia and Indonesia.

With such diversity in the "Five Dragons," it is important to carefully delimit the role of Confucianism in economic development. What Confucianism needs is to adapt itself to changing historical circumstances. In addition, in the study of Confucianism, current research should not be confined to the area of philosophy and history but should relate Confucianism to business, thereby creating a business ethic that can truly merge Confucianism with modern management.

This relates to a second point of interest. Shibusawa's thought really represents a balance between righteousness and profit. Though devoting his whole life to capitalism, Shibusawa discovered certain problems in modern capitalism. These include rising materialism among the general populace and seeking profit by the capitalists at the expense of social responsibility. Facing these, Shibusawa thought it necessary to use Confucianism to reshape society. In advocating the idea of "moralized profit-making," he sought a union of business development and social responsibility. Successful businesses, he believed, must assume responsibility for improving social welfare, education, and the environment. A stable society, harmonious labor relations, healthy social environment, and widespread education—these are conditions leading to a healthier and more prosperous economic development. Many leftists in Japan might criticize Shibusawa for having served the interests of the bourgeoisie, being himself a conservative business tycoon. But for a man coming out of the feudalistic Tokugawa reign, Shibusawa's accomplishment is extraordinary.

At present, while many East Asian countries are under the sway of commercialism and materialism, it is sobering to study Shibusawa's *The Analects and Abacus*. By embracing the moralism of Confucianism and the best of Western technology, these countries can achieve further economic successes without suffering from the social ills of Western capitalism.

NOTES

An earlier, abridged version of this paper was read before "The Conference on Confucianism and Modernization," August 17–19, 1986, Taipei, Taiwan. It also appeared as "*Jukyo Bunka Ken Ron No Ichi Kou Satsu—'Wakon Yousai' to 'Chutai Saiyo' no Wakareme*" [An Inquiry into the Theory of "The Confucian Cultural Area"—The Difference between "Japanese Spirit, Western Learning," and "Applying Western Technology within The Structure of Chinese Learning"], *Sei Kai* (December 1986) (published by Iwanami Shinsio), pp. 136–49.

1. Otsuka Hisao, *Otsuka Hisao saku shu zen ju san kan* [The 13-Volume Collected Works of Otsuka Hisao] (Tokyo: Iwanami Shinsio, 1969–1986).

2. See Otsuka Hisao, "Hikaku keizai shi no sho mondai" [Problems on the Comparative Economic History] in ibid., vol. 11.

3. For writings on the life of Shibusawa, see his *Ama yo gatari* [Conversations on Rainy Nights] (Tokyo: Iwanami Bunko, 1984); Takao Tsuchiya, *Shibusawa Eiichi den* [The Biography of Shibusawa Eiichi], 1st ed. (Tokyo: Kaizoshia, 1931); latest ed. (Tokyo: Toyo Shokan, 1955); Koda Rohan, *Shibusawa Eiichi den* [The Biography of Shibusawa Eiichi], 5th printing (Tokyo: Iwanami Shinsio, 1986).

4. The latest edition of *The Analects and Abacus* was published by Kokushio Kankokai in 1985. *Rango kogi* was incorporated into *Kou Dan Shia Gakujutsu Bunko* [Kuo Dan Shia Encyclopaedia], published by Kou Dan Shia in 1975.

5. *The Analects and Abacus*, pp. 1–2.

6. Irobe Yoshiaki, "Rango to dento Nihon" [The Analects and Traditional Japan] in *Yomigaeru Rongo* [The Analects Resurrected] (Tokyo: Tokuma Shoten, 1981).

7. *The Analects and Abacus*, pp. 2–3.

8. Tsuchiya, *Shibusawa Eiichi den*, pp. 188–89.

9. Chio Yukio, *Meicho—sono hito to ji dai—Seienhiyakuwa* [The Author and Times of a Celebrated Work—Seienhiyakuwa] *Economisuto* [The Economist] (published by the newspaper Mainichi), July 6, 1965, pp. 76–77.

10. Chio Yukio, Commentary in *Ama yo gatari*, p. 233.

11. Shibusawa, *Shibusawa Eiichi zen shu* [The Complete Works of Shibusawa Eiichi], vol. 1 (Tokyo: Heibon Shia, 1930), pp. 222–24.

12. *The Analects and Abacus*, pp. 102–05.

13. Irobe, "Rongo to dento Nihon."

14. Chio, *Meicho—sono hito to ji dai—Seienhiyakuwa*, p. 77.

15. Cf. Kato Jinbei, *Nihon kyoiku shiso shi kenkyu—Wakon Yousai setsu* [An inquiry into the Evolution of Japanese Educational Principles—Wakon Yousai] (Tokyo: Bai Fu Kan, 1926), pp. 316–46.

16. Cf. Nakajima Mineo, *Nijiu ichi seki wa Nihon, Taiwan, Kankoku da* [The 21st Century Belongs to Japan, Taiwan, and South Korea] (Tokyo: Dai Ichi Kikaku Shu Tsu Pan, 1986).

FIVE

The Divergent Economic Development of China and Japan

Edward F. Hartfield

Introduction

Five East Asian countries have attracted the attention of the world because of their strong and, in some cases, spectacular economic performance. These countries—Japan, Taiwan, Singapore, Hong Kong, and South Korea—are unique in the sense that they are among the very few non-Western nations having successfully industrialized and that they share a common, Confucian heritage. Some analysts have suggested that Confucian culture is largely responsible for the economic success of these countries.[1]

Yet this suggestion has raised a thorny question. If Confucianism is a positive influence on economic modernization, then we should expect a strong development experience in China—the source of Confucian culture. This was clearly not the case in modern China. And when we see the vastly different development experiences of China and Japan, we are intrigued by the question of why a common cultural heritage functioned so differently in the modernization of the two countries.[2] Japan, a country with 120 million people crowded on small islands with very few natural resources, has become one of the world's great economic powers. China, with over one billion people residing in the world's third largest national territory, struggles to feed her population and features a per capita income of about $300 per year in 1986, equalling the poverty level of Zambia.[3]

Historically, China and Japan possessed many things in common; it was only in the last hundred years that the two countries have moved in different directions. Just as modern Japan has assiduously imported technology and ideas from the West, Japan in the past borrowed almost wholesale her language, literature, arts, philosophy, and religion from China. Moreover, both countries enjoyed a comparatively isolated existence until the middle of the 19th century, when Western nations decided to impose "enlightenment" upon them. Western nations arrived in powerful ships, declared their right to trade whenever they wanted—and on their terms—and supported their demands with cannons and gunpowder.

The advent of the West awakened China and Japan to the need for modernization; yet the two countries had very different responses. This chapter will attempt to analyze the factors affecting the economic performance of the two countries in modern times. In doing so, this chapter will utilize a *multiple-factor, interdisciplinary approach.* The analytical framework will consist of four sets of factors: *internal factors, external factors, the role of government, and social/ cultural factors.*

The Literature

In general, the literature comparing the modernization experiences of China and Japan falls into three categories: theories that emphasize social/ cultural explanations; theories that emphasize economic variables, particularly the concept of imperialism; and theories that emphasize various, discrete factors.

A leading proponent of the social/ cultural explanations is Marion J. Levy, Jr. In his work entitled "Contrasting Factors in the Modernization of China and Japan," Levy attributes the varying economic performance of the two countries to the differences in the social structures of the two countries.[4] He suggests that in Japan the process of modernization has not diluted, but has been facilitated by, the traditional system of social control. In China, by way of contrast, the tumultuous changes the country experienced in modern times have decimated the traditional system of social control and have made it impossible to create a new mechanism for social coordination. China floundered on the path of modernization.

Theorists using economic variables to explain the case of China and Japan may best be exemplified by Frances Moulder. In her book *Japan, China, and the Modern World Economy,* Moulder adopts the premise that Japan was able to function independently within the world economy, while China could not maintain her economic autonomy but was subject to the oppressive effects of imperialism.[5] Moulder analyzes how China and Japan interacted with the Western world in terms of four variables: trade, investment, political incorporation, and missionary penetration.

In the area of trade and investment, Moulder notes that the Western nations were involved to a much greater extent in China than in Japan. The West exchanged Western manufactures and Indian opium for Chinese primary products; the West controlled major investments in China, including shipping, manufacturing, mining, railroads, and financial institutions. But the West made only limited investments in Japan and conducted a much smaller volume of trade. Consequently, Japan enjoyed a greater freedom and a greater capacity for shaping her own economic development strategy.

The political presence of the West contributed, Moulder suggests, to the weakening and ultimately the decline of China's imperial bureaucracy, whereas in Japan the advent of the West ushered in Western technology without Western subjugation. Finally, with respect to missionary penetration, Moulder observes that China's exposure to Christianity, which had been greater and longer than Japan's, may be a factor reducing Chinese receptivity to Western ideas.

Another proponent of the economic interpretation of Japan's modernization—and by implication, China's underdevelopment— is William Lockwood. His study of the economic growth of Japan from 1868 to 1938 carefully documents the key economic variables affecting that country's incipient industrialization program. Lockwood also addresses the applicability of the Japanese experience to the developing nations of Asia.[6]

Proponents of a *multiple-factor* explanation of the economic development of China and Japan identify forces that often are unrelated. Illustrative of scholars of this approach are Edwin O. Reischauer, John K. Fairbank, and Albert Craig. In their work *East Asia, The Modern Transformation,* they attribute the economic difference of the two countries to the degree of willingness to borrow and learn from abroad, the societal organization, pragmaticism versus doctrinairism, the military orientation of Tokugawa society versus the scholar/ gentry mindset of Manchu China, the size of the countries and the ease of change, internal economic factors, and the impact of feudalism on modernization.[7]

Another "multiple-factor theorist," Norman Jacobs, believed Japan's economic development could be attributed to the traditional institutions of exchange and property, kinship and descent, religion, and "integrative stability."[8] Huan-chang Chen attributes China's difficulty with modernization to her ethics, philosophy, educational system, social patterns, politics, economic heritage, and isolationism.[9]

Albert Feuerwerker has compiled two studies on the Chinese economy covering 1870–1911 and 1912–1949. After thoroughly examining the available data on the Chinese economy—agriculture, handicrafts, transportation, foreign trade, and investment—he concludes that it is difficult to isolate the economic variables from the myriad forces which besieged China. "The Chinese economy in the years covered by this essay, at least," he points out in his study on the latter period, "did not occupy center stage in the unfolding of the drama of Chinese history." This was so because of the

> ideological and political disequilibrium which was the most profound consequence of the impact of the West, and which for decades obstructed the emergence of a new political integration capable of replacing the Confucian imperial pattern of the past and taking advantage of the possibilities of economic development inherent in modern industrial technology.[10]

Internal Factors

It is useful to review briefly the historical setting of China and Japan in the middle of the 19th century, just before the two countries began their industrialization effort. Serious cracks began to appear in the veneer of the Chinese political system in the mid-19th century. The Chinese defeat at the hands of the British in the Opium Wars of 1839–1842 commenced a 60-year period in which China was continuously involved in wars with foreign nations—and always lost. Her defeats resulted not only in reparations to foreign countries of over 750 million taels of silver but also a loss of control of her customs, postal system, banks, and telegraph/ telegram services, along with much of her mining and railroad industries.

But Japan's initial exposure to the West could be described as comparatively tame. "No wars were fought, no smuggling trade developed, no territory was forfeited. Not a single man was killed on either side during Perry's expedition to Japan, and the commercial treaties were negotiated amicably around a table."[11] Subsequent contact between Japan and the West prompted Japan to initiate modernization without losing her autonomy and become an imperialist power herself.

With the historical context in mind, we can begin to examine several *internal factors* which hindered economic development in China: the lack of unity, the lack of financial resources, and the scarcity of managerial talent in public service. Of course, these factors would have adversely affected China's economic development even if Western imperialism had not occurred. Conversely, a set of contrasting internal factors in Japan greatly facilitated the development of that country.

The lack of unity presented a substantial problem for the Chinese. In the latter half of the 19th century, rebellions posed a serious threat to the Ch'ing government; in the early 20th century, warlords controlled much of the country. Even when the Kuomintang came to power in 1928, it only exercised full control over four provinces. Kiangsu Chekiang, Anhwei, and Kiangsi. The enormous size of the nation and the regional diversity, with its accompanying provincialism, further exacerbated the situation. As Reischauer, Fairbank, and Craig have observed, even the Chinese culture in general was unconducive to national unity: "The Chinese commitment to their traditional way of life, their 'culturalism,' served less well than Japanese feudal loyalty (even in the less centralized Tokugawa state) to produce the unity necessary for a modern nation."[12]

The lack of unity would later manifest itself in the deep division between the Kuomintang and the Chinese Communist Party, which seems to continue to plague China in the remainder of the 20th century. The struggle for power by the two parties in the 1930s and 1940s not only caused China to neglect economic development but also led to a loss of precious economic resources in the ensuing warfare.

The lack of financial resources stemmed at least from two directions. First, rebellions dissipated economic resources; warlords wasted much of the local tax revenue they controlled on their personal and military pursuits. Then, Western and Japanese imperialism robbed China of substantial income from her mining, manufacturing, and railroad industries; from postal and communication services; and from customs duties.

The scarcity of managerial talent in public service reflected the fact that traditional Chinese civil servants—members of the scholar/ gentry class—were trained more in Chinese classics than in modern economics. In the latter half of the 19th century when China began its modernization effort, the bureaucracy remained the haven of the tradition-bound scholar-officials; little new administrative talent was recruited to deal with the issues and problems with which a modern, rational, and economically knowledgeable government had to cope. An illustration of that problem can be seen in the formulation of a modern legal code. China had long sought to free herself from the unequal treaties the West had imposed; one of the prerequisites for the modification or removal of these treaties was for China to develop a system of law governing the relations of her citizens and foreigners.[13] Yet China was woefully incapable of handling such a task, despite the great importance China attached to the abolition of the unequal treaties.

In contrast, Japan's internal situation when she commenced her industrialization program was decisively different. While China faced continuous internal disunity, Japan notably maintained her national cohesion in the face of the Western threat. As Reischauer, Fairbank, and Craig have observed,

> Despite the mutual hostility between Japanese political units, no *han* and few, if any, individual Japanese ever thought of making common cause with the foreigners against the rest of Japan. Inter-*han* rivalries dominated the domestic politics...and were to remain important for the next half-century, but the national interest took precedence over *han* loyalties or personal interests. Having the key ingredient of a nationalist sentiment, the Japanese were well on their way to becoming a modern nation-state.[14]

Here, Japan's relatively small size and compactness facilitated a sense of unity, as did the homogeneity and cohesiveness of Japanese society.

Lack of revenue did not pose a great problem for the Japanese, largely because they retained control of their industries and tariff-producing customs system. The relative peace and stability during the Tokugawa Period paved the way for a substantial growth in agriculture, industry, and trade. With economic growth, there rose gradually an entrepreneurial class, and the traditional disdain of the ruling class for commerce insulated business from government control. All these conditions created an environment conducive to investment and savings.

Similarly, the Japanese did not experience *a scarcity of managerial talent and expertise.* Rather, both the *samurai* class, which amounted to five times the proportional equivalent of the scholar/gentry class in China, and the merchant class constituted a significant pool of talent and experience from which the Meiji Government could draw to manage the massive and complex industrialization program.[15] From this context we can see the beginning of a very close working relationship between government and business—a phenomenon that has remained to this day a key element in the Japanese pattern of growth.

External Factors

External factors believed to have a significant impact on the speed and direction of Chinese and Japanese economic growth may include the Sino-Japanese War of 1895, Western imperialism, and the availability of foreign economic assistance.

The significance of China's defeat by her cultural protégé in the Sino-Japanese War cannot be overstated. The war brought to China not only a territorial loss of both Korea and Taiwan but also a severe damage to China's self-confidence and morale. The "master" had been defeated by the "student"—a crushing and humiliating experience. Moreover, Japan's victory revealed the rising importance of Western technology and the declining relevance of Chinese culture to the process of modernization. And the defeat distracted China from the essential task of modernization. If Chinese culture could not stand up to Western science and technology, what was to become of China? What would be the guide for China's future?

The role of imperialism obviously had negative results for China. As mentioned earlier, imperialist nations dealt China humiliating military defeats and robbed her of scarce capital resources at a time when she needed them most. Western nations and Japan were intent upon colonizing China (made evident in the Paris Peace Conference in 1919 over the Shantung question).

These developments generated so much Chinese hostility toward Western nations that they made it difficult for China to assimilate the best of Western cultural elements.

Some analysts have seen the negative impact of the West in a different light. They have argued that while China's net capital losses to the West were not as large as was commonly believed, China's continuous dependence on foreign loans proved to be a disincentive for China to deal effectively with her own financial problems.[16] Some Western observers believed that China was never seriously engaged in a careful self-scrutiny of her resources and liabilities so as to formulate a national strategy for economic development; nor did she impose on herself a strong discipline for the implementation of any development strategy she did adopt. Without an overall sound economic policy or effective implementation of any specific economic program, China faltered on the road to modernization.[17]

Just as the Sino-Japanese War damaged China's confidence severely, it provided a great boost for Japan. What Japan learned from this war was that Western technology was powerful. The validity of a national policy in favor of Westernization—a policy first adopted at the beginning of the Meiji Reform of 1868—was now confirmed by the victory over China in 1895. An indication of the degree of confidence that the victory instilled in Japan is her assault and conquest ten years later of another great empire, Russia. By then Japan had become an imperialist nation herself.

Unlike China, Japan did not suffer any substantial amount of capital loss to the West. On the other hand, she systematically absorbed Western technology before the Second World War and became a recipient of Western economic assistance after the war. Indeed, the post-war Japanese economic miracle, many observers have agreed, is largely attributable to external factors: American economic assistance and military spendings during the Korean and Vietnam Wars and a world market that was until recently willing to take in Japanese exports and ignore Japanese restrictions on imports.

Role of Government

The next factor deserving our attention is *the role of government* in modernization. This subject is fascinating because in pre-industrialization China and Japan the roles were exactly opposite and they were completely reversed later when both nations embarked on modernization.

Following a long tradition, the Ch'ing government played a very active role in the Chinese economy. In pre-modern China, as Norman Jacobs has pointed out, the emperor's obligation to provide for the welfare of his people entitled him to intervene in economic transactions.[18] The government constructed and managed many public projects including roads, water transport, irrigation, flood control, and reclamation.[19] Other government economic activities included subsidies to agricultural production, distribution of farm products, and maintenance of a nationwide granary system.[20]

The government also was a manufacturer of many products it consumed. As Charles O. Hucker observes, in the Ming Dynasty "Peking abounded with armories, textile factories, metalwork shops, leatherwork shops, saddlery shops, paint shops, apparel factories, wineries, and the like...."[21] The Ch'ing government simply carried on the tradition of producing much of what it needed. Furthermore, the government supervised or managed a portion of the country's porcelain industry and operated large-scale weaving and dyeing operations in various cities. Essential commodities such as salt, iron, wine, silk, matches, tea, as well as mining and finance were strictly regulated by the Ch'ing government.[22]

One generally would expect that with these extensive economic activities, the Ch'ing government would play an active role in the process of industrialization. But such was not the case. To begin with, by the late 19th century, when China had come to a full realization of the need for modernization, the governmental machinery was already in substantial decline. Graft and corruption had spread throughout the imperial bureaucracy, rendering it largely ineffective. Moreover, the mandarin bureaucrats possessed neither the training nor the disposition to deal with the kind of economic issues with which they were confronted, even if the corruption problem had been less severe.

Ironically, in the opinion of some, the extensive governmental involvement in the Ch'ing economy may have adversely affected China's long-term economic development, for an economically active government may have suppressed the need for an entrepreneurial class, which was crucial to the success of China's industrialization effort. If the government managed to provide so many goods and services, there was that much less incentive for private individuals to do the same. In the opinion of Huan-chang Chen, the Chinese government, in a sense, adopted socialist policies too soon and interfered with commerce and manufacturing too much to permit the emergence of an entrepreneurial spirit.[23]

In contrast to an economically active Ch'ing government in pre-industrialized China, the Tokugawa regime in pre-modern Japan played a limited role in the economy. Their intervention was primarily regulatory in nature, involving little direct management of public projects or the productive process.[24] Indeed, in exercising its regulatory function, the Tokugawa government largely intended to preserve agriculture's dominant position in the economy. As a Japanese economic historian has observed: "The central authorities in Edo [Tokyo] sought to protect agriculture against the inroads of commerce and industry by trying to regulate the location of industry. Their primary aim was to confine industrial enterprise and to prevent the movement of industry to the countryside."[25] Robert T. Holt and John E. Turner also have observed that most of the Tokugawa government's attempts at regulation failed miserably. Enforcement of the various policies was irregular and inconsistent.

Ironically, the disdain of the Tokugawa regime for commercial activity, combined with the rigidity of the feudal system, induced some members of the less privileged classes—townspeople and peasants—to seek social status through business activity, leading to the emergence of a viable and talented merchant class. By the end of the Tokugawa Period, the merchants had become so successful that they had gained direct access to political power, as many members of the ruling class were in great debt to them. When the Meiji government came to power, it assumed leadership for the purpose of managing the modernization process. It created a comprehensive industrial infrastructure; it provided managerial talent and industrial manpower through systematic recruitment and training; and it developed basic manufactures.[26]

While proceeding full speed to absorb Western technology, the Meiji reformers deliberately retained traditional values to promote modernization. Thus Joseph Saniel observes:

> Indeed, the Meiji social engineers manipulated the concept of the emperor system to effect a strong central government in Japan with powers symbolically concentrated in the emperor. The transfer of allegiance from the feudal lord to the nation-state, usually requir-

ing time, was facilitated by substituting for the abstract idea of nation-state, the concrete idea of the emperor as the father of the nation. Within a society undergoing revolutionary changes, as Japan was during the Meiji Period, the father image of a divine emperor also provided the people with an unchanging fixed source of authority which aided the centralization of political control.[27]

The centrality of the economic role of the government, initiated by the Meiji reformers, remains a distinctive feature of the Japanese economy today, and the close, cooperative relationship between the government and the private sector is a vital force bringing forth the Japanese economic miracle.

Social/Cultural Factors

Social/cultural factors comprise the final group of factors in this analysis. Perhaps it is useful to begin with a discussion of the social structure of the two countries. Marion J. Levy Jr. maintains that one of the critical distinctions between the 19th-century Chinese and Japanese societies is that China did not have a feudal society. In Levy's opinion, a closed class system—that is, a system not permitting inter-class social mobility—is a primary distinction of feudalism. In China, people of peasant origin could and in fact did join the ruling class by passing the civil service examination.[28] In that sense, China's social structure was flexible.

In contrast, a Japanese would retain the social status into which he was born. Aspiring peasants and townspeople had no hope of becoming members of the ruling class; they could only transfer to a class of comparable social status, people in commerce. Toward the end of the Tokugawa Period, the merchant class flourished; through commercial and money-lending activities, Japanese businessmen carved out a useful niche for themselves in society; eventually they grew to wield a substantial amount of influence over the *samurai.* Some lower-ranking *samurai,* unable to support themselves on the low stipend they received from their *daimyo* (fief), left the *samurai* class altogether to join the new entrepreneurs, sometimes selling their rank and status to the merchants.

In China, however, traditional hostility toward merchants was so ingrained that an elevation of the social status of business never took place. Some merchants considered commerce only a temporary occupation, and successful businessmen often sought to purchase land in order to become members of the gentry. Ideally, their sons were expected to enter the imperial bureaucracy, not to follow their fathers into the family business. Hence, no substantial entrepreneurial class emerged; instead, a veritable flight of talent and capital from the business professions persisted.[29]

Similarly, the traditional family systems of China and Japan have had a different impact on economic development. Frances L.K. Hsu has advanced the theory that Japan's primogeniture rule affected the evolution of Japanese business organizations. Since the eldest son received everything, other siblings often had to look outside the family for their employment and livelihood. If they engaged in business, they would create or join business organizations that were structured like family.[30] Joseph Saniel concurs, noting that working outside the family for wages in Tokugawa times was a favorable condition for the evolution of a social structure appropriate to industrialization in the Meiji Period.[31] Moreover, if a Japanese family did not have a male heir, it would adopt a daughter's husband or—when it did not have a female offspring—someone totally unrelated to the family. This development existed in both peasant households and in the great commercial houses such as Mitsui and Mitsubishi. In short, the flexibility of the Japanese family system enabled the country to create family-like social organizations useful to large-scale economic operations.

The primogeniture rule did not exist in the Chinese family system. The eldest son might receive a larger share of the inheritance, but other siblings also received some portions. China was not as successful as Japan in transforming the family model into an effective, rational, decision-making organization. Most businesses remained family owned and small in scale. In the opinion of Marion Levy, Jr., Chinese business organizations were affected by sentimental factors, particularistic in structure, and diffuse in functions; whereas Japanese business organizations were characterized by "highly rational universalistic, and functionally specific relationships."[32] Saniel shares this opinion:

> The [Japanese] family system was opened—in the sense of being made more universal, by such specific

family mechanisms as adoption of a talented outsider into the family system, a step towards the universalistic relations in modern bureaucracies and industries. The Japanese family system also lacked the rigid familial boundaries of the Chinese family system, a precondition for modernization. Yet, it maintained a strong, particularistic type of social control over non-conforming behaviour.[33]

Of course, both Japanese and Chinese family systems were shaped by the same Confucian values, and in terms of their operational characteristics, the family system and non-family social organizations of both countries were more alike to each other than they were to those of Western countries. Japanese anthropologist Chie Nakane has pointed out that in Western society group polarization often occurs in such organizations as unions, student groups, youth movements, men's clubs, and so on. Western groups set one against another: students against teachers, youth against parents, employees against employers, whereas in Japanese society group consensus is stressed. Sharing this view, Herman Kahn argues that in a Confucian society cooperation among different groups is facilitated by the fact that they are all based on the family model.

> Smoothly fitting, harmonious human relations in an organization are greatly encouraged in most neo-Confucian societies. This is partly because of a sense of complementarity of relations that is much stronger in Confucian than in Western societies.... There is emphasis on fairness and equity, but it is fairness and equity in the institutional context, not for the individual as an individual. Synergism—complementarity and cooperation among parts of a whole—is emphasized, not equality and interchangeability. The major identification is with one's role in the organization or other institutional structure, whether it be the family, the business firm, or a bureau in the government. Since the crucial issues in a modern society increasingly revolve around these equity issues and on making organizations work well, the neo-Confucian cultures have great advantages. As opposed to the earlier Protestant ethic, the modern Confucian ethic is superbly

designed to create and foster loyalty, dedication, responsibility, and commitment and to intensify identification with the organization and one's role in the organization. All this makes the economy and society operate much more smoothly than one whose principles of identification and association tend to lead to egalitarianism, to disunity, to confrontation, and to excessive compensation or repression.[34]

Writing in the early 20th century, Huan Chang Chen made an observation quite parallel to Kahn's: "[Chinese] trade guilds are different from American trusts. Although the guilds are organizations for the private interests of their members, they are not so selfish or individualistic as the trusts, and they also have social functions like clubs. The Chinese trade unions are about the same as those in America, but they do not interfere with the liberty of others. Therefore, although the guilds and unions have existed for many centuries, public sentiment is not opposed to them."[35]

The element of *social control* looms large in the overall scheme of development. Japan has been able to keep its traditional values intact. It has used devotion to family and emperor as a mechanism to maintain social control in the midst of dramatic and sometimes confusing social change.[36] In comparison, China had seen her traditional values questioned, her social institutions challenged, her imperial bureaucracy mired in decay and corruption—at the very time when the country needed an effective way to cope with traumatic upheavals.

The Chinese family, which traditionally had served as a cohesive force, gradually weakened as a means of social control as the country entered the 20th century. Wars and incipient industrialization were the centrifugal force pulling the individuals away from the family/ clan matrix. Rurally underemployed and underpaid peasant farmers now swarmed into cities attempting to find alternative sources of employment. Sons were no longer dependent upon fathers, women were somewhat freed from their usual dependent roles. While the basic economic unit was still the family, an "individualism by default" occurred in China.[37]

The traditional Chinese social control mechanism has lost its effectiveness.[38] Predictably, new ideas appeared. Influential thinkers such as Ts'ai Yüan-pei and Chen Tu-hsiu, both based at Peita (Peking University), argued vigorously for a reassessment of traditional Chinese culture. the latter severely criticized the Confucian ethics and values and glorified Western concepts of individualism, dynamism, and utilitarianism. Chen blamed Confucianism for China's decline, stating that "its social and familial obligations enervated the individual and its disdain of commerce and wealth impoverished the economy." He advocated an acceptance of "man's material self-interest as the basis of society" in China.[39]

Again, the contrast between China and Japan is striking: When facing modernization, China lost its traditional social control; Japan kept and made full use of its heritage.

Analysis

An examination of four groups of factors—internal, external, social/ cultural, and the role of government—on the economic development of China and Japan lends itself to a number of observations.

To begin with, *Confucianism, while possessing a core of values, was practiced in different Confucian societies in different ways.* The core values, as Herman Kahn has pointed out, include a strong emphasis on education; orderliness, as achieved through tightly structured social relations based on the family model; and perseverance and diligence in undertaking matters involving one's work, family, or social obligations." A properly trained member of a Confucian culture will be hardworking, responsible, skillful, and (within the assigned or understood limits) ambitious and creative in helping the group (extended family, community, or company). There is much less emphasis on advancing individual (selfish) interests."[40] But Confucian societies have their varieties. Kahn notes:

> Japan, of course, is in some ways the most formal and hierarchic modern society and has retained many of its other traditions. South Korea has traditionally been more Confucian than Confucian China. Even under the Japanese occupation and during the post-War turmoil, it did not lose this characteristic. Taiwan tries to be the cultural and political heir of Confucian China and consciously prizes its Confucian heritage. However, among Confucian societies, Taiwan is one of the most individualistic and competitive.[41]

One manifestation of the diversity of Confucian forms can be seen in the varying definitions of such concepts as *achiever* and *ambition*. In traditional China, aspiring individuals regarded membership in the scholar-official class as their career objective. "Since Confucius permitted everyone to raise himself to the higher classes," Huan-chang Chen has written, "everyone might consume more as his social standing became higher. Therefore, sumptuary regulations do not really prevent economic development, provided the individual is capable of elevating himself."[42] Success in scholarship was the key; it led to officialdom and to personal wealth. No similar accolade was given to the man who succeeded in business.

In traditional Japan, the *samurai* was the chosen class, not the scholar. Toward the end of the Tokugawa Period, however, the *samurai* were in debt to the highly successful merchants; some of them abandoned their once-prized status and joined the previously despised creditors. The merchant class became socially esteemed. One might say, therefore, that not only the social orientation of Confucian societies varied, but *even within the same society, the social orientation may change over time.*

When first facing change, all societies tend to resist them. New thoughts and practices are destabilizing. But obviously a society has to initiate a broad range of changes to accommodate economic modernization. How a society makes the necessary social changes while retaining its traditional values may determine the success or failure of a development effort.[43]

Second, *the forces of modernization affect different societies in different ways.* Societies, like individuals, develop at different rates of speed and respond in different fashions. As Edwin O. Reischauer and John K. Fairbank have pointed out,

> One cannot but be struck by the great differences among the various countries of East Asia in the speed and nature of their responses to the West during the past century. Manifold changes have brought a considerable degree of modernization to all these countries, but at decidedly different rates and in strikingly different ways. These variations in response must be attributed mainly to the differences in the traditional societies of the countries of East Asia. Only such differences can explain why a basically similar impact could have brought such varied initial results in China, Korea, and Japan—and

why relatively small Japan, for example, soon became a world power, while China sank to the status of an international problem, and Korea disappeared temporarily into the Japanese empire.[44]

Even one society may react to modernization differently at different times. China's xenophobic brand of conservatism in the 19th century seemed to have frustrated modernization. But today, as Herman Kahn has observed,

> the old rigidities and blocks have eroded and the cultural legacy is now positive. Since 1945, almost every neo-Confucian culture has, in its own way, been highly skillful at industrialization. The conventional wisdom of the late 19th and early 20th centuries that the Chinese simply could not learn how to industrialize has been turned inside out to read, "The Chinese can industrialize under any and all circumstances."[45]

Thus, even in socialist China the Deng Xiaoping regime appears to have removed the many cultural and political restraints hampering development. Deng is encouraging privatization of the market and use of individual incentives—techniques which just a decade ago would have been regarded as political heresy—to stimulate production. The Chinese experience confirms the notion that a society may learn to change its response to industrialization as circumstances demand.

Confucius himself has put it very well: "There are truly many paths leading up to every mountain, and many mountains lead to heaven." And Kahn is certainly correct when he says: "Industrialization cannot really be characterized as truly Western or Eastern, capitalistic or socialistic. Modernization seems increasingly likely to take different paths in different societies."[46]

Third, *economic development is caused by a variety of factors, and culture is one central factor inexorably linked to the development process.* Confucianism has exerted an enormous influence on the culture of many societies in East Asia in the past; today it continues to be a formidable force shaping the life of the people in that part of the world. Yet Confucianism remains only one force—changeable and adaptable under different circumstances—affecting such a complex process as industrialization.

Fourth, *at some stage of development, certain factors may play more important roles than others.* The five Asian countries mentioned above all have been shaped and influenced by a strong Confucian heritage, to be sure. But it is also fair to say that such external factors as foreign aid, foreign trade, and foreign investment have made their marks on the development process of these countries.[47]

Fifth, the importance of *selective adaptation* cannot be overstated. Rather than following a stringent, focused, literal interpretation of Confucianism as the Chinese did, Japan has made use of only certain aspects of Confucianism to advance modernization. It has successfully extended the concepts of loyalty, filial piety, and the familial structure to the larger and more modern business organizations without suffering from the negative consequences of family-run businesses that are evident elsewhere.

Finally, *Japan's selective adaptation of Confucianism has implications for Western countries.* Joseph Saniel has cited the following ingredients of Japan's modernization experience as particularly relevant for development: strong and responsible leadership, well-defined goals and persistence, a strong national group consciousness and solidarity, and a strong and stable political system.[48] This is not to suggest that all of Japan's values and accomplishments are worth emulating. As Herman Kahn so eloquently observed,

> Certain differences in outlook between predominantly neo-Confucian and predominantly Western countries unquestionably exist, and are growing more important with the economic growth of the neo-Confucian countries. But these differences are matched by various equally important differences among the predominantly neo-Confucian countries and among the predominantly Western countries. Many subtle and complex blends of Confucian and Western cultural elements and values exist in both neo-Confucian and Western societies—and more are likely to appear. Thus, the whole concept of a marriage of machine and garden in a postindustrial Japan is a dramatic example of a potential cultural synthesis.[49]

The most outstanding feature of the modernization experience of Japan and East Asia's other Confucian societies is the acceptance *of culture as a significant force shaping a human-oriented workforce in the service of industrialization. That may be the most important legacy of Confucianism for modern times.*

NOTES

1. See, for example, Herman Kahn, *World Economic Development 1979 and Beyond* (New York: Morrow Quill Paperbacks, 1979).

2. See Dwight Perkins, ed., *China's Modern Economy in Historical Perspective* (Stanford: Stanford University Press), pp. 3–4, for further insight as to the economic similarities between pre-modern China and Japan.

3. The World Bank, *World Development Report 1988* (New York: Oxford University Press, 1988), p. 222.

4. Marion J. Levy, Jr., "Contrasting Factors in the Modernization of China and Japan," in Simon Kuznets, Wilbert E. Moore, and Joseph Spengler, eds., *Economic Growth: Brazil, India, and Japan* (Durham, NC: Duke University Press, 1955), p. 496. For other studies emphasizing social/ cultural factors, see George C. Allen and Audrey G. Donnithorne, *Western Enterprise in Far Eastern Economic Development: China and Japan* (London: George Allen & Unwin Ltd., 1954); and Robert T. Holt and John E. Turner, *The Political Basis of Economic Development* (Princeton: D. Van Nostrand Co., 1966).

5. Francis V. Moulder, *Japan, China, and the Modern World Economy* (Cambridge: Cambridge University Press, 1977).

6. William W. Lockwood, *The Economic Development of Japan: Growth and Structural Change, 1868–1938* (Princeton: Princeton University Press, 1954).

7. Edward O. Reischauer, John K. Fairbank, and Albert Craig, *East Asia: The Modern Transformation* (Boston: Houghton Mifflin Co., 1965). Ibid., pp. 180–91.

8. Norman Jacobs, *The Origin of Modern Capitalism and Eastern Asia* (Hong Kong: Hong Kong University Press, 1958). Cited in Moulder, *Japan, China, and the Modern World Economy*, p. 11.

9. Huan-chang Chen, *The Economic Principles of Confucius and His School*, 2 vols. (New York: Columbia University, 1911), 2: 717–30.

10. Albert Feuerwerker, *The Chinese Economy, 1912–1949* (Ann Arbor: Michigan Papers in Chinese Studies, No. 1, 1968), p. 75. Feuerwerker's other study is *The Chinese Economy ca. 1870–1911* (Ann Arbor: Michigan Papers in Chinese Studies, No. 5, 1969).

11. Reischauer, Fairbank, and Craig, *East Asia*, p. 180.

12. Ibid., p. 181.

13. John K. Fairbank, *The United States and China*, 3rd ed. (Cambridge: Harvard University Press, 1971), p. 236.

14. Reischauer, Fairbank, and Craig, *East Asia*, p. 189.

15. Ibid., p. 185.

16. See Hang-sheng Cheng, "Historical Factors of China's Economic Underdevelopment" in the present volume. See also Arthur Young, *Wartime Finance and Inflation, 1937–1945* (Cambridge: Harvard University Press, 1965), pp. 118–20.

17. See Rhoads Murphey, *The Treaty Ports and China's Modernization: What Went Wrong?* (Ann Arbor: Michigan Papers in Chinese Studies, No. 7, 1970); and Paul A. Cohen, "Ch'ing China: Confrontation with the West, 1850–1900," in James B. Crowley, ed., *Modern East Asia: Essays in Interpretation* (New York: Harcourt, Brace and World, 1970).

18. Norman Jacobs, *The Origin of Modern Capitalism in East Asia*, pp. 30–32 and 48–50, cited in Holt and Turner, *The Political Basis of Economic Development*, p. 109.

19. Kung-chuan Hsiao, "Rural China and Imperial Control in the 19th Century," in Holt and Turner, *The Political Basis of Economic Development*, p. 105.

20. Ibid., pp. 105–06.

21. Charles O. Hucker, "The Traditional Chinese State in Ming Times," in in Holt and Turner, *The Political Basis of Economic Development*, p. 106.

22. Ibid., pp. 106–09.

23. Chen, *The Economic Principles of Confucius and His School*, vol. 2, p. 722.

24. Takao Tsuchiya, "The Development of Economic Life in Japan," in Holt and Turner, p. 112.

25. Takao Tsuchiya, "An Economic History of Japan," *Transactions of the Asiatic Society of Japan*, 2nd series, vol. 15, December 1937, p. 156, cited in Holt and Turner, *The Political Basis of Economic Development*, p. 113.

26. Hung-chao Tai, "The Human Factor and Japanese Economic Development" (Detroit: The University of Detroit, 1984), p. 65.

27. Joseph Saniel, "The Mobilization of Traditional Values in the Modernization of Japan," in Robert N. Bellah, *Religion and Progress in Modern Asia* (New York: The Free Press, 1965), p. 128.

28. Levy, "Contrasting Factors in the Modernization of China and Japan," p. 502.

29. Ibid., p. 504. See also Johannes Hirschmeier, *The Origins of Entrepreneurship in Meiji Japan* (Cambridge: Harvard University Press, 1964).

30. Frances L.K. Hsu, *Iemoto* (Cambridge: Schenman University Press, 1975).

31. Saniel, "The Mobilization of Traditional Values in the Modernization of Japan," p. 136.

32. Levy, "Contrasting Factors in the Modernization of China and Japan," p. 509.

33. Saniel, "The Mobilization of Traditional Values in the Modernization of Japan," pp. 126–27.

34. Kahn, *World Economic Development 1979,* pp. 121–22.

35. Chen, *The Economic Principles of Confucius and His School,* vol. 2, p. 724.

36. Hung-chao Tai has characterized the Japanese value system as consisting of a strong devotion to education, an emphasis on group cohesiveness and conformity, an eagerness to absorb the best from abroad, a strong competitive spirit, a propensity for frugality and savings, a work ethic devoted to perfection, deference to authority and reverence for the nation, and acceptance of an active role for government in the economy. Tai, "The Human Factor and Japanese Economic Development," p. 26.

37. See Marion J. Levy, Jr. "Some Aspects of 'Individualism' and the Problem of Modernization in China and Japan," *Economic Development and Cultural Change* 10 (April 1962): 225–40.

38. Reischauer, Fairbank, and Craig, *East Asia,* p. 660.

39. See ibid., pp. 662–63.

40. Kahn, *World Economic Development 1979,* p. 121.

41. Ibid., p. 123.

42. Chen, *The Economic Principles of Confucius and His School,* vol. 2, p. 717.

43. Herman Kahn concurs: "Perhaps the most important single variable both historically and at present is the extent to which the intruding culture is perceived as a threat to personal, class, national, or religious interests." *World Economic Development 1979*, p. 114.

44. Edwin O. Reischauer and John K. Fairbank, *East Asia: The Great Tradition* (Boston: Houghton Mifflin Co., 1958), p. 670.

45. Kahn, *World Economic Development 1979*, p. 119.

46. Ibid., p. 117.

47. Perkins, *China's Modern Economy in Historical Perspective.*

48. Saniel, "The Mobilization of Traditional Values in the Modernization of Japan," pp. 143–45.

49. Herman Kahn and Thomas Pepper, *The Japanese Challenge* (New York: William Morrow and Company), pp. 144–45.

SIX

Republic of China's Experiences with Economic Development

Yi-ting Wong

Taiwan's Economic Performance

Taiwan, the island bastion of the Republic of China, is one of the most densely populated areas in the world. It occupies an area of only 36,000 square kilometers but has a population of 19 million. About 25 percent of the island's land is arable, most of which is on the west coast.[1] The population growth rate varied between 3.0 and 3.6 percent in the 1950s and 1960s, but declined substantially in recent years, to 1.7 percent in 1982 and 1.0 percent in 1986.[2] Taiwan's goal is to lower the rate further, to 1.25 percent by the end of the present decade.[3]

Taiwan has very few natural resources. Small coalfields are scattered in the mountainous areas in the north-central part of the island. About 90 percent of its energy is imported.[4] It produces an insignificant quantity of crude oil, enough for two or three days' consumption, and a small amount of natural gas. Fluctuations in oil prices obviously have an immediate and important effect on the economy.

Taiwan's subtropical climate allows year-round, multiple-crop farming. Rice, the main staple food of the people, and a variety of vegetables and fruits are grown. Intensive farming in Taiwan has led not only to self-sufficiency in food but also an agricultural surplus for export. In the 1950s and the 1960s agricultural export provided the badly needed foreign exchange to sustain industrialization.

Taiwan's rapid economic development began in 1953 when the government initiated a series of economic plans. From 1952 to 1980 the Gross National Product (GNP) increased 11 times in real terms, from NT$130 billion to NT$1,450 billion, with an average annual growth rate of 9 percent (the exchange rate between NT$ and US$ was stable throughout this period, at about 40:1).[5] This is about twice the 4 percent average annual increase in industrialized nations during the same period and well above the 5.2 percent average growth rate of the developing nations. Taiwan's per capita GNP also experienced fast growth, rising from NT$15,500 in 1970 to NT$141,700 (or US$3,751) in 1986.[6]

In the early stage of Taiwan's economic development, savings were at a low level, as most personal income went for basic necessities. Between 1953 and 1960, savings accounted for only about 5 percent of the national income, a small amount for capital formation.[7] Of the total investment in that period 60 percent was from domestic sources, with the rest coming from foreign financing. By the time United States economic aid was phased out in 1965, the rate of savings (savings as a percentage of national income) had increased to 16.5 percent. In 1972 it rose to 31.6 percent, a level sufficient to meet the needs of massive investment and rapid growth.[8] In 1980, Taiwan's savings rate reached 27.4 percent—the highest in the world (well above Japan's 21.2 percent, the Republic of Korea's 16.0 percent, West Germany's 11.9 percent, and the United States' 5.6 percent).[9]

The Changing Economic Structure

The initiation of industrialization in Taiwan in the early 1950s has brought about very substantial changes in Taiwan's economic structure. In 1952, agriculture generated 35.9 percent of the National Domestic Product (NDP); industry, 18 percent; and the remaining economic sector including services, 46.1 percent.[10] In 1986, 34 years later, the agricultural sector of NDP declined to a mere 6.6 percent, the industrial sector increased to 47.3 percent, and the remaining sector including services was stable, at 46.1 percent.[11]

Structural changes also took place within the industrial sector. In the 1950s, industrial investments were aimed at the production of import-substitutes and daily necessities.[12] Besides the traditional sugar extraction, tea processing, and pineapple canning industries, such manufacturing industries as textiles, plywood, cement, and glass were developed. Beginning in the early 1960s, industrial development efforts were centered on export expansion to lay a foundation for a trade-oriented economy. Among the more important products developed in the 1960s were home appliances, electronic products, plastics, and synthetic fibers.

The 1970s saw the beginning of backward integration and the development of petrochemical intermediates. There also was a shift toward the production of heavy industrial products and more sophisticated items, such as machine tools and motor vehicles. In the early 1980s, machinery manufacturing and the information industry received a top priority for development. These are considered "strategic industries" by virtue of their linkage effects, technology intensiveness, and low energy intensity. Their development will speed up industrial restructuring, essential to the long-term growth of Taiwan's economy.

As is evident from the economic changes described above, Taiwan has gradually developed capital-intensive, sophisticated industries. Now, with such industries as petrochemical intermediates, iron, steel, shipbuilding, and auto manufacturing fully in place, Taiwan has become a Newly Industrialized Country.[13] In more recent years the growth of computer-related products has been especially rapid. Today, Taiwan has become one of the leading world suppliers of computer peripherals, after the United States, Japan, and several European countries.

With such a rapid pace of economic development, the price level of Taiwan understandably underwent great changes too. These changes occurred in five stages:

The first stage, from 1945 to 1952, was a period of recovery from the ravages of civil war and the rampant inflation from mainland China. The annual inflation rate reached an extraordinary 4,000 percent shortly before the currency reform in Taiwan in June 1949, and in 1951 it dropped to 60 percent.[14] The second stage, from 1953 to 1962, was in the early years of industrialization, when a still moderately high inflation rate, 7.6 percent, remained.[15] The third stage, from 1963 to 1972, saw Taiwan expand significantly its export market, but, with the then-stable world economy, the island experienced a low inflation rate, averaging 1.8 percent.[16] In the fourth stage, between 1973 and 1981, under the impact of the oil crisis, Taiwan's inflation rate gyrated to 47 percent in 1974 but fell back to 5 percent the following year and rose to 16 percent in 1981.[17] In the present stage, in the aftermath of the oil crisis, the inflation rate has declined, to 1.36 percent in 1983 and 0.70 percent in 1986.[18]

Industrialization has also significantly changed the composition of the labor force. In 1962, 72 percent of the labor force was male and 28 percent female; in 1982, the corresponding figures were 66 percent and 34 percent.[19] Parallel to this change was an increase in education for the employed, especially males, and enhanced job opportunities for females. In 1962, women held 28 percent of all jobs; but that had risen to 34 percent 20 years later. In 1962, almost twice as many women as men were unemployed; in 1982, the unemployment rates both for men and women declined to about 2 percent.[20]

The sectoral distribution of employment also changed markedly. The share of agricultural employment dropped substantially, from 50 percent in 1962 to 19 percent in 1982. Industrial employment rose from 21 to 41 percent, and services' employment rose from 29 to 40 percent in the same time period. As the fastest growing sectors of the economy, industry and services are expected to see a continual increase in their shares of employment in the years to come.[21]

Foreign Trade

Like other newly industrializing countries, Taiwan relies on foreign trade as the main driving force behind its economic development. Over the years the island has considerably expanded its overseas markets and attracted a great deal of foreign investment.

Until 1949, the central government in Nanking on mainland China administered both the foreign trade and foreign exchanges of Taiwan. In 1950, when Taiwan charted its own course in foreign trade, it emphasized the export of such primary products as sugar, rice, camphor, and timber and the import of capital goods and industrial raw materials.[22] Quality control was poor; per capita GNP was low; trade volume was small; and the trade deficit was relatively large. In 1952, for instance, total trade volume was US$303 million, with US$116 million in exports and US$187 million in imports. The deficit stood at US$71 million, more than 60 percent of exports.[23] In the eight years, from 1952 to 1959, annual trade volume did not exceed US$400 million, with a deficit every year.[24]

Under this situation, Taiwan exercised rigid import controls, using its scarce foreign exchange primarily to purchase needed raw materials and industrial equipment. U.S. aid covered much of the deficit; without it, Taiwan's economic takeoff would have been delayed at least a few years. The U.S. aid program started in 1951 and terminated in 1965. In the first four years, from 1951 to 1954, American farm surplus aid (PL 480) amounted to US$900,000, and general economic aid wàs US$374.3 million.[25] For the same period, the two types of aid had a combined amount of US$375.2 million, a little under US$94 million per year on average.[26] The U.S. aid program was slightly expanded in 1955, averaging about $100 million until 1965 when it ended. For the entire aid period, from 1951 to 1965, U.S. aid totaled US$1,482.2 million (a small portion of which reached Taiwan after 1965).[27]

Major exports. U.S. aid not only stabilized Taiwan's economy but also helped the island launch its export program. Labor-intensive, export-oriented industries began to grow in the mid-1960s, and Taiwan's external trade broke the US$1 billion mark in 1965. It soared to nearly US$40 billion in 1980.[28] Since 1971, the annual trade balance has turned in Taiwan's favor. Subsequently, except for 1974 and 1975, when the world was in economic recession, Taiwan has enjoyed a comfortable trade surplus.[29]

In the 1960s, agricultural products were the mainstay of Taiwan's exports. These consisted of sugar, rice, tea, bananas, pineapple, mushrooms, asparagus, and processed agricultural products. These brought prosperity to rural communities and helped accelerate the process of industrialization. To develop industrial exports, Taiwan first concentrated on textile products, which until 1984 consistently ranked first among Taiwan's exports. In 1982, they amounted to US$4,788 million, or 21.56 percent of total exports.[30] During the late 1970s, export of electronics rose very rapidly, at 25 to 100 percent a year. In 1982, electronics export volume reached US$4 billion, becoming the second largest export item. The strong growth in electronics continued in the 1980s; with a growth rate at 20 percent a year, electronics has become Taiwan's biggest foreign exchange earner, overtaking textiles for the first time in 1984.[31] In addition to electronics, Taiwan has in recent years given high priority to the development of machinery manufacturing and the computer industry for export.

With the strong performance of industrial exports, there has been a basic shift in the composition of Taiwan's exports. In the 1980s, industrial products constituted more than 90 percent of total exports. Of these, heavy industrial products constituted about 18 percent, compared with only 12 percent in the 1970s.[32] In contrast, light industries have declined in importance. In fact, plywood and wood products exports declined in 1980.[33] Agricultural exports (including farm, forest, fishery, and livestock products) experienced a more severe decline, accounting for less than 10 percent of Taiwan's total export in the early 1980s.[34]

Major imports. As an island economy with very limited natural resources, Taiwan imports a large quantity of agricultural and industrial raw materials and capital equipment. The payment for oil alone was US$4 billion in 1982, about 25 percent of the total import bill. Electrical machinery (US$2 billion) and other machinery (US$1.96 billion) each accounted for over 10 percent of the imports.[35] Other major import items were basic metals, chemicals, transportation equipment, logs and lumber, corn, soybeans, and wheat.

Factors Conducive to Economic Development

Taiwan's economic performance in the last 20 years has led to a significant improvement in the living standard on the island. Calorie intake per person per day rose from 2,078 in 1952 to 3,000 in 1981. Average residential space increased from 75.6 square feet per person in 1965 to 183.6 square feet in 1981. Availability of household electrical appliances has approached the level of developed nations. There are 900 refrigerators per 1,000 households, one telephone for every four persons, and 1,030 color television sets per 1,000 households. And, most important of all, life expectancy increased from 58.6 years in 1952 to 71 in 1981.[36]

Taiwan's economic accomplishment has been duplicated in other East Asian countries such as South Korea, Hong Kong, and Singapore. What happened to these countries, as noted elsewhere in this volume, raises questions about certain long-accepted assumptions about the causes of economic progress. In the past, rich natural resources and a large domestic market were considered essential to economic success. Yet Taiwan, South Korea, Hong Kong, and Singapore had very little in the way of natural resources. All four countries were densely populated—in the 1950s and 1960s, Taiwan had 13 million people; South Korea, under 30 million; Hong Kong, less than three million; and Singapore, a little more than one million—but none had as large a labor force as the largest industrialized countries.[37] Nevertheless, they have overcome all these limitations and become industrialized.

It also was once believed that developing countries could not successfully compete with developed countries in the realm of industry. Even in the 1950s, most people in developing countries, including those in Taiwan, were convinced that in their trade relations with the West, these countries' best course of action was to develop the so-called import-substitute industries to protect domestic products. Practically no one foresaw that in less than 20 years these countries could compete head-on with the West in such industrial manufactures as electronics, machinery, and steel.

Furthermore, the four countries have adopted different strategies of economic development. On the whole, Taiwan, South Korea, and Singapore have seen their governments play a strong role in industrial development, while Hong Kong has followed a basically laissez-faire policy. Thus, these four economies fall into two opposite categories of political economy. Even within each category, there are differences. For example, government intervention in the private sector has been significantly more active in South Korea than in Taiwan.

In monetary matters, Hong Kong and Singapore have long been well established financial centers of the world, with little or no government control of foreign exchanges and interest rates; and both Hong Kong dollars and Singapore dollars are convertible currencies. In this respect, both Taiwan and South Korea have a different policy. For 30 years, the governments here have exercised rigid control of foreign exchanges and interest rates.

Hong Kong and Singapore are free ports with few trade restrictions. Taiwan and South Korea, on the other hand, practice trade protectionism. Indeed, in spite of their persistent trade surplus and of the strong pressure from the United States for trade liberalization, both countries do not appear ready to abandon their trade controls.

The four countries also have very different policies toward wages. The Hong Kong government has never directly interfered with the wage-setting process, except indirectly in 1962–63, when its rather lenient policy toward the inflow of refugees from mainland China permitted the island to hold down wages. Singapore, in contrast, follows stringent immigration policies and maintains high wages. In recent years, it even raised wages by law in order to stimulate technological progress.[38] Both Taiwan and South Korea tend to discourage the rise of wages, which they consider as undermining the international competitiveness of their products.

It is indeed surprising that the four economies, given the similarity of their resources, populations, and domestic markets, would adopt such different strategies and still arrive at similar achievements.[39] On the other hand, countries with better natural endowments may not have fared so well. For example, there are two countries that are rich in natural resources and large in area, and have an appropriate size of population, but are poor economic performers: Colombia and Indonesia. In terms of the size of population, Colombia is roughly like Britain, while Indonesia compares with Japan.[40] The geographical location of these countries is an object of envy for many developing countries. However, neither has developed rapidly.

Climate has been considered by many historians to be one important factor affecting the progress of human society. Indeed, intense heat or severe cold tends to inhibit human activities, particularly in the early stages of development when neither wealth nor technical capability is adequate for overcoming these obstacles. Under such conditions, it is difficult for a culture to take root and grow. But modern science and technology have been helpful in overcoming these limitations. Iceland, Scandinavia, Canada, and the Soviet Union are located in very cold regions, and Singapore is close to the Equator. But all of them are now industrialized. Thus, climate clearly is not a decisive factor in economic development.

One further factor said to affect economic performance is the form of government or political institutions. Communist East Germany has a faster pace of development than capitalist Caribbean nations. Stalin's Russia saw faster economic growth than the more liberalized Russia of today. Germany and Japan have had both totalitarian and democratic systems of government in the last 40 years. Both have experienced economic growth under free and non-free government. And a politically stable Burma under General Ne Win does not bring more economic progress than a Pakistan under turmoil.[41] A peaceful Sri Lanka does not do better than a civil war–ridden Cyprus.[42]

Clearly, the factors that usually are said to have a decisive influence on economic performance often are found to be inappropriate in specific circumstances. In this connection, we may have to consider certain cultural and social factors that impinge on economic development.

Social Discipline

To the extent that the four fast-growing East Asian industrial economies share a cultural background in the form of Confucianism, one factor that may account for their performance is the sense of social discipline.

Since the beginning of Chinese civilization, there has been a strong inclination toward establishing an ordered society. The Confucian ideal in social relations is based on a hierarchy of well-defined roles, which has been well epitomized by the statement, "Emperor must act as an emperor; ministers, ministers; fathers, fathers; sons, sons." What this statement means is that an emperor can be respected as an emperor only when he follows certain rules of conduct appropriate to an emperor, that ministers are treated as ministers when they follow their rules, and so on. These traditional concepts can now have their modern applications. Many East Asians have come to accept the present relationships between the government and the people, between the employer and his employees as something equivalent to those between the emperor and his ministers, and between the father and his sons. What these concepts attempt to achieve is social harmony.

"For every one to act properly" means that the individual exerts his maximal effort in discharging his social responsibilities. Hence, observance of rules, industriousness, and diligence have long been the social traits of East Asians. Today, as the East Asian societies have become industrialized, the maintenance of these social traits is especially important to their continual progress. For in a modern complex economy, social discipline is the only force that can bring together millions of individuals—with their divergent interests and beliefs—for common economic action.

The social traits of East Asians are the functional equivalent of what Max Weber called the Protestant ethic, but they do have their peculiar characteristics. First, in Taiwan as in other East Asian societies, social discipline and group identity are inseparable. In Confucianist terms, individuals must strive to uphold the interest of an entity larger than themselves, be it a family, a social organization, or the nation. Second, in the Confucianist concept of human relations, social discipline entails thrift and frugality, which, in the context of today's economic development, facilitate capital formation needed for industrialization. And third, social discipline means a commitment of the society as well as individuals to a disinterested pursuit of education, which has long been a Confucian tradition. It is this tradition that enables East Asian societies to acquire the knowledge and skills necessary for modernization.

The economic experiences of Taiwan and other East Asian countries suggest that today's developing countries can acquire the requisites of industrialization—capital, technology, and markets—with relative ease. The development of a social ethic to sustain industrialization is, however, a very difficult process, and it has to come from the social and cultural traditions of the countries concerned. With social discipline all countries can sooner or later achieve industrialization; without it no country can.

NOTES

1. Taiwan had a population of 18,700,538 in 1982 and occupies an area of 36,179.12 square kilometers, including the offshore islands. Republic of China, Executive Yüan, Directorate General of Budget, Accounting & Statistics, *The Statistical Summaries* (Taipei, 1984), pp. 30–31.

2. Taiwan's annual rate of population growth was 3.51 percent from 1952 to 1960 and 2.73 percent from 1961 to 1969. Republic of China, Executive Yüan, Council for Economic Planning and Development, *Taiwan Statistical Data Book 1987* (Taipei, 1987), p. 4.

3. Republic of China, Executive Yüan, Ministry of the Interior, *Laws and Regulations on Population Policy* (Taipei, January 1983), p. 3.

4. Republic of China, Ministry of Economic Affairs, *Operational Report on the Utilization of the Special Fund for Energy Studies* (Taipei, 1984). Taiwan's dependence on imported energy has been rising very rapidly, from 27 percent in 1961 to 89 percent in 1984.

5. *The Statistical Summaries*, pp. 525–27.

6. *Taiwan Statistical Data Book 1987*, p. 29.

7. Ibid., p. 56.

8. Ibid.

9. Ibid., p. 325.

10. Ibid., p. 41.

11. Ibid.

12. In the 1950s, manufactured products, such as man-made fibers, PVC products, plate glasses, and bicycles made their appearance but were insignificant in quantity. Ibid., p. 92.

13. China Steel Corporation was established in 1972. Petrochemical and automobile plants were established between 1969 and 1978.

14. The inflation rate reached 3,884.66 percent in 1949 but dropped to 56.93 percent in 1951, a year and a half after the monetary reform promulgated on June 15, 1949. Taiwan Provincial Government, Accounting Department, *Monthly Statistics of Prices* (Nantou, Taiwan: February 1959), Table 2.

15. *Taiwan Statistical Data Book 1987*, p. 181.

16. Ibid.

17. Ibid.

18. Ibid.

19. For data on employment by sex, see Republic of China, Executive Yüan, Directorate General of Budget, Accounting & Statistics, *Survey Report of the Labor Force of Taiwan* (Taipei, 1984).

20. Ibid.

21. *The Statistical Summaries*, p. 89.

22. In 1952, agricultural and processed agricultural products accounted for 90.5 percent of the total export, and industrial products, 9.5 percent. Ibid., p. 199.

23. Ibid., p. 194.

24. Ibid.

25. Ibid., p. 235.

26. Ibid.

27. Ibid.

28. Ibid., p. 194.

29. Ibid.

30. Ibid., p. 214.

31. Ibid., pp. 214–15.

32. Ibid., p. 194.

33. Ibid., pp. 214–15.

34. Ibid., p. 199.

35. Ibid., pp. 224–25.

36. For calorie intake, see ibid., p. 285. For other data, see Republic of China, Ministry of Economic Affairs, *Economic Development—Taiwan, Republic of China* (Taipei, 1984).

37. In 1957, in its first official census, Singapore had a population of 1.4 million. *Encyclopedia Britannica*, Book. XVI (15th edition, Helen, Hemmingway, Benton, Publisher, 1973–1974), p. 781. In 1952 the population of Hong Kong was 2,250,000, and of Korea, 21,144,000. United Nations, Department of International Economic and Social Affairs, Statistical Office, *Monthly Bulletin of Statistics* (December 1961).

38. See *Ching Chi Jih Pao (The Economic Daily News*, Taipei, Taiwan), June 2, 1981, and June 14, 1983.

39. See Republic of China, Ministry of Economic Affairs, *Comparison of Economic Growth of R.O.C. and Other Asian and Major Industrial Nations* (Taipei, 1981).

40. United Nations, Department of International Economic and Social Affairs, Statistical Office, *World Statistics in Brief* (New York, 1979), pp. 29, 48, 65, 73, and 142.

41. See ibid.

42. See ibid.

SEVEN

Entrepreneurial Role and Societal Development in Taiwan

Wen-lang Li

Introduction

Taiwanese billionaire Y.C. Wang was on the front cover of the July 15, 1985, issue of the business magazine *Forbes*. For a Chinese who until age 13 did not even have shoes to wear, this is indeed an extraordinary honor. Wang's success story is a legend. His enterprise currently yields about US$3.2 billion a year; it has beaten such multinational corporations as Du Pont and B.F. Goodrich in the race to be the world's largest producer of polyvinyl chloride.

Y.C. Wang's personal success exemplifies the dramatic growth of Chinese entrepreneurship. Many other Taiwanese business owners are now ranked among the world's richest persons. They invest handsomely in various industries in the United States and Southeast Asian countries. Behind the dramatic success of these entrepreneurs is the hyper-rapid growth of Taiwan's economy. With fewer than 20 million people, Taiwan is currently ranked 16th in international trade among all countries. It is the fifth largest trade partner of the United States. The per capita income in Taiwan was US$3,751 in 1986.[1]

Taiwan's success is not unique among Asian countries. Many others—such as Singapore, Hong Kong, and South Korea—have experienced similarly impressive development. Their rates of economic growth in the last decade have ranged up to 10 percent per year. These so-called Newly Industrializing Countries (NICs), along with Japan, are the constituents of the Pacific Basin economic force, which has a more dynamic economic performance than the European Common Market.

The institutional factors behind the growth of the Pacific Basin economy are a fascinating research topic for social scientists.[2] Why was there a dramatic surge of economic development among these countries in the last three decades? In the search for some common denominators, one may agree with Nathan Glazer and attribute success largely to culture.[3] Since these Pacific Basin countries share to a certain extent the same Confucian ethics and religious belief, it appears reasonable to propose that the Confucian tradition is the one common underlying institutional factor behind the dramatic economic growth of Japan and the NICs.[4]

This proposition, however, is not consistent with the classical writings of Max Weber on society and economic development.[5] As is well known, Weber considered Confucian ethics and doctrines inimical to the *rise* of capitalism, but he believed that "the Chinese in all probabilities would be more capable than the Japanese of *assimilating* capitalism."[6] This latter supposition is clearly erroneous. In the light of the economic performance of all Pacific Basin countries, one wonders how valid is Weber's general proposition on the subject.

In all fairness, Weber's study of the interplay between traditional institutional factors and economic development is insightful and stimulating to contemporary social research. His emphasis on the importance of cultural factors to economic development is widely accepted by scholars of Chinese society.[7] What can be examined, in this connection, is whether Chinese traditional norms and values, on the one hand, and the traits of effective entrepreneurs, on the other, are compatible.[8]

This chapter attempts to address a critical question raised by Max Weber, that is, What is the relationship between traditional norms and entrepreneurial development in a growing economy? There are two important schools of thought following the Weberian model. One emphasizes that entrepreneurship, which is essential to capitalistic enterprise, can occur in any traditional society. Another school argues that entrepreneurship is a composite of rather nonconformist, nontraditional personal traits. It puts entrepreneurship studies in the context of a psychological framework. In this chapter we will use empirical data to demonstrate that, at least in the case of Taiwan, entrepreneurial roles are traditionalistic, conforming to some of Confucius' normative expectations. In addition, we would like to argue that entrepreneurship is not necessarily the independent variable in capitalistic development. It is the change of societal environment that will induce the entrepreneurial traits to surface and become functional in a capitalistic economy.

Two Approaches in the Study of Entrepreneurship

The role of entrepreneurship is of profound importance in the study of economic development. Entrepreneurship is traditionally considered to be one of the four fundamental economic factors critical to capitalism, in addition to land, labor, and capital. Some economists emphasize that economic development is made possible primarily through entrepreneurs' risk-taking initiative and industrial drive. Without the entrepreneurial spirit, an economy will stay stagnant, unable to mobilize the factor inputs for purposeful economic change. A transition from a traditional economy to a modern one by necessity implies promotion and encouragement of entrepreneurship. Thus, an examination of entrepreneurs' origins, recruitment, and functions is indispensable to the study of economic development.

Joseph Schumpeter was among the pioneer economists who closely examined the role of entrepreneurship in economic development.[9] His research concluded that entrepreneurship, more broadly defined as "creative response in business," primarily accounted for the accelerating growth of Western economies. Without it, technological progress is virtually impossible. He has succinctly delineated the function of entrepreneurship as follows:

> ...the function of entrepreneurs is to reform or revolutionize the pattern of production by exploiting an invention, or, more generally, an untried technological possibility for producing a new commodity or producing an old one in a new way, by opening up a new source of supply of materials or a new outlet for products, by reorganizing an industry and so on.[10]

Unfortunately, managers with "creative responses" have become an endangered species as Western economics has passed its initial growth stage.[11] Society at large is by definition intolerant of the egotistic drives of particularistic groups. The increasing bureaucratization in Western societies thus threatens the very existence of entrepreneurship. On the other hand, in the developing societies, the role of entrepreneurship has not yet been fully recognized. Some economists have taken the position that scarcity of entrepreneurship is a primary characteristic of current underdeveloped economies. For example, Nathaniel H. Leff observed:

> Scarcity of entrepreneurship was among the barriers to development proposed as explanations. Entrepreneurship could indeed be seen as the most crucial scarce input, for it could be the case as the "prime mover necessary to initiate the development process by mobilizing supply of other prerequisites.[12]

David McClelland also can be considered a major contributor to the theoretical study of entrepreneurship. Schumpeter was not interested in explaining entrepreneurial behavior. Instead, he used entrepreneurship as an independent variable to explain economic development. McClelland, on the contrary, treated entrepreneurial behavior as endogeneous in his theory of economic development.

In his *The Achieving Society*, McClelland firmly establishes the linkage between entrepreneurship and economic growth.[13] Persons with a high need of achievement are shown to be more attracted to business occupations, because they perceive such work as calling for the characteristics which they possess. These include risk-taking, achievement satisfaction, knowledge of results of action, long-range planning, and coordinating abilities. McClelland stresses the influence of parents on the entrepreneurs. Parents who continually instill high, achievable standards on their children and who do not interfere, but share emotionally, with their activities will produce entrepreneurs.

McClelland's work has had a profound impact on subsequent studies of entrepreneurship. Ralph M. Stogdill, for example, in attempting to extend McClelland's ideas, found that the achievement motive for entrepreneurs is very closely related to a strong desire for freedom of action.[14] This desire is frequently cited by entrepreneurs as the reason why they are not satisfied with working in large businesses. In a cross-cultural investigation of achievement values and entrepreneurship, Leticia Vincente-Wiley concluded that the values held by entrepreneurs are inconsistent with those of traditional societies.[15] Entrepreneurs are significantly more individualistic and active than the average people in a traditional society.

Everett E. Hagen has advanced a theory of status withdrawal to explain the emergence of entrepreneurial behavior.[16] Hagen considered the distinction between an authoritarian personality and a creative personality critically important to the understanding of how entrepreneurs emerge. Under normal circumstances, the child-rearing practices of traditional societies tend to create an authoritarian personality whose characteristics are incompatible with innovative entrepreneurial action. Certain external disturbances—such as social discrimination or the death of one's father in early life—may so affect the child-rearing practices that, under certain conditions, a creative personality results.

Charles B. Swayne and William R. Tucker have expounded on the Hagen thesis: "As the child matures, the society around him attempts to block his advancement. This social blockage produces eventual entrepreneurial behavior—*one who is a creative problem-solver, who has a high need for achievement, and who has an air of order and autonomy.*"[17] In fact, the presence of a strong father figure is believed to inhibit entrepreneurial propensity. A group of business researchers have noted that entrepreneurs are often orphaned or half-orphaned.[18] A similar observation was obtained in a study of entrepreneurs in the Philippines. Vincente-Wiley found a quarter of the entrepreneurs there had lost their fathers during boyhood.[19]

The theories advanced by McClelland and Hagen are based purely on the behavioral approach. Their conclusions illustrate that entrepreneurship is characteristic of the marginal groups—the groups that have suffered from some withdrawal of status or have never enjoyed status. McClelland and Hagen, in short, have developed the social marginality concept to explain entrepreneurship.

Both McClelland and Hagen have failed to examine the economic conditions within which the entrepreneurial capacity has been evident. They merely view entrepreneurship as something analogous to psychological capacity for musical or poetical talent. Granted, personality factors are important in determining occupational success or achievement, but they are by no means the most significant. Obviously, persons who experience status withdrawal do not necessarily become entrepreneurs; in fact, many may be emotionally or socially damaged before they reach adulthood. We cannot suggest that persons with high achievement values are natural candidates for entrepreneurship. Perhaps the traditional Chinese society is a good case to refute this perspective; in that type of society persons with high achievement values tend to strive for Mandarin or bureaucratic status rather than entrepreneurship. Entrepreneurship cannot emerge unless social structure changes and business opportunities become available. Consequently, when exploring the roots of entrepreneurship, the term must be defined in relationship to a business institution.[20]

A Theoretical Proposition

The structural approach perhaps can provide more meaningful interpretations of entrepreneurship.[21] That approach examines the environmental or sociological context in which entrepreneurship emerges. In this sense, entrepreneurs will no longer be viewed as a deviant or marginal group in society; instead, they are conformists who struggle to catch emerging social opportunities. The essentials of the structural approach are well delineated by William Glade:

> Although it is clear, for example, that not all cultural deviants or socially marginal men seek, or succeed in realizing, expressions of their deviance in entrepreneurial roles (e.g., Gypsies, Amish, etc.), it might be worth the effort to ascertain and specify the circumstance under which the presence of deviant groups or individuals does eventuate in such an outcome. In like manner, it is germane to explore the conditions under which those who are, broadly speaking, conforming rather than marginal to the dominant cultural norms, fulfill the entrepreneurial role.[22]

If entrepreneurs are viewed as a conformist group, our focus of research will necessarily turn to an examination of the kind of conforming mechanisms that shape entrepreneurial roles. Before we specify the underlying mechanisms, it is helpful to point out that the theoretical gap in previous studies of entrepreneurship. Surprisingly, previous researchers have rarely attempted to relate their studies to the voluminous literature on social elites. In our judgment, entrepreneurs are but a particular group of business elite; they are businessmen who excel in bringing innovative measures to industrial pursuits. As leaders of the business world, entrepreneurs should unquestionably be the carriers of societal norms and values. In this sense, entrepreneurs are indeed social conformists, not deviants.

Let us now examine the kind of conforming mechanisms that prevail in Chinese society in general and in the business community in particular. Two personal qualifications that are highly valued in the Confucian culture appear to be a prerequisite for the Chinese elite: seniority and education. The significance of these two factors in traditional Chinese society is well known.[23] In fact, the importance of these two qualifications also can be observed in other Asian societies highly influenced by Confucianism, such as Japan and South Korea.

It is our theoretical proposition that entrepreneurs basically are a social conformist group; thus their personality characteristics are not substantially different from other elite groups. Whether our theoretical proposition can be accepted depends on the results of empirical testing. The empirical data should definitely establish the fact that in the Taiwan business environment those who are young and less educated have less chance of achieving entrepreneurship. On the surface, it would seem that our hypothesis might be wrong; for entrepreneurs normally emerge from small businesses which require not so much maturity and education as hard drive and innovation. However, if our hypothesis is proven valid, it would seem that the conjectures about nontraditional risk-taking entrepreneurship should be cast aside.

The emphasis on traditional personality traits is only part of the theoretical proposition. We would also argue that the business opportunity structure is an indispensable prerequisite for entrepreneurship. One may question whether entrepreneurship is an independent factor for economic development. Entrepreneurial roles emerge only as a response to the changing business environment. In other words, when an economy is rapidly developing, some persons excel in making the most of the available opportunities. The extent to which entrepreneurship exists distinctively and the amount of independent contribution entrepreneurs can make to economic development remain puzzling issues.

Thus, this chapter sets forth to examine Taiwanese entrepreneurial roles from two perspectives. On the behavioral side, we are interested in examining whether modern entrepreneurship carries the same personality qualifications as those of the traditional elite. On the structural side, we intend to ascertain whether the entrepreneurial role is a function of a changing industrial structure.

Conceptualizing Taiwan's Entrepreneurship

Before we venture into an empirical analysis, we need to define entrepreneurship. We fully recognize the ambiguity of the entrepreneur concept; it means different things to different researchers. The word entrepreneur comes from the French word "entreprendre"—to undertake. An entrepreneur is a person who undertakes to organize and manage a profit-making business and who assumes risk for it.[24] Because in large businesses the function of enterprise is normally performed by many people rather than by one person, entrepreneurs are not usually associated with large businesses. In fact, an entrepreneur is often defined as the owner of a small business who performs all or most of the business functions personally.[25]

In examining our theoretical proposition, we intend to use the data from the Taiwan Labor Force Survey conducted in May 1979. The survey is fairly large in scale, covering nearly 50,000 persons, about 0.3 percent of the total population. The survey asked the respondents to identify their "employment status." For those who worked in the private sector, it asked them to specify if they were self-employed, employed by others, or were employers. For employers, the survey collected information about the number of workers under their management. Thus, our analysis can compare business owners by size of employment. This comparison may lead to some assessments about the growth of entrepreneurship. For this study, we focus on a subsample of 25,589 persons who were engaged in labor force pursuits as of May 1979. The original data, stored on computer tape, were made available for this research by the Taiwan Labor Force Survey Commission, Directorate-General of Budget, Accounting and Statistics.

A preliminary tabulation of the data shows that 1,052 persons, or 4.1 percent, of our subsample were owners of business enterprises; they will be considered entrepreneurs in our study.

Taiwanese Entrepreneurs

In the Western cultural context, the stereotyped image of an entrepreneur is that of an ego-driving and incentive-seeking personality—characteristics commonly associated with young persons. One may assume that because Taiwanese society has undergone rapid social changes under heavy Western influence, the emerging Taiwanese entrepreneurs might share the same characteristics as those of the Western type. Some observers have claimed this to be the case.[26]

The ego-driving and incentive-seeking type of young entrepreneur, however, is not considered consistent with the image of the traditional Chinese business elite.[27] Among the criteria for career advancement in traditional Chinese society, seniority is perhaps the most important. Inexperienced young people seldom can elevate their social status no matter how hardworking or inventive they may be. Thus, it will be of interest to examine the Taiwan labor survey data to see if there is an emerging class of young entrepreneurs.

The data in Table 1 appear to show that traditional Chinese norms and values of business success persist in Taiwan today. Young and "inexperienced" businessmen are decidedly in the minority among the age-groups of entrepreneurs (i.e., "employers"). Among young adults (age 15–39) the proportion of entrepreneurs is 3.3 percent; among middle-aged adults (ages 40–54) 5.3 percent; and among older adults (55 +) 6.4 percent. It is obvious, then, that seniority does constitute a major criterion for Taiwan entrepreneurs.

Education is another important channel of upward mobility in Chinese society. In fact, in traditional Chinese society, education was the only means through which young people could raise their social status, regardless of their family origin. This pattern of social mobility has recently declined, but we may expect education to continue to be a major criterion for status attainment.

Education, however, is not regarded as an important component of entrepreneurship in Western societies. For example, William Copulsky and Herbert W. McNulty observed that college business education, especially at the graduate level, appears to discourage entrepreneurship.[28] Kenneth R. van Voorhis concluded that "successful small business owners have typically been poor students in school."[29] One simple reason for the noncorrelation between education and entrepreneurship is that education is generally aimed at preparing people to work for others, whereas entrepreneurship involves self-directed, self-centered activities.

Our data appear to refute this generalization. Table 2 shows that higher education does not handicap entrepreneurship in

Table 1
Employment Status by Age

Employment Status	15–39	40–54	55 +	Total
	— (in percent) —			
Employer	3.3	5.3	6.4	4.1
Self-employed	12.2	37.3	47.1	22.1
Employed	64.0	33.9	25.0	52.4
Government	9.8	16.5	16.5	12.2
Unpaid	10.7	7.1	5.0	9.2
Total	100.0	100.0	100.0	100.0
	— (total in number) —			
	16,473	6,721	2,395	25,589

Table 2
Employment Status by Education

Employment Status	None	Primary	Junior High	Senior High	Junior College	College	Total
	— (in percent) —						
Employer	1.3	4.1	3.7	4.9	4.5	9.1	4.1
Self-employed	41.4	30.6	12.1	8.4	4.6	4.1	22.1
Employed	36.6	50.9	66.0	57.3	44.6	37.5	52.4
Government	5.3	5.0	8.0	22.3	42.9	48.1	12.2
Unpaid	15.4	9.3	10.2	7.2	3.3	1.2	9.2
Total	100.0	100.0	100.0	100.0	100.0	100.0	100.0
	— (total in number) —						
	2,831	11,207	4,829	4,470	1,168	1,084	25,589

Taiwan. On the contrary, those who have no formal schooling have little chance of becoming entrepreneurs; as the level of education increases, the likelihood of becoming entrepreneurs improves; the most highly educated (college level) have at least twice the chance of the less educated to become entrepreneurs (9.1 percent v. 4.1 percent).

One additional observation can be made. The relationship between education and entrepreneurship is not monotonic from

primary school level to junior college level. The proportion of
entrepreneurs is 4.1 percent among primary school graduates and
4.5 percent among junior college graduates. Two factors may
intervene to hold down the number of entrepreneurs. One is the
overlapping effects of age and education. Young people tend to
attain higher levels of education than older people but are less
likely to become entrepreneurs, as previously observed in Table 1.

The other factor has to do with the fact that junior colleges
primarily provide vocationally-oriented training. Their educational perspective is narrow and specialized. As a result, their
graduates are more likely to work for others than for themselves.
This is clearly shown in Table 2. A larger proportion of junior
college graduates (87.5 percent) work for others (i.e., "Employed"
and "Government") than any other education group. This observation raises an important issue in educational policy: Does a
vocationally-oriented curriculum reduce students' chances of
becoming entrepreneurs?

In Table 3 we present data on entrepreneurs by their fields of
study at junior colleges and four-year colleges. Engineering and
business are the two major disciplines popular to entrepreneurs:
10 percent major in business and 7 percent in engineering.
However, when the proportion of entrepreneurs for each field of
study is computed, graduates of business and engineering
schools no longer have a higher likelihood of becoming
entrepreneurs than those in other fields. In fact, graduates from
the humanities and sciences have even greater chances of engag-
ing in entrepreneurial activities than those with business and
engineering backgrounds. This fact suggests that a liberal arts
education may not be as useless as generally perceived.

Industrial Pursuits and Entrepreneurship

In the previous section we dealt mainly with the supply side of
entrepreneurial roles—the qualifications of those who have become entrepreneurs. However, personal qualifications alone may
not be sufficient. The changing demands of the economy may be
an even more important factor. As explained previously, the rise
of entrepreneurship may be a function of societal development.
People with entrepreneurial propensities exist in every type of
social environment, traditional or modern. Their abilities and
propensities are channeled to various types of occupational roles,
depending on the state of societal conditions.

Table 3
Field of Study by Employment Status

Field of Study	Entrepreneurs	Others	Entrepreneur proportion
	— (in percent) —		
Humanities	1.4	1.0	5.8
Social sciences	0.5	0.4	5.5
Business	10.0	7.8	5.2
Sciences	0.5	0.3	6.1
Engineering	6.8	5.4	5.1
Agriculture	2.2	1.5	5.9
Medicine	2.5	0.8	12.0
Military	1.2	0.9	5.3
Education	0.5	1.3	1.5
NA	74.4	80.6	3.8
Total	100.0	100.0	100.0
	— (total in number) —		
	1,052	24,537	

Social science literature often delineates the economic development of a society in three stages.[30] The first stage is the predominancy of primary industries. The general mode of livelihood is agriculture, hunting, or direct utilization of natural resources. In the second stage of development the importance of primary industries declines, and the manufacturing sector becomes the prevailing mode of industrial pursuit. A high population mobility is observed; rapid social changes occur. This is called the industrial revolution or the beginning of the modern era. In this stage, industrial entrepreneurship emerges. The third stage of development is characterized by the rise of the service sector and the decline of manufacturing. Many popular writers call this stage the Third Wave or the post-industrial society. In this stage entrepreneurship will become more salient.

This theory will be tested with Taiwan's data. Table 4 appears to demonstrate the theory's validity. The proportion of entrepreneurs is only 0.8 percent in the primary sector. The proportion drastically increases to 4.5 percent in the manufac-

Table 4
Employment Status by Industry

Employment Status	Primary	Secondary	Tertiary	Total
	— (in percent) —			
Employer	0.8	4.5	5.8	4.1
Self-employed	54.2	3.1	23.6	22.1
Employed	17.0	87.9	37.4	52.4
Government	4.4	5.0	25.6	12.2
Unpaid	23.5	2.5	7.7	9.2
Total	100.0	100.0	100.0	100.0
	— (total in number) —			
	5,888	10,641	9,060	25,589

turing (or the secondary) sector. Finally, in the service (tertiary) sector the proportion of entrepreneurs rises to 5.8 percent.

What are the types of industrial pursuit that give rise to the entrepreneurial role? We have seen that the emergence of the industrial revolution tends to induce and expand the size of entrepreneurship. But industrial revolution is a grandiose term and more specificity is required to characterize the effects of the industrial expansion process on entrepreneurship. Table 5 presents data on the top ten industries that produced entrepreneurs; together they account for approximately 63 percent of all entrepreneurs in Taiwan.

The retail industry alone claims 16 percent of all entrepreneurs. However, it should be noted that the retail industry is also the major type of industrial pursuit among all Taiwanese workers. The proportion—the ratio of entrepreneurs to other workers for each industry—is also shown in Table 5. We note that the import-export industry has the highest proportion of entrepreneurs, about 19 percent. The second highest is the wholesale industry, about 13 percent. These figures suggest that the dramatic growth of Taiwan's international trade in recent years has expanded the role of entrepreneurship. There are many forces that induce the growth of Taiwan's international trade, and the explication will involve political as well as economic theories.

Table 5
Entrepreneur Proportion by Top-Ten Industries

Top Ten industries	Entrepreneurs	Others	Ratio
1. Retail	16.0 (168)	9.5 (2,343)	6.7
2. Personal Services	9.2 (97)	4.1 (1,006)	8.8
3. Machine tool	6.7 (65)	2.7 (661)	8.9
4. Import-export	5.8 (61)	1.1 (258)	19.1
5. Wholesale	4.7 (49)	1.3 (315)	13.5
6. Furniture	4.6 (48)	2.8 (678)	6.6
7. Construction	4.6 (48)	6.6 (1,614)	2.9
8. Machinery repoir	4.2 (44)	17. (426)	9.4
9. Restaurant	4.0 (42)	2.3 (565)	6.9
10. Plastic	3.7 (39)	2.5 (606)	6.0

Note: Figures in parentheses represent sample size.

The phenomenon is so complex that we can hardly appeal to entrepreneurship as the predominant explanation. It will be more convincing if we treat entrepreneurship as the dependent, rather than the independent, variable in its relationship to the growth of international trade in Taiwan.

The Successful Entrepreneurs

The Taiwan data provide an opportunity to examine entrepreneurship by size of business enterprise. From an analysis of business size one can draw inferences as to the success of entrepreneurs. As always, some enterprises have become multinational while others remain small. What are the determinants? What are the explanations in light of our theoretical propositions? Our focus of analysis is 1,052 entrepreneurs.

Table 6 presents data on the size of business establishment by entrepreneur's age. Most of the entrepreneurs are small-business owners, about 78 percent of them employing fewer than 10 workers. The scale of Taiwanese business establishments is, of course, much smaller than that of a highly developed country like the United States. But Taiwan was a predominantly underdeveloped country just 20 years ago, and its recent rapid industrialization already has led to an expansion in the average size of a business establishment. In our sample, 6 percent of the business owners were found to employ 30 or more workers.

Table 6
Size of Establishment by Entrepreneur's Age

Size of Establishment	Entrepreneur's Age			Total
	15–39	40–54	55 +	
	— (in percent) —			
Under 10	82.9	73.4	70.5	77.9
10–29	13.6	18.1	18.8	15.8
30–49	2.8	4.5	4.0	3.4
50–99	0.8	3.1	5.4	2.3
100 +	0.2	0.8	1.3	0.6
Total	100.0	100.0	100.0	100.0
	— (total in number) —			
	546	354	152	1,052

The variables we used earlier to explain the emergence of entrepreneurship are still valid in the context of entrepreneurial success. The size of the entrepreneurial establishment steadily grows with the increase of the entrepreneur's age. Young entrepreneurs (ages 15–40) employ on the average 8.2 workers; middle-aged entrepreneurs (ages 40–54), 11.1 workers; senior entrepreneurs (ages 55 +), 13.9 workers. Clearly entrepreneurial success is correlated with entrepreneurs' years of experience.

We can probably infer from Table 6 that the educational attainment of entrepreneurs and the type of industrial pursuits they have are also highly correlated with the success of an enterprise. In order to validate this generalization we will use the technique of multivariate analysis. Two points should be made: This analysis will deal with only nonagricultural business owners, as agricultural entrepreneurs are relatively few; the variable of establishment size has been transformed into logarithmic form because of its highly skewed distribution.

Let S denote the size (or success) of entrepreneurial business, I the type of industrial pursuits (0 for the manufacturing and 1 for the service sector), A for age or seniority, and E for educational attainment. We can then specify a multivariate model as follows:

$$\mathrm{Log}_e\ S = b_1 I + b_2 A + b_3 E + e$$

Table 7
**Correlation Matrix of Establishment Size (In Logarithm)
Industry, Experience, and Education**

	Size of Establishment	Industry	Seniority	Education
Size of Establishment	1.000	–1.197	0.144	0.129
Industry		1.000	0.122	0.141
Seniority			1.000	–0.075
Education				1.000
X	1.813	0.519	25.2	8.9
S.D.	0.833	0.500	11.0	3.8

Note: The sample size is 1,004, including only nonagricultural industries. Industry is coded 0 if secondary and 1 if tertiary. Experience refers to the number of years beyond age 15. Education is coded in years of schooling.

Note that b_1, b_2, and b_3 represent respectively the proportional effect of each independent variable on the size of the establishment.

Table 7 presents the results of correlational analysis among the independent and dependent variables. With a sample of 1,004, most of the Pearsonian correlation coefficients are statistically significant at the 5 percent level. Note both seniority and educational attainment are positively related to the success of business enterprise, although both independent variables themselves tend to be negatively related. Another interesting observation is that the type of industrial pursuit is negatively related to the size of business enterprise. Entrepreneurs tend to employ fewer workers in the service sector than in the manufacturing sector.

From the results in Table 7 we can derive the following regression model:

$$\text{Log}_e S = 1.321 - 0.408I + 0.014A + 0.039E$$
$$(0.051) \quad (0.002) \quad (0.007)$$
$$R = 0.313$$

The results show that different industrial pursuits, from manufacturing to service, will reduce the average size of a business enterprise by roughly 41 percent. On the other hand, an increase of one year in seniority (age) will increase the average size of an enterprise by 1.4 percent. And an increase of one year of schooling will also increase the average size of the enterprise by 3.9 percent. In the light of the relatively small standard errors, it is clear that type of industrial pursuit, seniority, and level of educational attainment all have independent effects on the size of business enterprises.

Conclusion

In this chapter we have attempted to assess the determinants of the entrepreneurial roles and the success of entrepreneurial business enterprises. We interpreted the phenomena in terms of three independent variables: seniority, educational attainment, and type of industrial pursuit. The theoretical proposition underlying our inquiries is that the proper study of entrepreneurship should be approached from both the behavioral and the structural sides. Seniority and educational attainment represent the behavioral characteristics of entrepreneurial qualifications, whereas the changing mode of industrial pursuit represents a structural force that has impact on entrepreneurial roles.

Taiwan serves as an ideal social laboratory for the study of entrepreneurship. It inherits traditional Chinese normative and value systems that are quite different from those of Western societies, from which most of the current theories of entrepreneurship are derived. On the other hand, Taiwan is undergoing rapid industrialization, in which the functions of entrepreneurship are dynamic and visible.

Our analysis of Taiwanese data provides the following two general conclusions:

First, contrary to the theories of McClelland and Hagen, we have shown that entrepreneurs can hardly be characterized as a deviant group who have suffered status withdrawal or have never enjoyed status. Two traditional qualifications for "success" in the Confucian society—seniority and educational attainment—are still distinct characteristics of today's Taiwanese entrepreneurs.[31] The conjectures about entrepreneurs being nonconformist or poorly educated are not supported by our empirical analysis.

Second, Taiwan's recent industrial transformation, from an agrarian to a trade-oriented economy, apparently has had great impact on the emergence and success of entrepreneurial roles.

Some challenging types of industrial pursuits, such as international trade, have opened up promising opportunities for entrepreneurship. From the results of this study we would propose that entrepreneurship is perhaps more appropriately viewed as a dependent, rather than an independent, variable in the course of Taiwan's economic development.

This chapter has taken an almost impossible task of challenging two prevailing theoretical propositions in entrepreneurship studies. On the one hand, it attempts to refute the psychological school which generally regards entrepreneurship as a reflection of nonconformist, nontraditional characteristics. Our empirical data from Taiwan have shown the contrary. In fact, as a footnote, the feature article in *Forbes* also reported that Taiwanese tycoon Y.C. Wang still lives with his 90-year-old mother, and reports to her every morning. The story appears to be quite consistent with our research findings.

On the other hand, this chapter raises an issue with the Schumpeter school, which claims entrepreneurship as a unique characteristic of capitalism. We argue that entrepreneurial traits can be discovered in traditional, noncapitalistic societies, though their existence might be more latent. It is the structural change of a society that promotes entrepreneurial roles. Therefore, entrepreneurship should not be regarded simply as an independent variable in the context of economic development.

NOTES

An earlier version of this chapter appeared in *Journal of Chinese Studies* 3 (April 1986): 77–96.

1. See Tables 1 and 3 in Chapter 2. See also Wen L. Li, "Structural Development and Behavioral Modernity in Taiwan," in Hungdah Chiu and Shao-chuang Leng, eds., *China: Seventy Years After Hsing Hai Revolution* (Charlottesville, VA: University of Virginia Press, 1984), pp. 457–88.

2. Albert O. Hirschman, *The Strategy of Economic Development* (New Haven, CT: Yale University Press, 1958).

3. Nathan Glazer, "Social and Cultural Factors in Japanese Economic Growth," in Patrick Hugh and Henry Rosovsky, eds., *Asia's New Giant: How the Japanese Economy Works* (Washington, D.C.: The Brookings Institution, 1976), pp. 813–52.

4. Cf. Thomas A. Metzger, *Escape from Predicament: Neo-Confucianism and China's Evolving Political Culture* (New York: Columbia University Press, 1977).

5. Max Weber, *The Religion of China: Confucianism and Taoism*, trans. from the German by Hans Berth (Glencoe, IL: Free Press, 1951), and *The Protestant Ethic and the Spirit of Capitalism*, trans. from the German by Talcott Parsons (London: Allen and Unwin, 1930).

6. Weber, *The Religion of China*, p. 248; italics added.

7. See Huan-chang Chen, *The Economic Principles of Confucius and His School* (New York: Columbia University); Derk Bodde, "Harmony and Conflict in Chinese Philosophy" in Arthur Wright, ed., *Studies in Chinese Thought* (Chicago: University of Chicago Press, 1953); and Lucian W. Pye, *The Spirit of Chinese Politics* (Cambridge, MA: MIT Press, 1968).

8. Dwight H. Perkins, "Growth and Changing Structure of China's Twentieth-Century Economy," in Dwight H. Perkins, ed., *China's Modern Economy in Historical Perspective* (Stanford: Stanford University Press, 1975), pp. 115–65.

9. Joseph A. Schumpeter, *The Theory of Economic Development* (Cambridge, MA: Harvard University Press, 1934).

10. Idem, *Capitalism, Socialism and Democracy*, 3rd ed. (New York: Harper and Row, 1950), p. 132.

11. William H. Whyte, Jr., *The Organization Man* (Garden City, NY: Simon and Schuster, 1956).

12. Nathaniel H. Leff, "Entrepreneurship and Economic Development: The Problem Revisited," *Journal of Economic Literature* 17 (1979): 43.

13. David McClelland, *The Achieving Society* (Princeton, NJ: D. Van Nostrand Co., 1961), especially chaps. 6 and 7.

14. Ralph M. Stogdill, *Individual Behavior and Group Achievement* (New York: Oxford University Press, 1969).

15. Leticia Vincente-Wiley, "Achievement Values of Filipino Entrepreneurs and Politicians," *Economic Development and Cultural Change* 27 (1979): 467–83.

16. Everett E. Hagen, *On the Theory of Social Change* (Homewood, IL: Dorsey Press, 1964).

17. Charles B. Swayne and William R. Tucker, *The Effective Entrepreneur* (Morriston, NJ: General Learning Press, 1973), p. 29 (original italics).

18. Orvis F. Collins, David G. Moore and D.B. Unwalla, *The Enterprising Man* (East Lansing: Michigan State University, Bureau of Business and Economic Research, 1964).

19. Vincente-Wiley, p. 482.

20. Arthur H. Cole, "Meso-Economics: A Contribution from Entrepreneurial History," *Exploration in Entrepreneurial History*, 2nd Series, 6 (1968): 3–33.

21. Paul H. Wilken, *Entrepreneurship: A Comparative and Historical Study* (Norwood, NJ: Ables Publishing Corp., 1979).

22. William P. Glade, "Approaches to a Theory of Entrepreneurial Formation," *Explorations in Entrepreneurial History*, 2nd Series, 4 (1967): 249.

23. See Pye, *The Spirit of Chinese Politics;* and Robert H. Silin, *Leadership and Values: The Organization of Large-Scale Taiwanese Enterprises* (Cambridge, MA: Harvard University Press, 1976).

24. See William Copulsky and Herbert W. McNulty, *Entrepreneurship and the Corporation* (New York: Amacom, 1964).

25. Israel M. Kirzner, "The Entrepreneurial Process" in Calvin Kent, ed., *The Environment for Entrepreneurship* (Lexington, MA: Lexington Books, 1984), pp. 41–58.

26. Stephen M. Olsen, "The Inculcation of Economic Values in Taipei Business Families," in W.E. Willmott, ed., *Economic Organization in Chinese Society* (Stanford: Stanford University Press, 1972), pp. 261–95.

27. Margery Wolf, "Child Training and the Chinese Family" in Maurice Freedman, ed., *Family and Kinship in Chinese Society* (Stanford: Stanford University Press, 1970), pp. 37–62.

28. Copulsky and McNulty, *Entrepreneurship and the Corporation,* p. 34.

29. Kenneth R. van Voorhis, *Entrepreneurship and Small Business Management* (Boston: Allyn and Bacon, Inc., 1980), p. 22.

30. Hirschman, *Economic Development.*

31. Cf. Alan P. Lui, "T'ui-tung ching-chi fa-chan ti chi'i-yeh-chia chieh-ts'eng" ("The Social Backgrounds of Entrepreneurs Promoting [Taiwan's] Economic Development,"), *Chung-kuo lun-tan (China Forum),* no. 260 (July 25, 1985), pp. 20–25.

EIGHT

The Impact of Chinese Culture on Korea's Economic Development

Young-iob Chung

Introduction

Economic development depends upon human endeavors to exploit natural resources. Three of these endeavors, as W. Arthur Lewis has suggested, are especially important: the effort to economize, the increase of knowledge and its application, and the accumulation of capital.[1] The success of these endeavors, in turn, depends upon a cultural environment motivating individuals to increase the production of goods and services.

For some time is was primarily the Western countries that were thought to have provided a cultural environment highly favorable to the productive process. Now, with many Asian countries achieving unprecedented economic growth, the effect of non-Western cultural traditions on economic development is the subject of much discussion. The purpose of this chapter is to examine the impact of the Chinese cultural tradition on South Korean economic growth in the last 100 years. We will scrutinize how certain elements of this tradition retarded Korea's industrialization in the past but more recently have positively contributed to economic growth. Korea is one of a number of Asian countries with its cultural roots predominantly in China. A study of the relationship between culture and economic performance in South Korea will help identify matters of common interest to other Asian countries. It will also shed light on the kind of issues that the Third World countries in general have to face in their search for appropriate development strategies.

Korea's Record of Economic Development

Like its neighbors China and Japan, the "Hermit Kingdom"—as Korea was once called—did not start its effort at modernization until about 100 years ago, when Western nations forcibly opened its door to foreign trade. At that time, Korea's economy was more backward than Western Europe at the end of the Middle Ages. Though accurate information on the income of Korea is unavailable, inferences from existing data suggest that in the 1880s Korea's per capita income was about $140 in 1983 prices, and the Gross National Product about $1,800 million.[2] The society's elite, *yang-ban*, had a relatively comfortable life, but most of the people lived at the subsistence level.

The economy then was stagnant, with a low ceiling on the level of attainable output per worker. Underdevelopment permeated all fields of economic endeavor. Agriculture absorbed more than 85 percent of the population, most of whom worked on small, near-subsistence farms; commerce involved no more than transactions of such essential goods at salt, clothes, utensils, and agricultural products between itinerant merchants and consumers on infrequent, though regularly scheduled, market days; and industry and mining were minimally developed.

In the late 19th century, Korea lost her sovereignty to Japan, after the war of 1894–1895. To the Japanese conquerors, the Koreans needed nothing but "the whip and the spur" to get the country's resources mobilized.[3] Though Korea may be said to have started then the process of modernization, sustained economic progress proved elusive during the half century of Japanese rule. Even in the 1950s, after the country had regained independence, South Korea was in the eyes of many Americans "a hopeless and bottomless pit."[4] She survived only on the massive economic assistance from the United States.

In the 1960s South Korea finally embarked on a path of rapid growth. In 1983 its GNP reached $70 billion, a nearly 39-fold increase since the 1880s; its GNP per capita stood at $1,750, almost thirteen times what it was a century ago.[5] Given what the country has accomplished in the past twenty years, it is not surprising to read the government's prediction that South Korea's per capita income will reach $7,700 in 1991, about what Britain achieved in 1975.[6] In the last two decades, the structure of the Korean economy also has changed. Agriculture's share of the total domestic product dropped from more than 80 percent to less than

20 percent, while the industrial sector rose from an insignificant size to nearly 40 percent (see Chapter 2, Table 2 of this volume).

After such a rapid transition from agriculture to industry, Korea is now poised for the age of high technology, starting to export cars to North America in 1985 and racing to get into the field of supercomputers. With a severely damaged economy at the end of the Second World War and the ensuing Korean War, and carrying a heavy military burden in the tense, divided Korean peninsula, what South Korea achieved in the last two decades is astonishing indeed. Along with other East Asian countries, South Korea has maintained an economic record that is nothing short of miraculous.

Chinese Culture's Negative Impact in the Past

With Korea's long historical association with China, the Chinese cultural tradition has been a persistent and powerful force permeating all phases of the country's social life. As Edwin O. Reischauer and John K. Fairbank have observed, "In fact, Korea during [its pre-modern] period seemed at times even more Confucian and traditionally Chinese than China itself."[7] However, very few people have studied the impact of this tradition on Korea's economy, and their writings consist of largely casual and incidental remarks.

I will therefore attempt to relate the past and present economic performance of Korea to what I perceive to be the relevant elements of Chinese culture. Insofar as Korea's pre-modern economic experience is concerned, the Chinese cultural tradition generally had a negative impact, as can be seen in four areas critical to economic development: economic aspiration, innovation and entrepreneurship, attitude toward work and specialization, and capital formation.

Economic Aspiration

In traditional Korea, the highest personal accomplishment was to become a "cultured man." Those who passed the civil service examination in Confucian classics were idolized. They served in the government, and returned to their villages to enjoy "old age," being able to take a noontime nap in their summer cottages, perhaps attended by a young servant. The cottage was situated in a wooded hill overlooking a creek, surrounded by chirping birds, serene cranes, and aged pine trees. This caricature in a painting by a well-known Korean artist, Lee Chae-Gwan, 1783-1837, was a popular characterization of the traditional social ideal of Korea as well as China.

Well educated in Confucianism, the cultured man lived by the moral standards set by the ancient sage and strove to cultivate such "cardinal virtues as patriotism, filial piety, loyalty, and valor." For the Koreans, only the cultured man could be raised to a position of true dignity. That is, in their spiritual and social life, the Koreans regarded the cultured man as an end unto himself, and he reached such an elevated position not by birth but by self-cultivation and study.[8] To the cultured man, the highest goal in life was to secure an appointment to a public office, the level of appointment depending on his performance in the civil service examinations. Leading a virtuous life, he was entitled to political power, social respect, and personal wealth. His achievements would glorify his ancestors and his posterity.

Contrary to what has been generally assumed, such a Confucianist did not necessarily disdain wealth but considered it a means to achieve a higher end, i.e., to lead a virtuous life.[9] The pursuit of wealth, however, should never be regarded as an end in itself; otherwise, the Confucianist felt he would lose the equilibrium of "the genteel soul."[10] "The gentleman understands what is right; the inferior man (so-in) understands what is profitable." The Koreans accepted this Confucian adage and had over the centuries greatly popularized this concept, as illustrated in the following Korean sayings: "One should not seek for gold, jade, and suchlike valuables; rather desire that each one's descendants be virtuous." "Men should warn against covetousness, for wealth thus coveted would provoke the wrath of heaven." "Gold and silver are but vain things; after death how could they remain in one's hands?" "Wealth is but dung; benevolence and righteousness are worth thousands of gold pieces." "It is better to understand the classics than to amass riches."

Confucian teachings rejected training in economics for the pursuit of wealth and held business people in low esteem. The ruling elite, yang-ban, did not allow themselves to participate in profit-making enterprises. As the society's consummate Confucianists, they considered the management of economic affairs below their dignity. Even Korean laborers, as a foreign observer discovered, would not render their services purely for pecuniary gains, for they regarded their work as part of their *social* obligations as well.[11] Obviously such an aversion to the pursuit of profit dampened Koreans' economic aspirations.

Innovation and Entrepreneurship

The heart of the Confucianist (and Taoist) doctrine was to maintain the immutable harmony, tranquility, and equilibrium underlying both the universe and human society; man could not conquer nature; he could only use his reason to adjust his circumstances to the cosmic and social order. In other words, the Confucianist accepted the world "as given," implicitly sanctified tradition, and demanded that the individual adapt to it. The structural core of this social order was the so-called "five cardinal relations" *(oh-ryun)*, namely, the relations between king and subject, father and son, husband and wife, elder and younger siblings, and friend and friend. To conduct themselves properly in these five relations, individuals had to observe *li*—a set of norms governing human conduct in all social situations.

The Confucianist also considered it important to avoid extremes in handling human affairs, preferring to follow a "middle-of-the-road" *(choong-yong)* approach. He deemed conformity of universal value; he stressed the fulfillment of one's family obligations as fundamental to all social virtues.[12] An individual acting according to these Confucian precepts was believed to be able to achieve social harmony, some wealth, and a good name after death—the Confucianist's ultimate objectives. These traditions were perpetuated by the patriarchal family-centered mode of life, and any deviance from them would lead to social ostracism. Clearly, Confucianism neither believed in man's ability to transform this world nor considered it desirable to alter tradition. As one Korean author has put it, "...human power is so slight compared with the great power of nature" that any attempt to manipulate nature was out of the question.[13] Considering all events as prearranged by fate, the Koreans had to seek contentment from what was given.

Confucianism deemed loyalty and obedience as virtues central to all human relations; it required the subordination of the son to the father, the wife to the husband, and the subjects to the rulers. This is especially evident in family relations. The young generation was expected to adopt the same customs and values of the old; females were raised to be filial daughters before marriage, faithful wives following marriage, and wise mothers after bearing

children.[14] Thus, traditional Korean culture accepted, as one anthropologist has noted, "familism" as its most important characteristic.[15] The government was in a way patterned after the family. It was centralized in structure and administration, and the people habitually followed governmental policies like children obeying their father's decisions. The law, which was devised primarily to preserve social order rather than to protect the rights of the individual, was secondary in importance compared to social ethics. As a Korean social scientist has observed, "the soul of the Korean culture is *ui li*—a deeply held system of morality, integrity, loyalty, and sense of obligation developed in the context of interpersonal relations. This idea of *ui li* supersedes the idea of self...."
[16] Competition among individuals was discouraged, for it was considered inimical to group cohesion.

Yet, economic growth depends upon competition, for it requires the acquisition of a variety of knowledge that only a reasoning, questioning, and experimental mind can bring about. The questioning mind can best function in situations where society encourages free, competitive thinking and the sharing of experiences. None of these situations existed in traditional Korea. The prevailing social values restricted creativity to the exhortation of official doctrines and discouraged individuals from seeking change or innovation. While these values obviously made it difficult for the development of entrepreneurial talent, Korea's class structure also stifled economic innovation. The *yang-ban* neither had the ability to initiate economic enterprise themselves nor encouraged others to do so. Korea's middle class *(Choong-in)* was small in size, consisting of people of modest means (accountants, artisans, small merchants) with little capacity for capital accumulation. The lower class, the *sang-in* (commoners), was the least likely group to develop entrepreneurial skills, as its members were uneducated, heavily taxed, and poor.

As can be imagined, there was little mobility between classes or occupations in traditional Korea. In fact, the government, it seemed, deliberately maintained a rigid class structure by setting up a board to allocate the number of workmen in each occupation. With the exception of the nobility, the *yang-ban*, and certain members of the middle class, the population was distributed among different occupations recognized by the government, and jobs were inherited from generation to generation.[17] Though studies on family lineage in the Yi period (1392–1910) indicate some deviation from this rigid occupational pattern in the last phase of traditional Korea, the lack of social mobility remained a persistent phenomenon throughout most of Korea's history.[18] Conservatism and resistance to change were the dominant traits of the Koreans when they were brought into contact with foreign influences beginning in the late 19th century.[19]

Work and Specialization

One of the conditions critically affecting economic performance is the people's attitude toward work and specialization. Individuals' willingness to devote their labor to work and society's encouragement of specialization are the conditions conducive to modern economic development. Korea's idealization of the cultured man, however, made it difficult for these conditions to emerge. The cultured man sought only to attain moral ideals, not to labor for any functional end; he was a humanist and generalist, not a specialist performing a technical job.[20] To the *yang-ban*, the experts should not be raised to a position of dignity; their job befitted only that of the clerical staff.[21] This condition obstructed specialization in bureaucratic functions and rational development of economic enterprises. In addition, it caused a neglect of studies in engineering, agriculture, and medicine.

In reality, work is not only a means of producing goods and services, but also a way of life. Though many individuals may regard working as a nuisance, others consider it a virtue. The men of the Confucian-oriented Korean society undervalued work, especially manual labor. The *yang-ban* regarded themselves a privileged group, chosen to rule society, and not required to work to make a living. In fact, even *yang-ban*'s sons were forbidden to engage in physical labor.[22] They preferred to consider themselves "not employed," so as not to soil their hands with gainful employment.[23] While the *yang-ban* had a low regard for manual labor, most of Korean commoners were noted for being "very hard working," and "diligent."[24] With an average farm size of 2.5 acres, the peasants toiled most of the year just to survive. Similarly, many of the small merchants, fishermen, and artisans had to work strenuously to eke out a livelihood.

Capital Formation

In traditional Korea, business investment stayed at an insignificant level, just about enough to support a small increase in population during normal times; it experienced a decline during times of war and natural disasters. The lack of productive investment had much to do with the society's low regard for business and the pursuit of profit. Most of the people had a marked reluctance to take risks in business expansion or new ventures. The *yang-ban* had the resources for investment but were not supposed to meddle with "such sordid matters as manufacture and merchandise."[25] In reality, they frequently argued against investment in any technical invention, which they considered to be an unnecessary expenditure to society. The *yang-ban* used their savings primarily to educate their young, to have them trained for the civil service examinations, and to help them gain entrance to the officialdom. But as the number of those who took and failed the examination increased, the education of the young *yang-ban* placed a heavy financial burden upon the family and the society as a whole.

When the relatively well-to-do Koreans did make investments, it was less for the development of productive enterprises than for non-productive purposes such as the purchase of gold, jewelry, and land; the construction of mansions and religious monuments; and the establishment of usury funds. Some savings were poured into various forms of gambling.[26]

Limited amounts of productive investment did go into farming, handicrafts, and small-scale commerce.[27] Insignificant investment showed up in the purchase of sampans and carts, the construction of roads, bridges, irrigation and drainage facilities, and the development of virgin lands. But the overall magnitude of these investments was not sufficiently large to sustain any long-term growth.

The level of savings in traditional Korea was obviously low; yet some of the savings were lavishly spent for fulfilling family duties. Dictated by Confucian ethics, the Koreans went farther than the Chinese in the development of elaborate ceremonies and rituals to honor their family members—from the celebration of the birth of a baby to the cult of the dead.[28] And they set up numerous organizations, i.e., *kye*, to conduct these ceremonies and rituals.[29]

Most Korean families observed four major rites *(sa-rye)*—*investure, wedding, funeral, and ancestor worship.* Of these rites, the demonstration of filial piety was the most important, and the Koreans were said to have been "more set in their ancestor-worship than the Chinese."[30] To provide for decent burials for their deceased elders, descendants would conduct elaborate ceremony and spare no expense. Ironically, some funerals assumed a festival air, giving "an impression of gaiety rather than grief."[31] Some in the procession might be neither relatives nor friends but people "bent on having a good time and drinking all the free wine they wanted."[32] One estimate has put the total funeral expenses incurred in traditional Korea at far more than one percent of the GNP.[33] On each recurring anniversary of the death of an ancestor, a sacrificial feast had to be given. The custom was for the Koreans to enshrine the tablets of the dead in their homes for four generations and to honor those of more remote generations at the family burial ground. On these occasions, all of the sons and daughters and other relatives were expected to attend. These events called for much drinking and eating, and many village "loafers" had a good time.[34] The grieved host who could afford the biggest spread at these annual feasts would be the man receiving the highest esteem of his neighbors.[35] A person could conceivably spend more on these rites than on his household needs, and he might go into debt because of them.[36]

Other occasions for social spending were also very costly. For a person reaching the 60th birthday *(hwan-gap)*, who had nothing remaining for him to do but to rest and reminisce, his children and relatives had to "strain every nerve" to provide a party for the occasion.[37] Wine and meat in great abundance were provided for the relatives, friends, neighbors, acquaintances, and even strangers.[38] Then, parents had to marry their children well; an inexpensive wedding in 1897 was estimated to cost about 75 yen, about two and a half times the annual per capita income at the time.[39] According to a Korean saying, "Those who have three daughters cannot keep even their utensils." For boys attaining manhood, investure ceremony was expensive, often causing families to go beyond the limit of their purse to provide for the festivity.[40]

In Korea, as in China, the place of the individual in society was negligible, and more emphasis was placed on the group, which took on the character of a corporate body, particularly in family relations.[41] Many Koreans considered it a great virtue to respect and maintain a sense of brotherhood; some, as foreign observers have noted, were almost "hospitable to a fault among themselves."[42] Thus, Koreans of all walks of life considered social entertainment one of their "sacred duties."[43] A person of ordinary means would not spare any expense to entertain his friends. The *yang-ban* often kept at their expense many "permanent guests" *(moon-kaik)*—as many as 200 to 300 per *yang-ban* family in certain cases.[44] They lived in relative luxury, but provided little useful service to the host.[45]

This corporate responsibility extended well beyond the limits of kinship, reaching to villagers, friends, and to some extent strangers.[46] Thus, the prevailing customs and values strengthened family and group cohesion, but the cost to society was out of proportion. These traditions not only placed a heavy burden upon family finances, but, more significantly, drained off savings and prevented capital formation.

The Contemporary Korean Economy

In the preceding pages I have identified and evaluated the negative economic impact of the Chinese cultural tradition on Korea. Today, South Korea, along with other Asian countries, has emerged from economic dormancy and experienced a dynamic growth that challenges not only the industrial West but even Asia's own economic giant, Japan.

This dramatic turnaround results from a fundamental shift in the Koreans' social orientations combined with certain factors external to the country. The shift of social orientations perhaps can be illustrated by identifying "the idolized person" in today's Korea. In contrast to the cultured gentleman of the past, the esteemed person in contemporary Korea would be a prominent corporation executive or a high-ranking government technocrat, aged 45, having studied abroad, with a cosmopolitan outlook.

This characterization of the idolized person reveals a substantial change in the make-up, outlook, and attitude of the Korean people in the post-World War II years. This person still is a man, not a woman; he is well-educated in science or business, not in Confucian classics; he excels in technical skills, not in humanities; he seeks satisfaction through a busy schedule, not the contented life in retirement. More significantly, he treats the pursuit of wealth as a desirable objective in life, not downgrading its importance.

The change of Koreans' social outlook has been caused by many things, but certain foreign-introduced changes appear crucially timed. First of all, prompted by its strong growth-oriented policy *(fukoku-kyohei)*, Japan abolished during its 40-

year rule of Korea the traditional institutions inimical to economic progress. The Japanese reforms included modeling Korean government on the modernized Japanese system; the establishment of market-oriented economic institutions, including nationwide commercial and financial networks; the encouragement of free exchange of resources and labor; some rationalization of agriculture; the streamlining of the tax system; the effective enforcement of law and order; and the provision of essential public services. In addition, Japan made a financial contribution to the development of Korea's incipient social overhead and infrastructure.[47]

These measures by the Japanese colonial government induced the Koreans to adopt an attitude favorably disposed to economic growth. They enabled Korea to march down the path of modernization sooner. But they took place at a high cost, as Japan exacted from its colony huge human and material resources in the service of its expansionist policies, which led to a series of armed conflicts eventually culminating in the Second World War.

In the aftermath of the war, the United States proved to be an important agent introducing modernization to South Korea. The American presence in Korea and the flow of military personnel and businessmen between the United States and South Korea gave many South Koreans a first-hand opportunity to learn from the most advanced Western nation about the process of industrialization. Then, in the 1950s and the early 1960s, American foreign aid and direct private investment provided South Korea with the critically needed capital when the country was engaged in a massive reconstruction of its war-torn economy.[48] Subsequently, when the United States' foreign aid dwindled, foreign private loans, mainly from Japan and the United States, provided the capital needed for economic expansion. For instance, in 1975 foreign capital invested in South Korea was equivalent to more than 11 percent of the country's GNP, a very substantial share of its investment needs.[49] At the same time, because of the Korean government's policy curbing social spending, South Korea's domestic savings rate rose rapidly. As seen in Table 5 in Chapter 2 of this volume, from 1965 to 1986, South Korea's gross domestic investment as a percentage of gross domestic product rose from 15 percent to 29 percent, and the country's gross domestic savings as a percentage of gross domestic product jumped from 8 percent to 35 percent.

It is significant to note that some of the Chinese cultural traditions that had once been thought to hinder industrial growth have now become a boon to economic development. Probably the most important of these is the reverence for education. The Confucian emphasis on learning and competitive examination as a means of social achievement has long motivated the Koreans to pursue scholarly and educational endeavors, which are crucial to the acquisition and diffusion of knowledge—skills indispensable to development. Thus, when South Korea was on the verge of its economic take-off, the nation gave a top priority to education and training. "By 1965, Korea's human resource development had exceeded the norm for a country with *three* times its median per capita GNP."[50]

Another Chinese cultural tradition that apparently has facilitated Korea's recent economic development is the high prestige the Koreans attach to governmental positions, which enables the government to recruit well-qualified personnel for public services. No country can achieve economic progress without positive stimulus from an intelligent and concerned government. The post-World War II Korean regime has always possessed highly educated officials well versed in modern economics. Moreover, effective government also depends upon the willingness of the governed to accept and follow the government's policy. Under the Confucian tradition, the Korean people have long been used to looking to and accepting government leadership; thus, when South Korea decided in the 1950s to adopt high economic growth as a national objective, the government could put forward initiatives and expect them to be supported.[51]

Summary

Many of the Confucian traditions that once caused the economic stagnancy of Korea also contributed to the economic under-development of China. Yet, in some respects, the Koreans were perhaps even more steeped in these traditions than the Chinese themselves. Hence, the negative economic consequences of Confucianism may well be more pronounced in Korea than in China of the past age. This chapter has identified and examined these consequences in four areas: 1) the discouragement of economic aspiration, 2) the lack of emphasis on innovation and entrepreneurship, 3) the undervaluation of work and specialization, and 4) the disincentive for capital formation.

Korea's economy remained stagnant until the first half of the 20th century, when it showed a slow but firm growth; it was then followed by a very rapid development in the last two decades despite having to overcome the damage of devastating wars. The change of Korea's economic fortune resulted largely from the policies of foreign powers—Japan and the United States—which led to certain institutional reforms in Korea, a shift in the social orientation of the people, and a substantial foreign capital contribution to Korea's initial development effort.

These foreign-induced changes were accompanied by Korea's own effort to adapt two Chinese cultural traditions to the requirements of modernity. One of these was the emphasis on education, which facilitates the development of human resources needed for industrialization. The only required change here was to substitute science and technology for Confucian classics as the content of popular learning. Another Chinese tradition contributing to modern Korea's economic growth was the high prestige the Koreans attached to governmental offices and the obedient attitude of the people toward government. In the past, the government's role was primarily administrative; in modern times it is also managerial. In the latter capacity, the Korean government—like the government in the Republic of China—easily became an initiator and a coordinator of the modernization process.

Korea's developmental experience suggests that the transformation of a stagnant to a vibrant economy need not be long or difficult, and that cultural traditions that once handicapped industrial growth can be adjusted to facilitate the needs of modernization.

NOTES

1. W. Arthur Lewis, *The Theory of Economic Growth* (Homewood, IL: Richard D. Irwing, Inc., 1955), p. 11.

2. Young-iob Chung, "The Traditional Economy of Korea," *The Journal of Modern Korean Studies* (January 1984), pp. 6–9.

3. For a detailed discussion, see Chosen, Government-General, *Korean Reforms and Progress Reports, 1910–1913* (1910–1911), p. 59; Joon-ichiro Suenaga, *Chosen Shooho*, Toko Sosho by Toho Kyokai (Tokyo: Toho Shoten, 1895), pp. 124–25; Seizo Shikida, *Chosen Nogyo Yoran* (Tokyo, 1910), p. 143; James S. Gale, *Korean Sketches* (Boston, 1893), p. 58; George Kennan, "Korea: A Degenerated State," *Outlook* 81 (1905): 409 *et seq; Angus Hamilton, Korea, London, Heinimann* (Boston: J.B. Millet, 1910), p. 274; Shannon Boyd McCune, *Korea's Heritage* (Rutland, VT: C.E. Tuttle Co., 1956), p. 75.

4. W.D. Reeve, *The Republic of Korea: A Political and Economic Study* (London, 1963), p. 121.

5. The Bank of Korea reported that GNP and per capita GNP of Korea in 1982 were $65.7 billion and $1,671 respectively. *The Korea Herald,* August 2, 1983.

6. The Republic of Korea's Minister of Economic Planning made this estimate in 1978. *The Korea Herald*, January 26, 1978.

7. Edwin O. Reischauer and John K. Fairbank, *East Asia: The Great Tradition* (Boston: Houghton Mifflin Co., 1960), p. 426. See also H.J. Whigham, *Manchuria and Korea* (London: Isbister, 1904), p. 185.

8. Max Weber, *The Religion of China* (New York: The Free Press, 1951), p. 228.

9. Ibid., p. 245.

10. Ibid., pp. 245–46.

11. Homer B. Hulbert, ed., *Korean Repository*, Vol. III (Seoul: Trilingual Press, 1895), 479.

12. This situation was noted also in Ch'ing China by Tung-tsu Chu, *Local Government in China under the Ch'ing* (Cambridge, MA: Harvard University Press, 1962), p. 193.

13. Nang-nyung Lee, "The Korean's Way of Thinking," *Koreana Quarterly* 5:3 (1963): 114–16.

14. Seong-hi Yim, "The Problem of Human Metabolism in Korea," *Koreana Quarterly* 5:2 (1963): 57; for two series of articles on the Korean family system by Hyo-chae Lee and Jae-seuk Choi respectively, see *The Korea Herald,* January 18–February 9, 1978 and March 7–March 15, 1978.

15. Shin-pyo Kang, a paper presented at the Conference on U.S.-Korean Relations held at the University of Hawaii, jointly sponsored by the American Studies Institute of Seoul National University and the Center for Korean Studies of the University of Hawaii, May 21–27, 1982, reported in *The Korea Herald,* May 26, 1982.

16. Young-nok Koo, a paper presented at the Conference on U.S.-Korean Relations held at the University of Hawaii, noted above.

17. William Woodville Rockhill, *China's Intercourse with Korea from the 15th Century to 1895* (London: Luzac & Co., 1905), p. 51.

18. Edward W. Wagner, "Report on a Conference: Traditional Korean Society," *Items,* Social Science Research Council, vol. 29, no. 4 (December, 1975), 45–47.

19. Hae-jong Chun, "Korean Attitude toward Foreigners in Earlier Times," A paper presented at the Fourth Annual International Symposium on History and Culture of East Asia, sponsored by the Korean National Academy of Sciences, Seoul, Korea, October 26, 1976.

20. Weber, *The Religion of China,* p. 246.

21. Ibid.

22. J. Robert Moose, *Village Life in Korea* (Nashville, TN: Publishing House of the M.E. Church, South, 1911), pp. 54, 63, 99, 101–2, 123; Homer B. Hulbert, ed., *Korean Repository,* vol. V (Seoul: Trilingual Press, 1898), 2; and Charles Dallet, *Traditional Korea* (New Haven, CT: Behavior Science Translations, by Human Relations Areas Files, 1954; original publication in 1874), pp. 104–5.

23. *Korean Repository,* vol. V, p. 2; Moose, *Village Life in Korea,* p. 103; and Rockhill, *China's Intercourse with Korea,* p. 54.

24. *Repository,* vol. V, p. 230; and Suenobu Kato, *Kankoku Nogyo Ron* [Study of Korean Agriculture] (Tokyo, 1904), p. 168. This view is supported by contemporary observers, e.g., Chong-hae

Yu, "Unique Character Traits of Koreans," quoted in *The Korea Herald,* July 12, 1978.

25. Moose, *Village Life in Korea,* p. 54.

26. William E. Griffis, *Corea, The Hermit Nation* (New York: Scribner's, 1907), p. 295.

27. Man Kil Kang, "Yicho Fuki Sangup Chabon ui Sungchang" ("Growth of Business Capital in the Late Yi Period"), a paper presented to a seminar sponsored by the Asian Research Institute, Seoul, Korea, November, 1970.

28. Whigham, *Manchuria and Korea,* p. 185; Su Keun Chang, "Ku-Chung Seshi ki" ["Note on the Lunar New Year Festivities"], *The Kyong Hyang Shinmun,* January 31, 1976.

29. Young-iob Chung, "Kye: A Traditional Economic Institution in Korea," in Andrew C. Nahm, ed., *Traditional Korea—Theory and Practice* (Kalamazoo, MI: The Center for Korean Studies, Western Michigan University, 1974), p. 108.

30. Whigham, *Manchuria and Korea;* Chang, "Ku-Chung Seshi ki."

31. Isabella Bird Bishop, *Korea* (New York: Fleming H. Revell Co., 1897), pp. 286–87.

32. Moose, *Village Life in Korea,* p. 178.

33. According to a survey conducted by a governmental agency in 1971, the expenditures incurred for funerals in that year were as much as one percent of the GNP. In all probability, such expenditures in traditional Korea were far greater than that. *Hankuk Ilbo,* June 26, 1971.

34. See Bishop, *Korea,* p. 91; Dallet, *Traditional Korea,* p. 157; Rockhill, *China's Intercourse with Korea,* p. 52; Homer B. Hulbert, ed., *Korean Repository,* vol. IV (Seoul: Trilingual Press, 1897), 229, 447.

35. Moose, *Village Life in Korea,* pp. 197–98.

36. Bishop, *Korea,* p. 290.

37. Dallet, *Traditional Korea,* p. 162; Griffis, *Corea,* p. 296.

38. Dallet, *Traditional Korea,* p. 163.

39. Bishop, *Korea,* p. 117.

40. Ibid., p. 360.

41. McCune, *Korea's Heritage*, p. 74; Moose, *Village Life in Korea*, p. 64; James S. Gale, *Korea in Transition* (Cincinnati: Jennings & Graham, 1909), p. 111.

42. Griffis, *Corea*, p. 288; Homer B. Hulbert, ed., *Korean Repository*, vol. II (Seoul: Trilingual Press, 1895), p. 346.

43. Dallet, *Traditional Korea*, pp. 150, 156; Griffis, *Corea*, pp. 288–9; Gale, *Korea in Transition*, pp. 109–10. The Koreans take friendship very seriously indeed. Numerous Americans have reported, with some amusement, experiences in which a little help rendered to a young, or otherwise disadvantage, Korean was paid back decades later, in the most lavish and elaborate way. See James Wade, *The Korean Herald*, May 22, 1982.

44. *Korean Repository*, Vol. II, p. 367.

45. Bishop, *Korea*, p. 356; *Korean Repository*, vol. II, p. 368.

46. Dallet, *Traditional Korea*, p. 149.

47. Young-iob Chung, "Japanese Investment in Korea, 1904–1945," in Andrew C. Nahm, ed., *Korea Under Japanese Colonial Rule* (Kalamazoo, MI: The Center for Korean Studies, Western Michigan University, 1973); Young-iob Chung, "Korean Investment Under Japanese Rule," in C.I. Eugene Kim and Doretha E. Mortimore, eds., *Korea's Response to Japan: The Colonial Period, 1910–1945* (Kalamazoo, MI: The Center for Korean Studies, Western Michigan University, 1977).

48. Young-iob Chung, "U.S. Economic Aid to South Korea after World War II" in Andrew C. Nahm, ed., *The United States and Korea* (Kalamazoo, MI: The Center for Korean Studies, Western Michigan University, 1979).

49. Ibid., pp. 212–14.

50. Irma Adelman, "Annex: South Korea," in Hollis Chenery *et al.*, *Redistribution with Growth* (London: Oxford University Press, 1974), p. 281 (original italics).

51. "Bittul ou jin Kwanryo ui Kwanii" ("The Warped Authority of Officialdom"), *The Dong-A Il-bo*, April 19, 1977.

NINE

Modernization and Chinese Cultural Traditions in Hong Kong

Siu-lun Wong

Introduction

Hong Kong, by now, is quite modern.[1] At the same time, it remains essentially Chinese. Measured by most accepted indicators, Hong Kong qualifies as a newly industrialized region. Between 1960 and 1979, for example, its annual energy consumption grew at about 10 percent—a rate higher than those of all the industrial economies and most Asian countries except Singapore and the Republic of Korea.[2]

Hong Kong's productivity is high, ranking third in Asia after Japan and Singapore. Its GNP per capita grew at 10 percent annually in the 1960s and '70s; by 1986 its GNP per capita reached US$6,910.[3] In terms of employment, 49 percent of its labor force was engaged in manufacturing and construction, 47 percent in commerce and services, and just 2 percent in agriculture in 1981.[4] Its inhabitants, like those in Singapore, are keen participants in the mass media. Its annual average newsprint consumption per thousand people was 13,041 kg. in 1970 and 1971, well ahead of the Republic of Korea at 4,345 kg. and Mexico at 3,630 kg.[5] Population growth is also conforming to patterns common in industrialized countries, with a low birth rate of 1.69 percent, a low death rate of 0.5 percent, and a high life expectancy of about 75 years in 1981.[6]

The population of Hong Kong is made up predominantly of ethnic Chinese. A mere 2 percent of the residents trace their origins to places other than Hong Kong and China.[7] Most of the

Hong Kong Chinese still adhere to traditional Chinese mores on various aspects of social living; they have adopted many Western folkways but only in a superficial sense. In a recent survey, nearly all of the respondents stated that family solidarity was important. "Only about nine percent of the sample said that they would 'not care' if a member of their *nuclear* family had a quarrel with a non-relative," and most of them declared that they would actively intervene.[8] Significantly, "it is not only the middle-aged and elderly who consider the familial group to be of overwhelming significance, but this point of view also is the norm for young adults in Hong Kong."[9] In the realm of interpersonal relationships, "courtesy and face" remain important considerations.[10]

The Impact of Culture on Growth

The spectacular economic success of Hong Kong calls for an explanation. So too does the success of Singapore, Taiwan, and South Korea. The shared Chinese cultural heritage readily suggests itself, and a persuasive case has been made that the "neo-Confucian" or "post-Confucian" ethic is conducive to economic development.[11] If Confucianism is understood in a broad sense as a cultural ethos, then we may hypothesize that the Chineseness of Hong Kong is linked in some way with its industrial performance.

But it is paradoxical that not very long ago the prevailing view in academic circles was that traditional Chinese culture was inimical to industrial development. This shift in perception is captured well by Daniel Kwok: Confucianism alive, it inhibited capitalism; Confucianism dead, it facilitates modernization.[12] The former view leads us back to Max Weber. As is well known, Weber traced the compulsion to harness profit—the hallmark of capitalism—to the fundamental ideas of ascetic Protestantism. According to him, this religious doctrine postulated a direct relationship between the individual and a personalized god. A Protestant, unsure whether he was among those receiving God's grace, had to excel in a worldly calling so as to attain salvation. The pursuit of wealth could be a religious calling so long as one worked ceaselessly and systematically, eschewing dishonesty, avarice, and ostentation. But the cultural and religious values of China, in Weber's assessment, did not engender this capitalistic spirit. He found the dominant teaching of Confucianism, though rationalistic in form, lacking "an ethical prophecy of a supramundane God" and thus without "an inward core, of a unified way of life flowing from some central and autonomous value position."[13] Contrasting the mentalities of Confucianism and Protestant asceticism, he wrote:

> Confucian rationalism meant rational adjustment to the world; Puritan rationalism meant rational mastery of the world. Both Puritan and the Confucian were "sober men." But the rational sobriety of the Puritan was found in a mighty enthusiasm which the Confucian lacked completely.... The rejection of the world by occidental asceticism was insolubly linked to its opposite, namely, its eagerness to dominate the world.... Nothing conflicted more with the Confucian ideal of gentility than the idea of "vocation." The "princely" man was an aesthetic value; he was not a tool of god. But the true Christian, the other-worldly asceticist, wished to be nothing more than a tool of his God; in this he sought his dignity....[14]

Without the "religiously systematized utilitarianism" of the Protestant faith, the compulsive urge to re-invest earnings was said to be absent in traditional Chinese enterprises. But this conclusion was specific to the problem preoccupying Weber. He was concerned with the question of the emergence of an endogenous spirit of capitalism—not its subsequent diffusion to the other parts of the world. He indicated that the *adoption* of capitalism is a separate issue. "The Chinese," he said without elaboration, "in all probability would be capable, probably more capable than the Japanese, of assimilating capitalism which has technically and economically been fully developed in the modern cultural area."[15]

Why should the Chinese-culture areas be capable of assimilating industrial capitalism, more so than the peoples in other developing countries, as the post-war record seems to have demonstrated? Roderick MacFarquhar finds the answer in "their post-Confucian characteristics—self-confidence, social cohesion, subordination of the individual, education for action, bureaucratic tradition and moralizing certitude."[16] He puts forth this suggestive list to account for the economic performance of non-Communist East Asian states. I shall be more modest in my aim and focus my attention on the case of the Hong Kong Chinese.

Our stock of knowledge about Hong Kong's modernization process is limited, but I believe we can still discern four major Chinese cultural elements which facilitate the adoption of industrial capitalism—incorporative cosmology, high achievement motivation, pervasive familism, and utilitarian discipline.

Incorporative Cosmology

A cosmological gulf, according to Frederick W. Mote, separates Chinese from Western cultures; no creation myth exists in Chinese religious thought.[17] Deities and spirits abound in the Chinese heaven, but a personalized god in the role of a creator is absent. The behavioral consequences of this religious worldview for the emergence of the spirit of capitalism may well be negative. An inner tension fostered by the uncertain relation between men and their creator is lacking. The idea of synchronicity and adjustment dominates the Chinese mode of thinking. The Chinese try to live in harmony with nature, while Westerners believe that it is human nature to try to subdue one's physical surroundings. Yet the inherent eclecticism of Chinese cosmology enables the Chinese to become adept borrowers of foreign practices. Non-exclusive in faith, they are generally pragmatic in outlook. "[A] Chinese may go to a Buddhist monastery to pray for a male heir, but he may proceed from there to a Taoist shrine where he beseeches a god to cure him of malaria. Ask any number of Chinese what their religion is and the answer of the majority will be that they have no particular religion, or that, since all religions benefit man in one way or another, they are equally good."[18]

In Hong Kong, at least, this incorporative attitude apparently has encouraged the adoption of many foreign practices. For the Hong Kong Chinese as a whole, Marjorie Topley has formed the following impressions:

> ...people do not usually turn to Western ideas because they come to believe them more "true" than the traditional ones. Rather, they follow some Western practices because they find them effective in some circumstances and [follow] some Chinese practices for similar reasons. People may move in and out of Chinese and Western traditions, at least at the present time: the effect is the proof—if it works it is true.[19]

A recent survey on popular attitudes toward technological innovation discovered that most of the respondents held positive views. The majority of them regarded "the increasing number of cars, big factories and machines" *as necessary,* though fewer of them *liked* such trappings of modernity. It is significant that little variation in attitude was found among different age groups and socio-economic strata, as well as between rural and urban residents. "Technological development seems to be generally favoured right across the population."[20]

In my study of a group of owners and directors of cotton spinning mills in Hong Kong, I found a similar orientation. The majority of my forty odd respondents, about 70 percent, did not proclaim any religious affiliation. Only 20 percent of them were Christians. When asked to name a book that they would recommend to a young entrepreneur, they gave diverse answers ranging from the opinion that most books are useless to technical manuals and the works of Beaverbrook and Edward de Bono. None of them mentioned the Confucian classics. No Confucianists themselves in the strict sense, "they have successfully combined their origins with a totally cosmopolitan world outlook."[21] They have blended Western elements with their own tradition with apparent ease. Michel Oksenberg, for example, gives the following description of the interior decoration of one Hong Kong textile company:

> The decor of the president's suite was quite plush—thick carpets, elegant furniture, all in a French renaissance style. It is here that the Western visitor is often entertained. I then went to the mill and was greeted in the main sales room. This too was elegantly furnished, this time in Danish style. I went on to a meeting room where Westerners are sometimes taken but where members of the mill also sometimes assemble. The decor was also basically Western, but I began to note Chinese touches. Finally, I was ushered into the inner sanctum of the mill—the place where the mill supervisors meet almost daily to plan production teams. This is a place where Westerners rarely stray. The decor is fully Chinese: the monk chairs with circular marble inlays are pushed against the wall, the tablet with the picture of the founder of the firm stared down from one end of the room, the table with flowers placed beneath

it create the atmosphere of a shrine. The atmosphere is elegant but stark.[22]

In terms of technology, a substantial number of the spinners I interviewed, some 40 percent, had university degrees in textile manufacture or various fields of engineering. They showed pride in their flexible and innovative handling of machinery. One of my respondents said:

> In Hong Kong, we have a lot of information about new textile machines. We know their merits and drawbacks. So we choose the suitable parts and assemble them. But in our neighbouring countries, they usually order the complete set from one company, down to the last screw. That's why we are a step ahead of them.[23]

As early as the 1950s, when the Hong Kong cotton spinning industry had just been established, an official of the International Federation of Master Cotton Spinners and Manufacturers was already greatly impressed by what he saw in the Hong Kong mills:

> The machinery used emanates from almost all the textile machinery works of the world.... All the machinery in the mills is up to date and new. Their mills have air-conditioning and vacuum plants; trolley transport for the warp-beams; Toyoda automatic looms seem to preponderate. There are no ordinary looms—all are automatic....[24]

Achievement Motivation

Herman Kahn believes that two connected aspects of the Confucian ethic tend to promote economic growth—"the creation of dedicated, motivated, responsible, and educated individuals and the enhanced sense of commitment, organizational identity, and loyalty to various institutions."[25] With respect to the concept of achievement motivation, David McClelland has provided some evidence for both the Chinese mainland and Taiwan in the 1950s.[26] Though comparative data are lacking for Hong Kong, a survey of Hong Kong's school pupils indicates that about one-half of the children say that their parents value most their achievement outside the family and give top priority to their doing well in school. Values pertaining to "compliance and family-centered activities" as well as "social relationships with people outside the home" are, according to the respondents, relegated to secondary importance.[27]

But what are Hong Kong students striving for after they have left school? Are their goals relevant to economic pursuits? Various studies on Chinese economic values and conduct are pointing to a common goal among Chinese youth: self-employment is at a premium. To a certain extent this explains why entrepreneurs are in abundant supply in Hong Kong but are relatively scarce in many other Asian countries, especially in non-Chinese cultural areas.[28]

The norm on self-employment was vividly expressed by a small Hong Kong industrialist who reportedly said that "a Shanghainese at forty who has not yet made himself owner of a firm is a failure, a good-for-nothing."[29] Such a preference is not confined to small industrialists. Large textile-mill owners also hold similar views. Nearly two-thirds of those I interviewed preferred to be owner-managers of small firms to senior executives of large corporations, if such a choice was available to them.[30] They treasured autonomy and disliked hierarchy. Various schools of Chinese philosophy since the Warring States period have shared one basic premise: men are "naturally equal," i.e., men are born with common attributes at birth.[31] Social inequalities appeared because of differences in the efforts of individuals devoted to their work and because of differences in education. This conception of man was embodied in a peculiar system of social stratification in traditional China. A strictly hierarchical structure coexisted with an ideology exhorting individual social advancement.[32] No status, however high, was regarded as intrinsically beyond the reach of an individual. In order to maximize one's chances of upward mobility, one should not let one's ambition be suppressed.

The family system, particularly in its inheritance practices during the imperial period, reinforced the value of individual autonomy by treating brothers as equals and claimants of the family estate. Such a system affects Chinese economic behavior and results in several notable differences between Chinese and Japanese enterprises. Both the Chinese and Japanese cultural traditions extol, as social ideals, "complementarity of relations" and "harmonious human relations in an organization."[33] But in practice, joint action by non-family related individuals is much more difficult to achieve among the Chinese. My hypothesis is that the pervasive ambition of individuals to strike out on their own tends to deny Chinese industrial entrepreneurs of an adequate supply of dependable executives.[34] Loyalty of subordinates cannot be taken for granted. Thus, tight managerial supervision, little delegation of authority, and a highly personalized form of management are the main traits of Hong Kong Chinese firms. These enterprises also are unlikely to cooperate among themselves. Entrepreneurial independence is so jealously guarded that oligopolistic groupings are rarely found, and no equivalents to the Japanese *Zaibatsu* exist.[35]

Nevertheless, the absence of a stable and dedicated middle managerial stratum does not necessarily dampen the overall vitality of Hong Kong industry. One of the spinners I talked to attributed the success of his industry to the flexibility resulting from a prevalent desire for self-employment:

> Japanese and South Korean workers are very obedient. But Hong Kong workers are dexterous, and hard working. They are willing to work overtime. Our recent success in denim manufacture is an example. In the United States, large factories usually carry out the entire process of production. They cannot take on sudden increases in orders or special requests because everybody is an employee, and workers are not enthusiastic about overtime pay. In Hong Kong, there are numerous small owners. Therefore, Hong Kong can take on special production. It is beneficial to existing spinners. We can make goods of uncommon specification even for relatively small orders. Only Hong Kong can do this. After the yarn is spun, there are specialized factories to do the dyeing. Afterwards, we can take the dyed yarn to yet another factory to be knitted. The whole is divided into parts, and this increases our flexibility.

Pervasive Familism

How is familism expressed in economic conduct? It may appear, in various combinations, as paternalistic managerial ideology and practice, nepotistic employment, and family ownership of enterprises. The Chinese in Hong Kong are still very familistic, and familism is often seen as an obstacle to industrialization.[36] Yet it does have its positive aspects.

Let us first consider paternalistic management—a subject that has not yet been systematically studied in Hong Kong. My research on the cotton spinners has shown them to be patriarchal business leaders. They confer welfare benefits on their employees as favors, take a personal interest in their subordinates' non-job related activities, and disapprove of trade union activities. Such a managerial approach has been adopted, I believe, to cope with both cultural and economic problems. Personalized ties with subordinates are forged in an attempt to discourage managers from setting up their own firms and becoming rival competitors. For a business such as the spinning and weaving industry, which requires a stable workforce, benevolent paternalism also is one way of retaining workers.

Two main consequences appear to flow from Chinese paternalism. In the first place, paternalism demands formal obedience from subordinates. The emphasis is on outward deference to one's seniors in the organization. Eye contact, for example, is avoided by employees with their chief executive during board meetings.[37] Staff members may advance dissenting views and personal opinions—they may sometimes even be demanded to do so—but they must present their views at the appropriate moment so as not to contradict their superiors in public.[38] In the second place, paternalism can inhibit the growth of class consciousness by the formation of patron-client relations between managers and their staff. This does not necessarily mean an absence of friction in Chinese firms. Rather, conflicts tend to be manifested more often in individual actions, such as absenteeism and resignations, than in group actions, such as collective bargaining and confrontation. A prominent Hong Kong entrepreneur has commented:

> In a Western industrial society, paternalism is frowned upon; in Hong Kong it has been an instrument for industrial success and social equilibrium in a period of great social upheaval. Here again it is worth noting that in 1968, out of a total of about 170 million industrial man-days, only 8,432 man-days were lost through disputes.[39]

Chinese and Western scholars alike often regard nepotism—a preferential treatment of one's relatives—as a hindrance to industrial efficiency.[40] How widespread is nepotism in the Hong Kong economy? Among my sample of cotton spinners, nearly 60 percent said they had employed relatives in their mills. But they also emphasized that only "one or two" or "a few" relatives were engaged. Since these spinners had at least two hundred employees each, the percentage of kinsmen in their workforce was small. Other studies in the Colony have produced similar findings. John L. Espy interviewed the chief executives (owners) of 27 large Chinese industrial firms in 1969. Among the 23 from whom information was obtained, 14, or 61 percent, had "family members employed in their companies."[41] In our 1978 survey of 415 small-scale factories, about 47 percent of the factory owners had relatives in their workforce.[42] These findings suggest that nepotism probably exists in about half of the Chinese firms in Hong Kong, but relatives apparently make up a small portion of personnel, unless they are very small.

Two analytical distinctions need to be made before the probable effect of nepotism can be assessed. The first is between the immediate family or *jia* of the employer and his wider kin group. When the kinship statuses of the relatives employed by the cotton spinners in my survey are examined, it turns out that the overwhelming majority of them were *jia* members.[43] This pattern is confirmed by other studies; they support Maurice Freedman's observation that "outside the family, a kinsman has few specific economic claims,. and that in general we must not look to see preference being shown to a kinsman in economic matters on the grounds simply that he is a kinsman."[44] The other distinction is between nepotism in its active and passive forms. As a rule, it seems that Chinese industrialists in Hong Kong prefer to employ family members in key positions, but they take on other relatives only reluctantly or passively. This may explain why many of them say, as a generalization, that they are against nepotistic practices.[45] There is, probably, an inclination to shake off passive nepotism whenever circumstances permit, while accepting active nepotism because it can serve them positively. (Entrepreneurs would put their sons or other *jia* members in responsible positions in order to prevent the dissipation of family property and business profit to outsiders.) Espy's data on large Chinese industrial firms suggest that the inclusion of family members in management in all likelihood, has little harmful effect on the

performance of the company. Poor growth rates and the employment of family members are not correlated in his sample.[46] The
reasons are not hard to find. Hong Kong Chinese industrialists
usually take meticulous care to equip their family members for
top positions through education and on-the-job training. Therefore, kinsmen are not necessarily sub-standard employees. They
also tend to be more reliable and trustworthy, and may be
expected to work harder for less pay. For example, in our study
of small Hong Kong factories with relatives in the workforce, only
67 percent gave full pay to kinsmen-employees.[47] All these conditions may have contributed to the resilience and competitiveness of Hong Kong Chinese enterprises.

Preferential recruitment of kinsmen in Hong Kong factories, it
should be clear by now, is very much a phenomenon deriving from
the family mode of ownership. If a minimum of family ownership
of 50 percent is taken as the yardstick, nearly 60 percent of the
small-scale factories in our survey and at least half of all cotton
spinning mills in 1978 were considered family-owned
enterprises.[48] What effect does this concentrated family ownership have on the enterprises? Do these firms tend to be small and
conservative? Are they, as David S. Landes has observed, wary of
external intervention, hence likely to sacrifice growth for the sake
of security?[49] Scattered information in Hong Kong suggests that
this is not necessarily the case. In fact, Donald W. Stammer, a
researcher on Hong Kong's financial structure, has noted a
beneficial tendency: The fact that "much of commerce and industry consists of family-owned business and not public companies means that a high proportion of profits can be retained for
investment. Some sizable, progressive businesses have for some
years, used *all* their profits to finance expansion."[50]

As data on the use of profit by Chinese companies are hard to
obtain, it is difficult to determine whether Stammer's statement
is true. But it is conceivable that he describes the behavior of
family firms in a favorable economic climate while Landes deals
with firms in a less prosperous time. Moreover, Chinese family
enterprises in Hong Kong made use of outside capital sources
such as bank loans, which did not force them to relinquish
exclusive ownership. A prominent Hong Kong banker has pointed
out that in the 1960s, the ratio of equity to bank loans in the
Colony's firms was smaller than that in most other industrial
countries except Japan. The average borrowing of spinning and
weaving companies from banks amounted to 75 percent of

proprietors' funds.[51] But most important of all, the scale and growth potential of family enterprises should be seen developmentally in terms of the family cycle, which merits a close examination.

I believe there are three major phases in the evolution of Chinese family enterprise which correspond to generational shifts. In this model, I shall assume the existence of a self-made entrepreneur who starts the first phase. The main spur to his effort is provided by his family. A Chinese family head is in some ways a trustee of the *jia* property which ultimately belongs to his children. But in order to be a good trustee, he must create an endowment to the family estate to ensure that there are valuable assets to pass on. The more successful he is in enriching that endowment, the greater the social recognition and esteem that will accrue to him. As Dwight H. Perkins puts it, the continuation of the family line can be a powerful reason for savings.[52] Though the family head-entrepreneur is a trustee, he has the authority to make use of the assets as he sees fit as long as the *jia* estate is not yet divided. In the investment of family funds, he does not need the consent of his sons.[53] The combination of such powers and the urge to enlarge the *jia* estate tends to make the pursuit of vigorous growth and a forceful, highly personalized style of leadership the hallmarks of the initial phase of family enterprise.

But sooner or later the problems associated with succession will occur. Feeling responsible for future generations, the self-made entrepreneur is typically reluctant to relinquish control of the firm during his lifetime. For example, the cotton spinning mills I studied did have fixed retirement ages for the executives, but none of the owner-directors felt bound by these regulations. As long as they still held some shares, they would remain directors with the right to intervene in company affairs. The founder, so it appears, will continue to overshadow his successors as long as he lives, even though a formal transfer of responsibility may have taken place. Nevertheless, I think the formal change-over does mark the beginning of the second phase of the family enterprise.

The problem of succession has naturally attracted the attention of many observers. But I do not believe it constitutes a major crisis. Most of the difficulties associated with leadership succession—such as the transfer of staff loyalty from the founder to the successor, the conflict between a young leader imbued with new ideas and experienced employees set in their old ways—are common problems of managerial transition in business firms irrespective of the form of ownership.

Only two features may be unique to Chinese family enterprises. The first is the lack of cultural support for the role of an inheritor. In the Chinese system, the self-made man is accorded high social recognition; an inheritor of wealth is not socially esteemed until he can prove his own worth. That is why nearly all of the second-generation spinners I interviewed admitted some initial reluctance to join the family enterprise. The second feature is the rule of equal inheritance by sons—a rule that has been blamed for fragmenting the family estate and dissipating capital. This may well be the case for the agricultural society in pre-modern China. However, such a situation certainly does not occur in Hong Kong's cotton spinning industry. Equality in legal claims to the *jia* estate does not necessarily lead to a physical division of industrial property. Most family-owned mills have regulations to keep their capital intact. Shares cannot be freely sold to outsiders. If family members want to give up company ownership, they must first offer the shares to existing shareholders "at fair value." The regulations of the companies usually provide a further safeguard by giving the Board of Directors discretion to refuse to register transfer of shares to outsiders. There are also other obstacles to prevent an heir selling his inheritance. He must be concerned about social criticism of unfilial and unfraternal conduct. He must recognize the economic disadvantages of selling his shares. Because his inheritance includes company *assets* as well as *debts*, the "fair value" of his shares is substantially lower than the nominal value after the debts are accounted for. He also has to consider the loss of steady income that his shares may yield in future years. Therefore, the inclination to break up the family enterprise during the second phase is not as great as it usually is assumed to be.

Nonetheless, tension is building up among the succeeding brothers. Though all brothers have equal claims to ownership, only one can occupy the highest managerial position. The eldest, by virtue of his age, stands a much better chance to win that status. This will create discontent among the losing, usually younger, brothers.[54] How, then, are sibling rivalries contained? A common arrangement is for the brothers to agree on different spheres of responsibility. This separation gives maximum independence to participating brothers but often leads to a proliferation of departments, factory plants, or subsidiary companies within the family concern. Outwardly, there is an appearance of physical expansion; but internally, the organizational structure becomes less unified. Centralized decision-making and strong leadership by the new chief executive becomes more difficult. Institutional restraints are sometimes set up to limit the autonomy of the chief executive. Finding his hands tied, he may gradually resign himself to the role of a caretaker instead of an innovator. Thus, the physical expansion and segmentation of the company often results in reduction of reinvestment.

If the analysis so far is not mistaken, then I would predict that the most serious threat to survival of the family enterprise appears in the third phase, when the sons of the brothers in turn take over. At this time, the number of members in the family enterprise has greatly increased so that discord over the management of the enterprise is likely to multiply. In addition, the economic considerations that discouraged the sale of family shares are less powerful. The value of individual shareholding has become much smaller because of subdivision, and this reduces the attraction of the regular income derived from the shares. Moreover, since it is unlikely for brothers to have identical numbers of children, inheritance by the third generation will create unequal ownership among the shareholders. Brothers may still cooperate on a more or less equal footing as owners, but cousins with unbalanced portions of the company have less reason to do so. Those at a weaker bargaining position may decide to break off the economic ties to the family enterprise, especially when they are brought up with little emotional attachment to it. Family members as shareholders will then be more concerned with immediate, tangible benefits than with long-term business prospects. From this stage on, the family enterprise will be crisis-ridden.

Thus, viewed developmentally, the Chinese family firms in Hong Kong have definite economic strengths as well as weaknesses. Compared with their Japanese counterparts, they are more short-lived individually. But given the chance, they will quickly be re-born to replenish a collective vigor. In addition, a much stronger measure of trust exists among family members than among unrelated business partners. Consensus is easier to attain. The need for mutual accountability is reduced. This enables family firms to be more adaptable in their operations. They can make quick decisions during rapidly changing circumstances and can maintain secrecy in their operations by committing little to written records. As a result, they are well-suited to survive and flourish in situations where a high level of risk is involved, such as an unstable political environment, fluctuating business development, and the creation of a new line of business.

Utilitarian Discipline

Certain cultural traits, which I choose to call "utilitarian discipline," may help explain changes in the fertility rates among the people of Hong Kong (which have helped economic development). Virtually all available studies on post-war population trends in Hong Kong show a rapid decline in age-specific birth rates since the 1960s—approaching replacement levels in a relatively short time.[55] The most commonly cited reasons are "[urbanization], industrialization, improvements in social and economic status of women, and increased educational attainment among the population" as well as the role played by the Family Planning Association of Hong Kong.[56] Yet these factors do not seem to account for certain unusual features of Hong Kong's population changes. For example, Pedro P.T. Ng has found that Hong Kong Chinese couples are strikingly receptive to the idea of birth control, uniformly preferring to have two or three children.[57] Benjamin Mok has observed that in Hong Kong the "distribution of fertility rates by age of mothers was much less skewed, with its mode at the age group 25–29 instead of 20–24, than was usually the case with other countries."[58] The fertility pattern of Hong Kong is sufficiently close to that of Taiwan and Singapore to suggest that some common cultural factors might be at work. One of the likely factors, as Ronald Freedman suggests, is that "the people of the Sino-influenced cultures are to an unusually extent pragmatic-empirical, problem-solving, rather than submissive and fatalistic in a problematic situation."[59]

Another probable factor is a strong sense of discipline which MacFarquhar calls "social."[60] But the Hong Kong Chinese are known to be politically apathetic and generally put familial interest ahead of wider social obligations.[61] Therefore, "utilitarian discipline" probably is more descriptive. There exists a tendency among the Chinese to be keenly aware of cost and benefit calculations in both monetary and human investments.[62] They are prepared to adopt a long-term strategy to enhance the welfare of their families by deferring immediate gratification. In the past this disposed them to practice various forms of abortion and infanticide; nowadays, it inclines them to use contraceptives to maximize the economic interests of the *jia.*

The Situational Factors

The cultural elements identified so far cannot completely account for Hong Kong's modernization experience. For while some traits have been positive for development, some have been negative. Perhaps the task before us is to unravel the circumstances under which the positive cultural elements have come to the fore in the process of industrialization. "However important motivational factors may be," as Robert N. Bellah has reminded us, "they have proven time and again to be highly sensitive to shifts in institutional arrangements."[63] Chinese cultural values, transposed to Hong Kong with its peculiar social structure, have undergone significant mutations. Several situational factors in Hong Kong society have pushed cultural values in the direction of economic growth.

The first of these is the large component of refugees in Hong Kong's post-war population. During the Chinese Civil War, between September 1945 and December 1949, an estimated 1,285,000 refugees came to the territory from the Chinese mainland.[64] Against the "normal" pre-war population of 1,640,000 in March 1941, this influx brought about a doubling of Hong Kong's inhabitants within just a few years.[65] In the spring of 1950, the population figure exceeded the two million mark for the first time.[66]

The onrush of refugees, which greatly strained the resources of the administration, turned out to be an industrial asset. Mostly destitute, they formed a vast pool of cheap labor. They were not drawn mainly from the rural peasantry; a majority of the male immigrants came from urban areas and had been soldiers and policemen, professionals, intellectuals, clerks, or shop assistants. Within a few years in Hong Kong, many of them turned into industrial laborers, unskilled workers in the service sector, and self-employed craftsmen and hawkers.[67] Cut off from home by political events, they became stable resident workers instead of seasonal migrants, a change unknown to the Hong Kong government at first. "To begin with," wrote the then-Hong Kong Governor in his memoir, "little for them was done since we predicted, wrongly as it turned out, that as soon as the new regime in China had settled down and things got back to normal, they would return to their native villages."[68]

Among the immigrant wave was a small contingent of entrepreneurs from the Shanghai region. They chose Hong Kong as their sanctuary because of its accessibility, social stability, and relative absence of government regulations. They tended to be the young generations of the Lower Yangtse industrial families that had considerable experience in operating modern and capital intensive factories. Many of them were the eldest sons who were apparently charged with the responsibility of continuing the family business, and they brought with them technical know-how as well as capital assets—mainly in the form of machinery.[69] Their role as catalysts in Hong Kong's post-war development has been emphasized by later government officials:

> Hong Kong was fortunate in being able to develop industry earlier and quicker than other countries in Asia which had the same essential economic inputs to offer, e.g., abundant and cheap labour of a high quality. South Korea, Singapore, Taiwan, Thailand, Malaysia, and others, all had such labour. Some had other in- gredients attractive to industry but in all cases there were disincentives also—and *it was Hong Kong which received the injection of Shanghai experience and capi- tal. The economic importance of this cannot be over- stressed.* Hong Kong was given ten to fifteen years' start in industrialization over many other Asian countries as a result.[70]

The immigrants brought to their new home not just tangible factors of production but also a refugee mentality suffused with a deep anxiety not unlike that experienced by Weber's early Calvinists. They were troubled by a precarious existence, though the perceived threats were mundane, rather than religious—the proximity of the Chinese Communist regime from which they had recoiled, an uncertain political future, and a lack of natural resources in their new home island. Struggling to obtain a worldly "salvation," they also seemed to have unleashed a transformative social process. As employees, they were eager to learn new skills and to acquire qualifications so that their labor would increase in value. As entrepreneurs, they were keen to diversify their investments and maintain maximum liquidity. They sent their children abroad to acquire foreign education and passports. They set up subsidiaries in Southeast Asia, Africa, and South America. The Shanghainese among them refrained from investing in real estates, saying that "we had burnt our fingers in Shanghai. We learned that when political situations changed, we could not bring the land with us."[71] They preferred to make full use of modern credit facilities. According to a Chinese banker with intimate knowledge of the Hong Kong textile industry,

> Industrialists "made do" with minimum investments and borrowed as much as they could from the banks. They took out their profits for deposit or investment outside of Hong Kong. They did not hesitate to grow in order to meet their markets' demand, but they financed as much of their growth as possible through bank credit. In this way, if Hong Kong were suddenly taken over or lost its markets, the banks could have their business. On the other hand, if Hong Kong remained stable and prosperous and their business did well, they could reap the profits themselves.[72]

The colonial set-up of Hong Kong is the second situational factor that turned the cultural energy of the Chinese inhabitants into an economic force. Colonialism in Hong Kong promoted industrialization in two major ways. On the one hand, it led to the formation of a limited, law-abiding, yet aloof government. Following the British colonial tradition of indirect rule, the Hong Kong government refrained (and still refrains) from initiating changes in the social life of the indigenous population. In the post-war era when de-colonialization became a worldwide trend, and an extractive policy could hardly have been followed, the Hong Kong government was obliged to be self-financing. The government was required to practice conservative fiscal policies such as low taxation, provision of many government services at market prices, and minimal involvement in commercial activities. Yet by being an alien and non-elective regime, it did not have to cater to private interests among its subjects. It pursued policies in accordance with the judgment of its officials, who primarily were administrators rather than politicians.[73] Relatively unconcerned with popularity, it practiced free trade and liberal immigration policies, refused to grant privileges to either foreign or local investors, and resisted the urge to spend generously on welfare. The resulting political environment proved to be attractive to private Chinese capital. Hong Kong became an economic heaven not just for its inhabitants, but for the overseas Chinese as well. Overseas Chinese remittances to China were traditionally channeled through Hong Kong. They have declined since the establishment of the People's Republic, from over 40 percent of China's foreign exchange in 1950 to just a quarter in 1963; a substantial portion of these remittances appears to have stayed in Hong Kong.[74] The flight of capital from Southeast Asia, because of disturbances there, also tended to flock to Hong Kong, estimated to be around several hundred million Hong Kong dollars annually in the 1960s and 1970s.[75]

Colonialism in Hong Kong has created a pattern of social stratification different from that of traditional China. In the past, social status in China was determined "more by qualification for office than by wealth."[76] The promise of upward social mobility through the officialdom had probably led to the dissipation of mercantile capital and talents.[77] In Hong Kong, government service has been largely beyond the reach of Chinese residents. Those unversed in English have had few chances to enter the government except at the very lowest levels; and even those with knowledge of English have had relatively few political opportunities. Many talented Chinese, therefore, have sought advancement elsewhere—more than a few becoming small industrialists.[78] With the official route to social ascent blocked, wealth by itself has brought social honor—just as it has in other Southeast Asian Chinese communities.[79] With the fetters of "Chinese institutional arrangements for checking motives of gain" removed, the entrepreneurial urge has been given free reign.[80] A recent small-scale study of occupational prestige rankings in Hong Kong, for example, has shown that "shipping magnate" and "commercial manager" top the list—ahead of "colonial secretary" and "professor."[81]

The third situational factor conducive to Hong Kong's modernization may be called urbanism by default. Chinese cities traditionally have not been powerful motors of economic change.[82] The absence of a sharp rural-urban dichotomy in imperial China meant that there was no self-conscious urban middle class as an independent social force.[83] The treaty port system, being an urban form artificially grafted onto a weakened China, probably stimulated cultural and economic confrontation more than growth.[84] But Hong Kong, since the early 1950s, has become a politically detached metropolis. The border with China has been guarded vigilantly, and the movement of people across the border has been strictly regulated. Without a rural hinterland of its own, Hong Kong has created for itself a separate urban identity; it is quite different from the "embedded" cities across the border.[85] Such an isolated position engenders among its populace a feeling of solidarity and a common orientation toward economic achievement as a means of survival.

"Detached" Hong Kong, other than overwhelmingly urban, is also physically tiny, which constitutes its last situational factor. Latecomers to modernization, as Marion J. Levy points out, have to tackle four special problems: "(1) gaps and scale, (2) the lack of direct convertibility of assets, (3) running to keep up, and (4) coordination and control."[86] The magnitude of these problems depends at least in part on the size of the latecomer. The bigger the size of the economy, the more formidable are these barriers. In this sense, Hong Kong is more fortunate. It is less burdened with the problem of unbalanced regional growth, the threat of a breakdown of social control, and the depletion of economic resources through internal re-distribution and population pressure—all major headaches for the larger modernizing countries such as China. As an island with excellent port facilities, Hong Kong is able to adopt successfully an export-led strategy for growth. There is always room for it to snatch a minute bite of the international market to sustain a high rate of growth.

A Closing Remark

Hong Kong is often said to be unique. This may mean that its form of economic development is so atypical that it cannot serve as a "model" for other Third World countries—or that it is such a cultural hybrid that it is hardly worthy of academic attention except perhaps as a temporary stand-in before one can get to know the "real" China.[87] I don't believe it has to be exemplary or pure to be theoretically interesting. The main goal of this essay is to show that a consideration of Hong Kong can shed some light on significant problems about the modernization process and the nature of Chinese society. It is important, at this stage, to try to pose the right questions. We can then "go on feeding scraps of information into a gradually expanding picture," hoping that a full-scale study of the modernization of Hong Kong will take shape and that more comparative investigations of different Chinese cultural areas will emerge.[88]

It has been a standard view among both Chinese and Western scholars that traditional Chinese values are an impediment to modernization. But the unexpected vitality of some of those values, such as familism, as displayed in the industrial growth of Hong Kong, suggests that a reassessment of the role of Chinese culture in connection with modernization is needed.[89]

Will Hong Kong lose its developmental momentum as it approaches 1997? My analysis suggests that as long as the situational factors essential to its past economic success exist, the relevant cultural factors likely will continue promoting development. In the pursuit of modernity, is Hong Kong a model for the rest of China? The debate is open, but at least modernization with distinctive Chinese characteristics can be attained.

NOTES

An earlier version of this chapter appeared as "Modernization and Chinese Culture in Hong Kong," *The China Quarterly,* June 1986, pp. 306–25.

1. In this essay, I shall use the terms "modernization," "industrialization," and "economic development" interchangeably for stylistic reasons, though I am aware that they are not exact equivalents. With these terms, I am referring to the social process set in train by the growing dependence on inanimate sources of power in production in a society. I am also confining myself to one particular form of this process, namely the capitalistic mode, without implying that it is the only or best route to "modernization."

2. The World Bank, *World Development Report 1982* (New York: Oxford University Press, 1982), p. 123.

3. See Chapter 2, Table 1 of this volume.

4. Hong Kong, Census and Statistics Department, *Hong Kong 1981 Census Main Report, Volume 1: Analysis* (Hong Kong: The Government Printer, 1983), p. 33.

5. Roderick MacFarquhar, "The Post-Confucian Challenge," *Economist,* 9 February 1980, p. 70.

6. *Hong Kong 1981 Census,* pp. 18–24.

7. Ibid., p. 122.

8. Sheelagh Millar, *The Biosocial Survey in Hong Kong* (Canberra: Centre for Resources and Environmental Studies, Australian National University, 1979), p. 150.

9. Lau Siu-kai, *Society and Politics in Hong Kong* (Hong Kong: The Chinese University Press, 1982), p. 74. See also H.A. Turner, et al., *The Last Colony: But Whose? A Study of The Labour Movement, Labour Market and Labour Relations in Hong Kong* (Cambridge: Cambridge University Press, 1980), p. 156; and Robert L. Moore, "Modernization and Westernization in Hong Kong: Patterns of Cultural Change in an Urban Setting" (Ph.D. dissertation, University of California, 1981), p. 237.

10. See Turner, *The Last Colony,* pp. 176, 197; Moore, "Modernization and Westernization in Hong Kong," p. 238; Joseph Agassi and Ian C. Jarvie, "A Study in Westernization," in Ian

C. Jarvie and Joseph Agassi, eds., *Hong Kong: A Society in Transition* (London: Routledge and Kegan Paul, 1969), pp. 129–63.

11. Herman Kahn, *World Economic Development: 1979 and Beyond* (Boulder, CO: Westview Press, 1979), pp. 121–23; and MacFarquhar, "The Post-Confucian Challenge," pp. 67–72.

12. Daniel W.Y. Kwok, "Confucianism and Modernization," a talk given at the Royal Asiatic Society, Hong Kong Branch in 1983.

13. Max Weber, *The Religion of China, Confucianism and Taoism*, trans. from the German by Hans H. Gerth (Glencoe, IL: The Free Press, 1951), pp. 229–32.

14. Ibid., p. 248.

15. Ibid.

16. MacFarquhar, "The Post-Confucian Challenge," p. 71.

17. Frederick W. Mote, *Intellectual Foundations of China* (New York: Knopf, 1971), pp. 17–20.

18. Francis L.K. Hsu, *Americans and Chinese: Two Ways of Life* (New York: Abelard-Schuman, 1953), p. 237.

19. Marjorie Topley, "Some Basic Conceptions and Their Traditional Relationship to Society," in Marjorie Topley ed., *Some Traditional Chinese Ideas and Conceptions in Hong Kong Social Life Today* (Hong Kong: The Hong Kong Branch of the Royal Asiatic Society, 1966), p. 19.

20. Millar, *The Biosocial Survey*, p. 405.

21. Michel Oksenberg, "Management Practices in the Hong Kong Cotton Spinning and Weaving Industry," paper read at the Seminar on Modern East Asia, Columbia University, New York, November 15, 1972, p. 6.

22. Ibid., p. 5.

23. Wong Siu-Iun, "Industrial Entrepreneurship and Ethnicity: A Study of the Shanghainese Cotton Spinners in Hong Kong" (Ph.D. dissertation, University of Oxford, 1979), p. 155.

24. A.S. Pearse, *Japan's Cotton Industry* (Cyprus: Kyrenia, 1955), pp. 122–23.

25. Kahn, *World Economic Development*, p. 122.

26. David C. McClelland, "Motivational Patterns in Southeast Asia with Special Reference to the Chinese Case," *The Journal of Social Issues* 19:1 (1963): 11–17.

27. Robert E. Mitchell, *Pupil, Parent and School: A Hong Kong Study* (Taipei, Taiwan: The Orient Cultural Service, 1972), pp. 192–205.

28. See S.V.S. Sharma, et al., *Small Entrepreneurial Development in Some Asian Countries* (New Delhi: Light and Life Publications, 1979); and Victor F.S. Sit, Wong Siu-lun, and Kiang Tsin-sing, *Small Scale Industry in a Laissez-Faire Economy: A Hong Kong Case Study* (Hong Kong: Centre of Asian Studies, Hong Kong University, 1979).

29. Ambrose Y.C. King and D.H.K. Leung, "The Chinese Touch in Small Industrial Organizations" (Occasional paper, Social Research Centre, Chinese University of Hong Kong, 1975), p. 34. See also John A. Young, "Interpersonal Networks and Economic Behaviour in a Chinese Market Town" (Ph.D. dissertation, Stanford University, 1971), pp. 195–99.

30. Wong, "Industrial Entrepreneurship," pp. 206–10.

31. Donald J. Munro, *The Conception of Man in Early China* (Stanford: Stanford University Press, 1969), pp. 1–22.

32. Tung-tsu Ch'ü, "Chinese Class Structure and Its Ideology," in John K. Fairbank, ed., *Chinese Thought and Institutions* (Chicago: University of Chicago Press, 1957), pp. 235–50; and Ping-ti Ho, *The Ladder of Success in Imperial China: Aspects of Social Mobility, 1368–1911* (New York: Columbia University Press, 1962), pp. 1–91.

33. Kahn, *World Economic Development*, p. 121.

34. H.A. Turner et al. cast doubt on the pervasiveness of such an ambition among the industrial employees in Hong Kong. In their survey of 1,000 employees, it was found that less than a third (31 percent) of the respondents had seriously considered starting a business within the next five years which they considered to be a "surprisingly low figure" (p. 196). But at least three points should be taken into account in interpreting this. First, administrative, executive, and managerial workers were not included in the sample (p. 179). Second, the question was apparently directed toward the respondents' realistic appraisal of their opportunities within a definite timeframe of five years, which might not be the same as their unfettered aspirations. Third, whether 31 percent was a low figure still is a question.

35. Kahn, *World Economic Development*, p. 381.

36. Lau Siu-kai, "Chinese Familism in An Urban-Industrial Setting: The Case of Hong Kong," *Journal of Marriage and The Family* 43:4 (1981): 181–96; and Millar, *The Biosocial Survey*, pp. 148–53.

37. Robert H. Silin, *Leadership and Values: The Organization of Large Scale Taiwanese Enterprises* (Cambridge, MA: Harvard University Press, 1976), p. 66.

38. A good illustration can be found in a novel be Mao Tun, *Midnight* (Peking: Foreign Language Press, 1957), pp. 58–59.

39. Chau Sik-nin, "Family Management in Hong Kong," *Hong Kong Manager* 6:2 (1970): 21.

40. Kang Chao and Chung-yi Chen, *Chung-kuo Mien-yeh Shih [A History of The Chinese Textile Industry]* (Taipei: Lien-Ching ch'u-pan shih-yeh kun-szü, 1977), p. 185; Marion J. Levy, Jr., *The Family Revolution in Modern China* (Cambridge, MA: Harvard University Press, 1949), p. 354; and idem, "Business Development in China," in Marion J. Levy, Jr. and K.H. Shih, eds., *The Rise of the Modern Chinese Business Class* (New York: Institute of Pacific Relations, 1949), p. 12.

41. John L. Espy, "The Strategy of Chinese Industrial Enterprise in Hong Kong" (D.B.A. thesis, Harvard University, 1970), p. 174.

42. Sit, Wong, and Kiang, *Small Scale Industry*, p. 353.

43. Wong, "Industrial Entrepreneurship," pp. 275–76.

44. See Espy, "The Strategy of Chinese Industrial Enterprise," p. 175; See also Sit, Wong, and Kiang, *Small Scale Industry*, pp. 353–54, and Maurice Freedman, "The Family in China, Past and Present," in G. William Skinner, ed., *The Study of Chinese Society: Essays by Maurice Freedman* (Stanford: Stanford University Press, 1979), p. 243.

45. Ambrose Y.C. King and Peter J.L. Man, "The Role of [the] Small Factory in Economic Development: The Case of Hong Kong" (Occasional Paper, Social Research Centre, Chinese University of Hong Kong, 1974), pp. 41–42; Lau Siu-kai, "Employment Relations in Hong Kong: Traditional or Modern?" in T. Liu, R.P.L. Lee, and V. Simons, eds., *Hong Kong: Economics, Social and Political Studies in Development* (New York: M.E. Sharpe, 1979), pp. 71–72.

46. Espy, "The Strategy of Chinese Industrial Enterprise," p. 174.

47. Sit, Wong, and Kiang, *Small Scale Industry*, p. 355.

48. Ibid., p. 337; and Wong, "Industrial Entrepreneurship," p. 287.

49. David S. Landes, "French Business and the Business Man: A Social and Cultural Analysis," in H.G.J. Aitkin, ed., *Explorations in Enterprise* (Cambridge, MA: Harvard University Press, 1967), pp. 185–87.

50. Donald W. Stammer, "Money and Finance in Hong Kong" (Ph.D. dissertation, Australian National University, 1968), pp. 261–62; original italics.

51. P.A. Graham, "Financing Hong Kong Business," *Far Eastern Economic Review*, 17 April 1969, p. 152.

52. Dwight H. Perkins, ed., *China's Modern Economy in Historical Perspective* (Stanford: Stanford University Press, 1975), p. 15.

53. S. Shiga, "Family Property and the Law of Inheritance in Traditional China," in David C. Baxbaum, ed., *Chinese Family Law and Social Change* (Seattle: University of Washington Press, 1978), pp. 128–33.

54. Margery Wolf, "Child Training and the Chinese Family," in Maurice Freedman, ed., *Family and Kinship in Chinese Society* (Stanford: Stanford University Press, 1970), p. 53.

55. Ronald Freedman and K.C. Chan, "Hong Kong's Fertility Decline 1961–68," *Population Index* 36:1 (1970): 3–18; Pedro P.T. Ng, "Social Factors Contributing to Fertility Decline," in Ambrose Y.C. King and R.P.L. Lee, eds., *Social Life and Development in Hong Kong* (Hong Kong: Chinese University of Hong Kong, 1981), pp. 235–54; Benjamin Mok, "Recent Fertility Trends in Hong Kong," in L. Cho and K. Kobayashi, eds., *Fertility Transition of the East Asian Populations* (Honolulu: University Press of Hawaii, 1979), pp. 178–97.

56. Mok, "Recent Fertility Trends," pp. 190–94; Ng, "Fertility Decline."

57. Ibid., p. 246.

58. Mok, "Recent Fertility Trends," p. 183.

59. Ronald Freedman, "Overview," in Cho and Kobayashi, *Fertility Transition of the East Asian Populations*, p. 292.

60. MacFarquhar, "The Post-Confucian Challenge," p. 70.

61. See Lau Siu-kai, "Utilitarian Familism: The Basis of Political Stability in Hong Kong" (Occasional paper, Social Research Centre, Chinese University of Hong Kong, 1978).

62. Maurice Freedman, "The Handling of Money: A Note on the Background to the Economic Sophistication of the Overseas Chinese," *Man* 59 (1959): 64–65; Marjorie Topley, "The Role of Savings and Wealth Among the Hong Kong Chinese," in Jarvie and Agassi, *Hong Kong: A Society in Transition*, pp. 167–227.

63. Robert N. Bellah, "Reflections on The Protestant Ethic Analogy in Asia," in S.N. Eisenstadt, *The Protestant Ethic and Modernization: A Comparative View* (New York: Basic Books, 1968), p. 244.

64. Edward Hambro, *The Problem of Chinese Refugees in Hong Kong* (Leyden: Sijthoff, 1955), p. 148.

65. David Podmore, "The Population of Hong Kong," in Keith Hopkins, ed., *Hong Kong: The Industrial Colony* (London: Oxford University Press, 1971), pp. 24–25.

66. Irene B. Taueber, "Hong Kong: Migrants and Metropolis," *Population Index* 29:1 (1963): 4.

67. Hambro, *The Problem of Chinese Refugees*, pp. 168–70.

68. Alexander Gratham, *Via Port: From Hong Kong to Hong Kong* (Hong Kong: Hong Kong University Press, 1965), p. 155.

69. Wong Siu-lun, "The Migration of Shanghainese Entrepreneurs to Hong Kong," in David Faure, James Hayes, and Alan Birch, eds., *From Village to City: Studies in the Traditional Roots of Hong Kong Society* (Hong Kong: Centre of Asian Studies, University of Hong Kong, 1984), pp. 206–27.

70. Hong Kong, Commerce and Industry Department, "Memorandum for the Trade and Industry Advisory Board: Land for Industry" (Hong Kong: The Department, mimeographed, 1973), p. 2; original emphasis.

71. Wong, "Industrial Entrepreneurship," p. 117.

72. Ibid.

73. Ambrose Y.C. King, "Administrative Absorption of Politics in Hong Kong: Emphasis on The Grass Roots Level," in King and Lee, *Social Life and Development*, pp. 127–46.

74. Chun-hsi Wu, *Dollar, Dependents, and Dogma: Overseas Chinese Remittances to Communist China* (Stanford: Hoover Institution, 1967), p. 6.

75. Ibid., p. 88; Mary F.S. Heidhues, *Southeast Asia's Chinese Minorities* (Australia: Longmans, 1974), p. 20.

76. Hans H. Gerth and C. Wright Mills, eds., *From Max Weber* (London: Routledge and Kegan Paul, 1948), p. 416.

77. Marion J. Levy, Jr., "Contrasting Factors in the Modernization of China and Japan," in Simon Kuznets, Wilbert E. Moore, and Joseph J. Spengler, eds., *Economic Growth: Brazil, India, Japan* (Durham: Duke University Press, 1955), pp. 496–536.

78. Sit, Wong, and Kiang, *Small-scale Industry*, pp. 288–92.

79. William Skinner, *Leadership and Power in the Chinese Community of Thailand* (New York: Cornell University Press, 1958), p. 83; Wong Siu-lun, "The Economic Enterprise of the Chinese in Southeast Asia: A Sociological Inquiry with Special Reference to West Malaysia and Singapore" (B. Litt. thesis, University of Oxford, 1975), pp. 110–15.

80. Topley, "The Role of Savings," p. 187.

81. Moore, "Modernization and Westernization in Hong Kong," p. 66.

82. Gibert Rozman, ed., *The Modernization of China* (New York: The Free Press, 1981), pp. 158–60.

83. Frederick W. Mote, "The City in Traditional Chinese Civilization," in James T.C. Liu and Wei-ming Tu, eds., *Traditional China* (Englewood Cliffs: Prentice-Hall, 1970), pp. 42–49.

84. Rhoads Murphey, *The Treaty Ports and China's Modernization: What Went Wrong?* (Ann Arbor: Center for Chinese Studies, The University of Michigan, 1970).

85. Audrey Donnithorne, "Hong Kong as an Economic Model for the Great Cities of China," in A.J. Youngson, ed., *China and Hong Kong: The Economic Nexus* (Hong Kong: Oxford University Press, 1983), pp. 282–310.

86. Marion J. Levy, Jr., *Modernization: Latecomers and Survivors* (New York: Basic Books, 1972), p. 13.

87. Andre Gunder Frank, "Asia's Exclusive Models," *Far Eastern Economic Review*, 25 June 1982, pp. 22–23.

88. Freedman, "The Family in China," p. 254.

89. For a more extended discussion on the issue of Chinese familism and modernization, see Wong Siu-lun, "The Applicability of Asian Family Values to Other Socio-cultural

Settings," paper presented at the Symposium on "In Search of an East Asian Development Model" sponsored jointly by Asia and World Institute and Council on Religion and International Affairs, 28–30 June 1985, New York City.

TEN

Bridging Tradition and Modernization:
The Singapore Bureaucracy

Thomas J. Bellows

Introduction

The People's Action Party (PAP), which has ruled Singapore for more than a quarter century, has a firm faith in technocracy. It believes that rationalism and technical expertise are the best way to solve the country's social and economic problems. Socioeconomic development and nation-building, it is assumed, occur when the economic system and the government work closely together under the guidance of a rigorously selected and well trained "meritocratic" elite. Singapore is small—238 square miles with a population of 2.5 million—hence amenable to administrative centralization and supervision. It is a unitary state, and the only popular elections are for Parliament.

During the next ten years, there may be some modification of the present hierarchical organization dominated by Prime Minister Lee Kuan Yew. A more decentralized arrangement may emerge—for the progressively expanding second generation leaders, now nearing the end of political apprenticeship, will certainly strive to establish autonomous spheres of influence. But none of them appears to possess the same self-confidence, self-righteousness, and consummate skill to monopolize political power as the present Prime Minister. For nearly three decades the PAP elite has constantly affirmed that nation-building rests on active and extensive state intervention. Unquestionably, Singapore is an administrative state. The transition to a new generation of leadership is not likely to change the pivotal role of the civil service in the government.

.The Singaporean civil service is a British creation (although its elitist, meritocratic character and policy-making functions are consistent with Confucian tradition). From the sunset years of the colonial era (1954–59) to the internal self-government period (1959–63) to the time of federation with Malaysia (1963–65), elected Singaporean politicians have vigorously jockeyed for power. The PAP leaders, who formed a government in June 1959, learned first-hand that a bureaucratic apparatus was essential for political survival.

In 1956, a White Paper (Command 65) issued by the Singaporean Legislative Assembly called for nearly complete and rapid localization of the civil service. It was intended to assure that "Singapore will achieve, in advance of self-government, that control of its public service which is normally associated with self-government."[1] In 1956, the 408 top-level expatriates (i.e., the British) were offered an opportunity to continue their services for a year or more; a surprisingly large number—263 (64 percent)—chose to retire within a matter of months. By April 1959, the number of expatriate officers in the highest division of the bureaucracy was half of what had been planned.[2] Localization of the civil service had been completed by the time the PAP came to power in 1959.

At the same time, factional disputes within the PAP also strengthened the political role of the civil service. Shortly after the PAP won the May 1959 elections, the mass-based, pro-Communist faction of the party decided to separate itself from the non-Communist leaders to seize power. In July 1961, Barisan Sosialis or the Socialist Front came into being and began to challenge the government. The non-Communist PAP leaders, who held all the cabinet posts, immediately made overtures to the civil service. As Dr. Goh Keng Swee, a former high-ranking civil servant and then Minister for Finance, wrote in the party newspaper in January 1960: "The fact that a certain party faction had hoped to increase its mass popularity by attacking the English-educated and trying to maul the Civil Service should open the eyes of even the most foolish of the English-educated to the perilous situation in which they now are."[3] Astute political maneuvering and selective detentions by the PAP government neutralized the Barisan Sosialis by 1965.

Thus, prior to independence, the civil service performed a number of political tasks: to protect and strengthen its own position, to defeat the pro-Communists' attempt to control the government, and to make it probable that PAP leaders would remain in power after independence. In the post-independence period, the civil service remained in the center of the political process, with the following two key roles to play: 1) to initiate and nurture social well-being and economic development and 2) to develop national identity, to facilitate political integration, and to cultivate civic/ ethical behavior among the citizenry.

The Political Milieu

Singapore became an independent country on August 9, 1965 after separation from Malaysia. It has a parliamentary government popularly elected through a compulsory voting system. From 1968 to 1980, the PAP won every seat in the four national parliamentary elections and numerous by-elections. The December 1980 general elections saw the PAP win all 75 parliamentary seats and 75.5 percent of ballots cast in the 38 constituencies where opposition candidates ran. The pattern of the PAP's complete electoral victories was broken on October 31, 1981, in the Anson constituency by-election. A personable, Sri Lanka-born lawyer, J.B. Jeyaretnam, was elected to Parliament with 52 percent of the vote. This was the sixth parliamentary race for the Secretary-General of the Workers' Party.

The situation changed more dramatically in the December 1984 elections. The PAP won 77 of 79 seats in Parliament and garnered 64.8 percent of the vote in the 49 contested constituencies. Most observers, including some in the PAP, saw the 1984 returns as a political watershed. MP Jeyaretnam, running this time against a government employee of the Economic Development Board, again was victorious, with an increased majority. A second winning opposition candidate obtained 60.4 percent of the vote. The PAP's popular vote declined 12.9 percent from its 1980 level. The September 1988 elections saw the PAP vote remain nearly level at 63.1 percent of the popular vote in the 70 of 81 contested constituencies. PAP candidates won 80 of 81 parliamentary seats. Because he was convicted of party financial irregularities, J.B. Jeyaretnam was ineligible to run for parliament in 1988.

Singapore's elected officials now face the task of reconciling a regime that has long been accustomed to managing a unified society through a Mandarinate (top civil servants) with growing demands for more individual autonomy, political pluralism, and a leadership more willing to accommodate popular feelings on important issues.[4]

The 1984 elections ushered in a new team of leadership; ten of the thirteen members of the Cabinet as of May 1985 were second generation leaders. At the same time, a new electorate with a limited personal political memory emerged. It consists of voters who have seen only the PAP's successes after independence, with little knowledge of the travail the party experienced before. These new voters, ages 21–43, comprised nearly 69 percent of the electorate in 1988; 15 percent of the electorate then will vote for the first time.[5] Many of these voters will have to be won over, not simply retained in the fold.

The Economic Milieu

The economic achievements of the PAP government are sufficiently known that no extended description is necessary. Without a hinterland, the city-state has only two principal economic resources. The first is its geographic location. Situated at a strategic mid-point between East Asia and Europe, Singapore's location is enhanced by a geologic fault. The Sunda Shelf was once above water, and archipelago Asia was part of the mainland. Subsequent geologic changes created the seas, islands, and straits. The mountain ranges slope into shallow seas, and the Straits of Malacca are characterized as coastal seas, shifting sands, and variable channels.[6] There is no deep water port in the area except at the mouth of the Singapore river. Here, scoured and dredged constantly by the tides, is the port of Singapore, the second busiest in the world. Singapore's physical attributes, complemented by the historic European-Asian trade, had long made Singapore a great commercial center since its founding in 1819. Its entrepôt trade, which was once second in importance to Hong Kong in the British commercial operations in East Asia, brought prosperity to the colony and laid the foundation for its modern economy.

Its second principal resource, repeatedly pointed to by government officials, is its 2.5 million population—76.6 percent Chinese, 14.7 percent Malay, 6.4 percent Indian, and 2.3 percent others. The population is hard-working and productive, having created a growing economy while facing economic difficulties. Cut off from

Malaysia, without a hope of establishing a common market with its large neighbor, Singapore had to face in the early years of the new nation (in 1970–71) a closing of the extensive British military facilities, which directly and indirectly contributed to 20 percent of Singapore's GNP. Despite these economic challenges, the burgeoning, job-anxious population—the 1970 census indicated that 50.7 percent of the population was 20 years of age or younger—pushed the economy into continuous expansion through 1984, averaging a nearly 9 percent annual growth in real GNP.[7] Throughout the first half of the present decade, unemployment remained below 3 percent. Until 1985, the country had more than 150,000 foreign workers holding jobs Singaporeans generally rejected as too menial, arduous, or low-paid.

During the 1960s, the government concentrated on the creation of labor-intensive industries, which resulted in full employment in relatively low value-added factories. Stressing the government's pro-business attitude, the Minister of Finance once explained to a group of industrialists that the government's Economic Development Board would be "at the disposal of manufacturers." The government had to abandon its "refereeing" role because "in our present stage of development. the Government needs to be positive" in responding to the needs of industries.[8]

By 1965 emphasis was placed on the expansion of exports, which led to a labor shortage in the 1970s. In order to curtail the need for foreign labor while continuing economic growth, the government began to shift from light manufacturing to high technology and capital-intensive industries and exportable high-value services. To facilitate this economic transition, the government adopted a policy in favor of wage improvement. After a mild recession in the mid-70s, in which a "modest wage policy" was followed, "the higher wage policy was resumed [in 1979] in an intensified effort to restructure the economy based on high value-added manufacturing and service activities."[9]

The upward wage policy marked the launching of the Second Industrial Revolution (SIR) to replace labor-intensive with "brain" industries. Thus, Prime Minister Lee concluded an analysis of Singapore's 1981 economic performance with a characteristically direct statement: "All sectors of the economy have to mechanize, automate, computerize, and improve management; or relocate their factories."[10] Speaking to Parliament, Minister of Trade and Industry Goh Chok Tong emphasized: "Our job as a government is to set out our objective, direction, and *modus operandi* clearly and unequivocally and lead. The rest is up to Singaporeans to achieve and excel."[11]

Singaporean government, since the mid-1960s, has actively sought out foreign investment, even permitting wholly foreign-owned enterprises. But it was selective in terms of enterprises invited. A long list of investment incentives are administered by the Economic Development Board (EDB). A United States government analysis notes that the EDB's incentives "tend to be decisive in companies' decisions to locate in Singapore or elsewhere."[12] Prime Minister Lee explained that foreign investment made it possible "to acquire the know-how to develop the management and the market.... As it was, Singaporeans were paid whilst learning."[13] To demonstrate the wisdom of foreign investment, the Prime Minister indicated that foreign-owned businesses had a much lower failure rate than purely Singaporean-owned firms. From 1960 to 1978, for instance, of the wholly owned American, European, and Japanese export-oriented industries, 6.1 percent ceased operation; of the industries jointly owned by Singaporean and American, European, or Japanese firms, 7.3 percent ceased operation; but wholly Singaporean-owned export-oriented industries had a failure rate of 38.3 percent.[14]

Foreign investment continued to be the dominant catalyst of economic development as this decade began. In 1980, for example, foreign investment accounted for over 80 percent of investment in Singapore.[15] The value of fixed assets of foreign invested manufacturing grew from less than U.S. $100 million in 1965 to U.S. $1.1 billion in 1973 and to U.S. $4.97 billion in 1983. The United States is the single largest foreign investor in manufacturing, accounting for 33 percent of the total in 1983.[16]

Singapore has a mixed economy. The government provides for most of the infrastructure and exercises control over the pace and direction of development—no small feat in an economy so internationally dependent that its foreign trade is nearly three times its GNP in value. In fact, Singapore exports more than any other nation in East Asia except Japan. Much of the economic success of this "global city" can be attributed to the civil service, which has made Singapore, as the editor of *Euromoney* has commented, "the most governed of democratic states."[17]

Though Singapore has no comprehensive five-year plans, the civil service has adopted a "forward planning" approach to economic development. First laying out economic targets, the civil service then sets into motion a series of government activities to mobilize the private sector. It exhorts both the government and the private sector to emphasize discipline, productivity, commitment, effort, specialization, hierarchy, order, and effective chain-of-command. Prime Minister Lee once again brought to light how Singapore was treated as an administrative state as he commented during the closing hours of the 1980 election campaign: "Whoever governs Singapore must have the iron in him or give it up. This is not a game of cards. This is your life and mine. I spent a whole life-time building this, and as long as I am in charge, nobody is going to knock it down."[18]

Nature and Organization of the Bureaucracy

The Civil Service: An Overview

Under the PAP's rule, Singapore's bureaucracy has experienced rapid growth: "During 1960–64," Peter S.D. Chen has observed, "private consumption expenditure increased 264 percent while government consumption expenditure increased 532 percent at constant prices."[19] Subsequently, the number of bureaucrats quickly multiplied. Singapore's bureaucrats are divided into civil servants and non-civil servant public employees. The former is further divided into monthly rated posts and daily rated posts. In 1974, established monthly rated posts numbered at 63,012 as compared to 25,000 in 1960, an increase of 143 percent. Later, the growth of the civil service continued, though slowed. In 1979, the number of established monthly rated posts reached 65,350; in 1984, 73,400.[20] If we now add approximately 12,500 daily rated employees, civil service employees totaled about 85,900 in 1984.

Staff members of various statutory boards are public employees outside the civil service system. These employees also have increased substantially. They numbered 27,000 in 1969; 48,000 in 1974; 51,000 in 1979; and 58,600 in 1984. All totaled, the public sector employed about 145,000 persons in 1984 or 12 percent of Singapore's workforce.[21] For a Newly Industrialized Country, this percentage is fairly high, though it is below the average for the European Economic Community countries where civil servants constitute 16 percent of the working population and well below Great Britain's 21.3 percent.[22]

Table 1 below shows the basic organization of Singapore's Civil Service, in four Divisions. It has many of the characteristics of the pre-1970 British Civil Service, with minimal mobility between Divisions. Approximately 10 percent of the monthly rated employees are in Division I. Of critical importance is the Administrative Service within that Division; it currently has approximately 650 authorized posts, of which slightly below 500 are actually filled. Division II comprises approximately 34 percent of the civil service. The remaining 56 percent are in Divisions III and IV.

As previously noted, the PAP has depended on the civil service to keep itself in power as well as to build up the new nation. The initial complementary roles of the higher civil service and the political leadership eventually led to a nearly identical outlook and approach. Critical issues of "survival" then came to the fore. There was a shared belief in the cabinet and the higher civil service that it was necessary for a relatively few to give coherence and continuity to the vague, sometimes conflicting aspirations of the majority. These attitudes at times render the two groups indistinguishable in many respects.

The bureaucracy is largely responsible for drafting and promoting many of the government's policies and programs and, in the process, often helps the ruling party strengthen its political position. For example, the People's Association, a statutory board chaired by a top civil servant, was set up in 1960 to provide community services; in reality the Political Association was created to check the grass-roots programs sponsored by the pro-Communists. During 1963, a critical year of political struggle, 130 community centers were built and staffed principally by carefully screened pro-PAP, Chinese-educated personnel; they effectively curtailed leftist activities. In another example, the Housing and Development Board (HDB), the first statutory board created by the PAP, delivered public housing units to broaden the popular appeal of the government. Between 1960 and 1965, the HDB constructed 55,000 units to house 23 percent of the population. By 1988, 86 percent of Singaporeans lived in government-built housing. In 1964 the government launched the Home Ownership for the People Program, which, as of the end of 1984, helped 73 percent of the occupants of government housing to purchase the units they lived in.

There are many other statutory boards or para-government bodies, including the Citizen's Consultative Committees

TABLE 1
Civil Service of Singapore

Division I Officers

Administrative Service

Permanent Secretary
Deputy Secretary
Principal Assistant
  Secretary
Assistant Secretary
Senior Administrative
  Assistant

Professional Service

Medical Officers
Engineers
Public Prosecutors
Accountants
Foreign Service Officers
Education Officers
Customs, Immigration,
  Police

Division II Officers

General Executive Service

Higher Executive Officers
Executive Officers

Professional Service

Education Officers

Division III Officers

Clerical Officers
Stenographers

Division IV Officers

Typists
Peons
Messengers
Daily-rated Employees

Residents' Committees that have become important service-delivery mechanisms of the PAP. These agencies receive block grants from the government and funnel them to their constituencies; they are able to conduct their activities expeditiously without having to conform to rigid bureaucratic procedures.

The Heavenborn and Meritocracy

At the top of the Singapore government stand the political elite and the Administrative Service of the bureaucracy. The Minister for Finance pinpointed the policy role of top civil servants when he declared:

> The Administrative Service more than most [other] civil servants is concerned with the formulation and execution of government policy and with planning and running the administrative machinery of government—including management of trade and industrial enterprises, shipping, banking, and insurance.[23]

The preeminence of the Administrative Service dates back to the colonial days when Singapore was governed by the Malayan Civil Service; the Administrative Officers, known as AO ever since, were once dubbed "the heavenborn" or the "mandarinate." The elite status of the Administrative Service continues to this day. The "new Singapore mandarin," as a cabinet minister once described, is "more interested in being right than in being popular. He must tell the people the truth—which is that progress, peace, and prosperity can be achieved only if people are prepared to pay the price."[24] Technical expertise and administrative orientation in the Singapore cabinet encourage a close, professional working relationship between the highest level of the civil service hierarchy and the PAP leadership. This working relationship helps promote top civil servants to cabinet membership.

Table 2 summarizes the composition of the Cabinet before the 1984 general elections; it reveals that, of the total 17 ministers, 7 were senior members, having served 13 to 25 years; 10 were junior members, having served 6 months to 7 years. Of the former group, 2 were former civil servants; of the latter group—most of whom are being groomed to take over the reins of government in the future—5 had civil service backgrounds and 2 were also in government service—as faculty members at the National Univer-

TABLE 2
The Singapore Cabinet
(As of April 1984)

Name	Ministry	Age	YC*	Education	Prof. Background
Lee Kuan Yew	Prime Minister	60	25	Double, First in Law Cambridge University	Lawyer
Goh Keng Swee	First DPM and Education	65	25	London School of Economics, Ph.D.	Civil Servant
S. Rajaratnam	Second DPM	69	25	Raffles College King's College	Journalist
Ong Pang Boon	Environment	55	25	University of Malaya	Organizing Secretary of PAP
E.W. Barker	Law	63	19	Raffles College Cambridge University	Lawyer
Chua Sian Chin	Home Affairs	49	16	University of Malaya University of London	Lawyer
Hon Sui Sen	Finance	68	13	Raffles College	CS: Chairman, Econ. Develop. Board
Ong Teng Cheong	Without Portfolio**	48	6	Univ. of Adelaide	CS: Planning Development
Goh Chok Tong	First Min. of Defense; Second Minister of Health	43	5	Univ. of Singapore Williams College, USA	CS: Manag. Director, Neptune Orient Line
Teh Cheong Wan	National Development	56	5	University of Sydney	CS: CEO, HDB, Division I
Howe Yoon Chong	First Min. Health; Second Min. of Defense	61	5	Raffles College	CS: Head, Civil Service
Ahmand Mattar	Social Affairs (Acting)	44	7	U. of Singapore, Ph.D. Univ. of Sheffield	Faculty Member Univ. of Singapore
Tan Tony Keng Yang	Finance, & Trade and Industry	43	4	University of Singapore; MIT, M.S. Univ. of Adelaide, Ph.D.	Deputy Gen. Manager Overseas-Chinese Banking Corp., Lecturer, Univ. of Sing.
S. Dhanabalan	Foreign Affairs	46	4	University of Singapore	CS: Exec. VP, DBS, Dep. Dir. for Finance & Operation, EDB
Yeo Ning Hong	Communications	41	6 m	Cambridge Univ.; Stanford Univ.; Univ. of London; Ph.D., Chemistry	Manager, Pharmaceutical Co.
S. Jayakumar	Labor	45	6 m	Univ. of Singapore Yale University	Dean of Law Faculty, Natl Univ. of Singapore
Wan Soon Bee	Without Portfolio	44	6 m	Univ. of Pisa, Ph.D., Electronic Engineering	Division Manager, Olivetti, Pte. Ltd.

* YC—Years in Cabinet; the first PAP government was sworn in June 5, 1959;
** Secretary General of National Trade Unions Congress since May 1983
CS—Civil Servant

sity of Singapore. *All* cabinet ministers held advanced degrees from English-language universities.

Singapore is a demanding meritocracy, and the future leadership is recruited and tested according to rigid criteria. A meritocratic government may exhibit elitist or authoritarian tendencies, but the government strives to retain popular confidence through repeated explanations (heavy on facts and rational arguments), without having to resort to emotional appeals.

Singapore's leadership subscribes to the belief that the country's well-being depends on the abilities and performance of a limited number of administrators. The Prime Minister explained:

> Outstanding men in civil service, the police, the armed forces, chairmen of statutory boards and their top administrators have worked out the details of policies set by the government and seen to their implementation. These people come from different language schools. Singapore is a meritocracy. And these men have risen to the top by their own merit, hard work, and high performance. Together they are a closely-knit and coordinated hard core. If all the 300 were to crash in one jumbo jet, then Singapore will disintegrate. That shows how small the base is for our leadership in politics, economics, and security. We have to, and we will, enlarge this base, enlarging the number of key digits.[25]

The civil service's commitment to high performance standards, expertise, and planned change in the socioeconomic system has placed a premium on educational attainment as an entry requirement. The initial screening process excludes most of the island's citizens. The total number of persons with baccalaureate degrees or higher is less than 2 percent of the adult population, and given the government's policy to limit university enrollment, this percentage is unlikely to increase dramatically in the future. Initial recruitment as an Administrative Officer requires, with rare exceptions, a Second Class Honors university degree. As a result, a substantial portion of university graduates—as high as 50 percent—is recruited into government service.

Statutory Boards

An important mechanism by which the government extends its influence in Singapore is the statutory boards. The PAP, since it has come to power, has created 83 new boards. Controlling two-thirds of the more than U.S. $500 million annual development expenditure, these boards influence nearly every aspect of Singapore's economic development effort. Possessing a status as government corporations, they enjoy a greater administrative flexibility than regular government agencies, control their own salary scales, and "carry out business dealings or organize the sale of products without having to follow government procedures...."[26]

During the early 1970s, the Ministry of Finance estimated, the government possessed through the statutory boards 26 wholly owned companies with an authorized capital of U.S. $670 million and 33 partially owned companies involving $200 million in government equity capital.[27] At the same time, the government owned seven subsidiaries in Raffles Center: Development Bank of Singapore (DBS) Finance, DBS Reality, DBS Nominees, Singapore Factory Development, Singapore Tourist Industry, and shares in 50 other companies. INTRACO, the state trading company, held equity investments in 20 other companies. Temasek Holdings Ptd., Ltd., a government holding company created in 1974, had gross assets of U.S. $1.55 billion in 1978.[28]

The intimate relationship between the statutory boards and private companies has considerably enhanced the influence of the civil service, since Division I officers are placed in charge of the statutory boards. Many top civil servants also sit on the boards of directors of private companies to oversee government investments, loans, and interests. Through these arrangements, the influence of civil servants is effectively diffused throughout the entire economy.

The scope of economic power held by bureaucrats is analyzed in a 1971 study by Lee Yoke Teng.[29] He found a pattern of interlocking linkages between civil servants and the economic enterprises which they supervise; 188 government directors sat on the boards of 47 companies; some sat on several boards, giving rise to a complex, if not an unfathomable, maze of interdependencies and interlinking patterns of influence.

Over the years, questions about the implications of such linkages have often been raised. In 1976, for example, one PAP Member of Parliament circumspectly but succinctly admonished the government:

> The Government has invested large sums of money in
> some private enterprises as joint ventures in order to

promote industrialization and employment. There are also some large industries wholly owned by the Government. Many of these wholly owned industries form subsidiary companies and joint ventures on their own supporting services. While not criticizing such enterprising expansion of these companies, they should be told to be cautious of proper financial, supervisory and management control by the parent company.

Large sums of public funds are invested in these enterprises which are not accountable either to shareholders or, in this respect, to Parliament. This makes the responsibility of the Ministry of Finance, in respect of these enterprises, greater than we can reasonably expect. I hope the Minister for Finance will give very serious consideration to the possibility of having sufficient checks and balances in respect of the management of these Government enterprises.[30]

Irrespective of this implied criticism and other questions that have been raised, the government has chosen to place the responsibility for economic management in the hands of top civil servants. A 1975 government memorandum to Administrative Officers stated:

Government administration involves much more than personnel and financial management. Administration embraces a broad range of activities including banking and insurance, commerce and industry, operation of shipping lines and airlines, research and statistics, public transport and housing, city planning, land use and development, cultural and environmental work and numerous other activities. The successful operation of these diverse activities requires a variety of disciplines including specialists. However, overall policy formation and implementation including the identification and solutions of problems and policy coordination rests with management. The Administrative Officer is primarily responsible for long range and intermediate planning and for formulating and implementing policies.[31]

The result is that Parliament has scant oversight over the statutory boards, with little supervision or even awareness of many decisions undertaken by civil servants, except in cases of glaring mismanagement.

Institutional Control and Coordination

Singapore's political leadership has developed several institutions to assure its close supervision of the performance and management practices of the civil service. Effective December 1975 through 1981, all job assignments for Administrative Officers were handled through the Establishment Unit in the Prime Minister's office. This was previously handled through the Budget Division in the Ministry of Finance. Prime Minister Lee stated to Parliament that this change was necessary because there is "an urgent need to spot talent at the top. The few carry an enormously disproportionate burden of the load because they have been found reliable and able to get things done."[32] Indeed, recruitment of top civil servants is a thorough and persistent endeavor. Thus, *The Straits Times* reported Prime Minister Lee's remarks at the PAP's Twenty-Fifth Anniversary rally:

> Mr. Lee Kuan Yew has disclosed that the hunt for potential leaders now requires him and his senior colleagues to comb systematically all the top echelons of all sectors in Singapore for talent. They will cover every profession and every sector—commerce, manufacturing, trade unions and even sports associations.[33]

Once advanced to the highest level of the civil service—Division I—top civil servants are subject to the close scrutiny of the Public Service Commission, which is responsible for the training and career development of these top civil servants.

The Pyramid Club is another institution of coordination. Created in the mid-1960s, the Club facilitates contact among leaders of government, business, and, to a lesser extent, academia. Its membership, which ranges from 120 to 150, includes Ministers, Ministers of State, parliamentary secretaries (about one-third of the Members of Parliament), high rank civil servants, prominent military officers, leaders of business and professions, and leading academicians. Located on Goodwood Hill, the Pyramid Club provides facilities for meeting, dining, swimming, and tennis. Through regular formal/ informal discussions, the Club works to assure that the country's leadership groups are moving in tandem to achieve common goals.

Sill another agency of great influence is the Corrupt Practices Investigation Bureau (CPIB). Now also housed in the Prime Minister's office, the CPIB originally dealt with only civil servants. Under the Prevention of Corruption Act, the CPIB is today empowered to investigate *all* corrupt practices in both the public *and* private sectors. The CPIB has a staff of approximately 40, but its size in no way diminishes its role as one of the most effective agencies in Singapore. No individual, whatever his rank, is immune from investigation. It has numerous contacts, paid and unpaid, in the business community, and there is little that evades CPIB scrutiny. The CPIB also has the authority to review bank accounts/ transactions of suspected persons, even before they are aware they are being investigated.

If any civil servant is identified—with evidence—as corrupt, the CPIB will sue him in court. The Prevention of Corruption Act broadly defines offenses as corruptly soliciting or receiving gratification as an inducement for doing or forebearing to do any act pertaining to any official transaction. It provides punishment both for carrying out corrupt acts as well as conspiracy. The result is practically no corruption.

The CPIB is quite successful in eradicating bribery and eliminating most corruption from the government. The agency, which has made Singapore's civil service known as the most honest and efficient in Asia, is now a target of emulation in many other Asian countries.

Bureaucratic Roles and Objectives

Economic Development: The Effort to Insure Prosperity

Singapore lives on trade and commerce, first as an entrepôt economy, then as a haven for tourism, manufacturing, and international financing. Singapore's dependence on trade is extraordinary; the value of its trade is three times its Gross National Product, the highest such ratio in the world.[34]

Singapore's government pursues interventionist economic policies. To provide for a philosophical/ historical basis for the government's position, Dr. Goh Keng Swee—once the second highest leader in the PAP hierarchy—explained that the government "had to try a more activist and interventionist approach" because the laissez-faire policies of the colonial period "had led Singapore to a dead end, with little economic growth, massive unemployment, wretched housing, and inadequate education."[35]

The Singaporean government has devoted enormous resources to the creation of an attractive social and economic infrastructure for business investment. Government expenditure was 29.4 percent of Gross Domestic Product in 1984. With the additional expenditure of the statutory boards, the government's share of GDP reaches a staggering 52.4 percent. Augustine H.H. Tan, an eminent economist and a PAP Member of Parliament, believes that the existing governmental share of GDP is far "too large for the efficiency of the economy"; 35 percent, he suggests, would be more appropriate.[36]

Government initiatives have brought about massive foreign investment and participation in the Singaporean economy. These initiatives drew much of their inspiration from a 1961 United Nations study recommending that Singapore adopt a strategy "to supplement on a comparatively large scale during the initial period [of Singapore's industrialization] its own resources with those from abroad...."[37]

In 1961, the government set up an Economic Development Board to promote industrial investment and to finance and manage industrial parks. Foreign multinationals were wooed unremittingly. "Singapore is where it's happening," read advertisements in Western newspapers. "Yesterday shakes hands with tomorrow and it's yours—today!" With its inexpensive pool of labor (in the 1960s, the average Singapore factory worker earned one-ninth of his American counterpart), its efficient administrators, and its relative absence of red tape, Singapore proved to be an attractive place for foreign investors. The first industries created with foreign participation were labor-intensive ones—to relieve unemployment; they produced such items as nails, textiles, footwear, and paint. As industrial employment expanded (from 31,000 manufacturing workers in 1959 to 126,000 in 1970, to 322,000 in 1984), Singapore shifted away from polo shirts and plastic flowers toward more skill-intensive enterprises: chemicals, petroleum products, machine components, computer parts, etc. By the late 1970s, the island was producing everything from batteries to pharmaceuticals, engines and oil rigs. With its four refineries, Singapore was intent upon becoming the petroleum processing and distribution capital of Asia. Engrossed in economic pursuits, many Singaporeans forgot about politics. Economic man of the 1970s and 1980s largely replaced the political man of the 1950s and 1960s.

The generally hard-working labor force has been kept in line as the PAP has dominated the National Trade Union Congress—a conglomerate of almost all Singapore's unions. Rapidly expanding job opportunities and a massive public housing program were important contributors to the type of "good" labor conditions that attracted foreign investment. Man-days lost as a result of strikes dropped to near zero during most of the 1970s. To avoid labor disruptions, various restraining laws have also been passed, including a 1977 ordinance authorizing the Ministry of Labor to freeze a union's bank account if the union is being investigated for irregular activities by either the Registrar of Unions or the Ministry of Labor.

Singapore's active solicitation of foreign investors resulted in their domination of the manufacturing export market. One study reported that as of 1973 there were more than fifty multinational manufacturing firms in Singapore accounting for 83.5 percent of Singapore's total direct exports.[38] Another study indicated that the multinational share of manufactured exports in 1963 was 54 percent, climbing to 86 percent in 1981. By 1983, nearly 90 percent of net investment in the manufacturing sector was by foreign-owned or partly foreign-owned firms.[39] Foreign investment of this magnitude goes far to explain why a World Bank study of 24 developing countries has identified Singapore as having the highest ratio of total private foreign investment to GDP between 1971 and 1979.[40]

Ironically, local manufacturing firms seem at times to have been discriminated against, resulting in a low indigenous participation in important aspects of Singapore's economic development (even in retailing). A partial list of the often heard complaints from local enterprise includes: 1) tax incentives are directed particularly at pioneer industries with investments of over U.S. $1 million in priority export-oriented categories (the minimum dollar investment requirement favors large foreign investors, and in 1973, for example, only 16 percent of the paid-up pioneer capital was local); 2) the Economic Development Board directs almost all of its efforts toward foreign investors; 3) few local firms can afford or are encouraged to relocate to the new industrial parks because of high rent and utility costs; and 4) the ratio of local-to-foreign supplies to the multinational manufacturers is low, discouraging the growth of indigenous suppliers for multi-national firms (one of the lowest is the American electronics companies which, in the 1970s, took on average 10 percent of their total production inputs from Singapore firms).[41]

Despite this drawback, Singapore's economic performance is impressive. Real GNP growth has averaged nearly 8 percent annually between 1965 and 1984. The standard of living has consistently been pushed up, and in Asia Singapore's personal income and quality of life are second only to those in Japan. Singapore has now launched the Second Industrial Revolution (SIR), which, as mentioned earlier, has dramatically and deliberately increased wage rates. The purpose is to weed out marginal companies and to upgrade its economy from a lighter, labor-intensive industrial base to a more advanced industry of the 1980s—emulating the high tech strategies of Japan and Western countries.

A Downturn

The annual August National Day Speech by Prime Minister Lee Kuan Yew normally speaks of the need for maintaining a dis-ciplined, rugged society so as to sustain and continue the economic accomplishments of the nation. The Prime Minister's 1985 speech, however, acknowledged a negative growth rate for the second quarter of the year, a first since 1967. Lee called for an immediate two-year wage freeze in order to regain internation-al competitiveness. Singapore's economy has shown weakness before. In mid-1983, for instance, *The Asian Wall Street Journal* analyzed the island's economy in a lengthy article under the headline "Recession Reveals Fundamental Flaws in Singapore's Economic Structure."[42] A 1985 article in *The Far Eastern Economic Review* stated flatly that "Singapore's ills are mostly its own work."[43]

These ills have to do with Singapore's economic restructuring. SIR forced a premature exiting of many labor-intensive in-dustries, and with them the employment cushion. SIR simply failed to create sufficient new employment. The emphasis in the 1980s has been on oil refining, oil-rig building, shipbuilding, ship repair, and electronics. With the exception of electronics, all these relatively high value-added and export-oriented industries experienced—because of the changing world economy and the increase of competition from other East Asian economies—a severe downturn in recent years. As a result, Singapore's surplus capacity in all these industries except electronics is near 50 percent. In addition, overexpansion of construction, much of it stimulated by the government, contributed to the recession. In 1980–1984, construction grew *three* times as fast (22 percent per annum) as the rest of the economy. An indicator of this problem was the doubling of hotel rooms in five years, resulting in a hotel occupancy rate of 65 percent by mid-1985.

The 1985–86 economic difficulties were overcome because many of the fundamental problems noted above were addressed. An imaginative and intelligent government guided Singapore out of its economic difficulties, as it has in the past. Not surprisingly, the government has taken a series of steps to prime the economy and to reduce the costs of doing business in Singapore. One result was economic growth rates of 8 percent in both 1987 and 1988.

Will the Singaporean government be able to assure the country economic success in the future as it has in the past?[44] Perhaps in the remainder of this decade, Prime Minister Lee's oft-quoted statement that "the PAP has been synonymous with the government and the government is Singapore" will be subject to a crucial test.[45]

Confucius Reemergent

Singapore Incorporated has experienced 20 years of economic progress. Hard work, discipline, government guidance, and market forces are principal ingredients. Capable individuals with imagination and drive are assured of economic success. With such success, Singaporeans, like many people in other modernizing societies, are permeated with strong doses of self-centeredness, materialism, and self-gratification. On the other hand, the government has repeatedly called for the maintenance of a "rugged" society whose members are to be courteous, industrious, family-oriented, and patriotic.

Thus, the government subscribes to a neo-Confucian spirit, emphasizing hierarchy, order, reciprocity, loyalty, and rule by the ablest and the most virtuous. This spirit, in the Prime Minister's view, has contributed thus far to the political achievement of Singapore as a new nation: "The bulk of the population followed Confucian ethics. Is the Government good or is it bad? If the government is bad, it is out. But when it is good, [and] they say no, this opposition is rubbish. I am for the government. I vote for it."[46]

If a 2,500-year-old behavioral ethic could earn votes, could it not also create a better citizen? Perhaps a "good" society in the long run is even a more important goal than a "rich" society. Does economic modernization inevitably mean that a society is merely a functional association of self-acquisitive economic citizens, possessed by an idolatry for material things? The Prime Minister believes such a danger exists. In August 1980 two previously confidential government reports, which dealt with workers' attitudes, were released. They revealed that many employees were lacking in loyalty and proper spirit; job-hopping, reluctance to do shift work, and adherence to narrow job specifications were said to be characteristics prevalent among workers.

Government leaders forcefully called attention to these negative traits. The Prime Minister admonished the Singaporeans to develop a group orientation in its national culture: "We can build up this team spirit, this *esprit de corps*, where every individual gives of his best for the team. The team, the nation, in turn, takes care of the individual, fairly and equitably. The art of government is the art of building up this team spirit."[47]

The emergence of a Singapore ethos as a basis of its own identity is especially important to a country undergoing rapid modernization with its attendant social and economic changes. For example, in 1980, as much as 80 percent of Singapore's television programs, including the most popular, was imported.[48] Similarly, speaking shortly before the 1984 general elections, Second Deputy Prime Minister S. Rajaratnam, told National University undergraduates: "Singapore has no history to speak of. We can only show them Raffles' statue. But we have a future. I can tell people what we have achieved—tomorrow the MRT [the underground Mass Rapid Transit]. Yesterday? Maybe Lee Kuan Yew. That's all."[49]

In early 1982 the government earnestly began a campaign to promote a Singaporean ethos. It announced a religious curricular program to be implemented in the secondary schools with five options: Buddhist studies, Bible studies, Hindu studies, Islamic studies, and world religious studies. Confucian ethics, as a secular subject, was announced as the sixth option. Deputy Prime Minister Goh explained that the intent of this program "is to produce men of upright character." He further stated: "Confucianism is by far the most durable of human social institutions, and Confucius believed that unless the government is in the hands of upright men, disaster will befall the country. By the way, in this respect the PAP also believes the same thing."[50]

This concern with morality and ethics may help sustain popular support for the government. It is, however, simplistic to say that this is merely an electoral device. The six options open to students suggest no singular official orthodoxy, but in a nation that is nearly 77 percent Chinese, Confucianism may well have a predominant influence. The current promotion of Confucianism is not an attempt at something new, but is a reminder of something old and valuable that is selectively relevant to the future. No one has shown any desire to turn the teachings of Confucius into Singapore's "little red book." Selective presentation of Confucianism may facilitate a more productive society or may mitigate against tendencies weakening national consciousness and solidarity.

In 1982 the Singaporean government invited a number of foreign scholars on Confucianism to help adapt Confucian teachings to the country's school curriculum. One of the scholars suggested that filial piety be considered the centerpiece of all human activity and that the family be regarded as the basic organizing unit of the society whose values are to be extended to larger groups.[51] To a certain extent, the Singaporean government has accepted this suggestion. Application for public housing units, for instance, will be expedited if parents and grown children agree to live in adjacent flats. The extended family not only is part of an Asian tradition but also helps reduce state financial obligation for caring for the aged. Singaporeans aged 65 and above constituted 5 percent of the population in 1980; they will be 7 percent by 2000 and 19 percent by 2030.[52]

There are those who view with reservations the government's effort to promote Confucianism. A major role for the family does not necessarily guarantee creation of a stronger, more integrated nation. Emphasis on family orientedness may actually lead individuals to center their activities around the confines of the family.[53] Family-run businesses, which dominate Singapore's indigenous economy, also cannot compete effectively with the multinationals, which permeate so much of Singapore's economy. An overemphasis on Confucianism may impede rather than facilitate commonality, especially for Singapore's non-Chinese minorities. Some Chinese in Singapore also consider it ironic that the country, without outstanding Confucian scholars of its own, has had to recruit foreign experts to help the Confucian campaign get started.

Moral training, it is to be noted, is but one component of an educational system that focuses on building a harmonious nation and a prosperous society. Perhaps the emphasis on the well-oiled machine is occasionally too bluntly enunciated for many Singaporeans, especially the younger and better-educated. Such bluntness is apparent in the following quote from Prime Minister Lee. He urges Singaporeans: "Build in reflexes of group thinking, reshuffle the emphasis on various values, produce qualities of leadership at the top and qualities of cohesion on the ground."[54]

Singapore's leaders should not, however, be judged too quickly. There is no reason to presume that the nurturing of a moral national culture will lead to George Orwell's *1984*. A rereading of Plato's *Republic* might be more appropriate. The overall objective is clearly social, but Confucian teaching can be one variable which, under appropriate circumstances, facilitates economic development.

Politically, Confucianism may also reinforce a high level of public dependency on government policies and civil servants. The Confucian tradition that values an elitist, moralistic approach to public affairs is entirely congruent with the perceived role of Singapore's bureaucracy in a rapidly modernizing society. A sociology professor—also one of three female PAP Members of Parliament—commented that Singapore's

> "compressed growth syndrome" has led to an expectation of unlimited growth and of an ever rising standard of living, a very daunting task indeed for any government to fulfill....
>
> Social discipline, coupled with materialistic aspirations, has served as a powerful vehicle for economic growth; but it also resulted in a "dependency mentality" among the population.... The people have come to rely on the government for economic and social restructuring and for the betterment of their personal lives.[55]

Future Directions

Singaporeans have long expected their government to be a catalyst of change and improvement in society. The government's commitment to innovation and problem-solving and its sense of direction and efficiency are rarely equaled in other Third World countries. Yet recent economic problems have given rise to concerns about an overbearing government. For instance, Prime Minister Lee's son Lee Hsien Loong, now an MP and a PAP Minister of State, was questioned in 1985 at the National University of Singapore in ways which would have been out of line in an earlier time. He was asked: "Where do you find the confidence to know that the PAP is always right?" Criticisms such as "don't talk down to us" also were heard.[56]

The more numerous and varied the changes a government initiates, the more the government will need to build local linkages so as to explain policies, to generate support, and to be alert to significant shifts in public opinion. Citizen's Consultative Committees, Residents' Committees and other similar organizations have been somewhat effective thus far in accomplishing these objectives. The lack of popular input in the decision-making process and the emphasis on technical solutions rationally arrived at have, however, weakened the human, caring image of the government. Voters are now increasingly critical of officials who appear overly patronizing, impersonal, and unwilling to accommodate popular feelings. Acceleration of a refined and pervasive social engineering implemented by an elitist, technocratic bureaucracy could slowly erode the countless individual strivings and ambitions which have contributed so much to Singapore's progress. However, PAP rule is not imminently threatened, although the second generation leaders obviously will have to rely more upon accommodation and negotiation. The government will have to become more of a broker.

Economic, social, and political development requires autonomy and creativity as well as an effective, interventionist government staffed by highly qualified and dedicated civil servants. Singapore has come closer to achieving this mix in its effective nation-building efforts than most other Third World countries.

NOTES

1. Colony of Singapore, *Annual Report, 1956* (Singapore: Government Printer, 1958), pp. 278–79.

2. Ibid., *Annual Report, 1957* (1959), p. 7; and Kenneth Younger, *The Public Service in New States* (London: Oxford University Press, 1960), p. 63.

3. *Petir,* III, no. 7 (22 January 1960), p. 7. For an analysis of the Barisan's decline, see Thomas J. Bellows, *The People's Action Party of Singapore: Emergence of a Dominant Party System* (New Haven: Yale University Southeast Asia Studies, 1970), pp. 75–100.

4. A succinct listing of major voter dissatisfactions prior to the 1984 elections is found in Linda Lim, "Singapore: Social Engineering and Economic Growth," *Southeast Asia Business* 1 & 2 (Spring/ Summer 1984): 22.

5. Figures provided by Prime Minister Lee, see *The Straits Times,* 19 August 1985, p. 6.

6. For background on hydrographic surveys and navigational problems, see C.V. Das and V.P. Pradhan, *Oil Discovery and Technical Change in Southeast Asia: Some International Law Problems Regarding the Straits of Malacca* (Singapore: Institute of Southeast Asia Studies, Field Reports, Series No. 5, 1972), pp. 53–57.

7. Anne O. Krueger, "Import Substitution versus Export Promotion," *Finance and Development* 22:2 (June 1985): 21. After a 1985/ 86 recession, the GDP growth rate grew to 8 percent in 1988.

8. Dr. Goh Keng Swee, "Speech at the Annual Luncheon of the Manufacturers Association" (Singapore Government Press Statement, mimeographed, 26 May 1961), p. 1.

9. Ministry of Trade and Industry, *Economic Survey of Singapore, 1979* (Republic of Singapore: Singapore National Printers [PTE] Ltd., 1980), p. 55. Higher wages encouraged labor-intensive manufacturers to transfer facilities to lower-wage sites in Indonesia, Malaysia, Bangladesh and Sri Lanka, or to introduce more sophisticated machinery and to reduce the number of workers.

10. *The Mirror,* 15 January 1982, p. 1. Singapore's GDP increased 9.7 percent in 1981.

11. Ibid., 15 March 1980, p. 20.

12. U.S. Department of Commerce, International Trade Administration, "Investment Climate in Singapore," in *Investment Climate in Foreign Countries*, vol. III (Washington: Government Printing Office, 1985), p. 218. The numerous incentives are summarized on pp. 221–27.

13. "Extrapolating from the Singapore Experience," Special Lecture by Prime Minister Lee Kuan Yew at the 26th World Congress of the International Chamber of Commerce, Orlando, Florida, on 5 October 1978 (unpublished manuscript), p. 15.

14. Ibid.

15. Stuart Sinclair, *The Third World Economic Handbook* (London: Euromonitor Publications Ltd., 1982), p. 93.

16. U.S. Department of Commerce, "Investment Climate in Singapore," p. 214; and Augustine H.H. Tan, M.P., "Singapore's Economy: Growth and Structural Change," Paper prepared for a Conference on Singapore and the United States into the 1990s, at The Fletcher School of Law and Diplomacy, Medford, Mass., November 1985, p. 6.

17. Interview with Prime Minister Lee Kuan Yew, *Euromoney* (July 1978), p. 18.

18. *The Straits Times*, 22 December 1980, p. 1.

19. Peter S.D. Chen, "Elites and National Development in Singapore," in Arnold Wenmhoerner, ed., *Elites and Development* (Bangkok: Union Publishing Ltd., 1975), p. 80.

20. The above data are compiled from Peter Y.S. Tan, "Recruitment of the Civil Service," *Kesatuan Bulletin* 12 (July 1973): 3; Republic of Singapore, *1974 Annual Report* (Singapore: Public Service Commission, 1975), p. 16; Republic of Singapore, *Economic Survey of Singapore, 1979* (Singapore: Ministry of Trade and Industry, 1980), p. 37; statement by Minister for Finance, *Singapore Parliamentary Debates*, 20 March 1979, col. 885; and Republic of Singapore, *Economic Survey of Singapore, 1984* (Singapore: Ministry of Trade and Industry, 1985), pp. 52 and 56.

21. Sources listed as in note 19.

22. See "Mountains of Civil Servants," *The Economist*, 22 December 1979, p. 36. Workers who generate revenue (postal, rail,

etc.) were excluded from the EEC calculations but not from the Singapore data.

23. Hon Sui Sen, "Speech at Official Opening of Staff Training Institute" (Singapore: Mimeographed, 1974), p. 1.

24. S. Rajaratnam, "Mandarins of a New Order," *The Mirror,* 7 September 1970, p. 1.

25. *The Straits Times,* 28 April 1971, p. 3.

26. *Singapore Parliamentary Debates,* 19 August 1975, cols. 1212 and 1218.

27. See Lee Boon Hiok, *Statutory Boards of Singapore* (University of Singapore, Department of Political Science, Occasional Paper Series, No. 20), 1975.

28. *Business Times* (Singapore), Special Supplement, 2 October 1978, p. IV.

29. "Foreign Borrowing and Investment Policy in the Public Sector" (University of Singapore, Bachelor of Social Science Honors Paper, 1974).

30. *Singapore Parliamentary Debates,* 15 March 1976, col. 226–27.

31. Memorandum from the Singapore government to Administrative Officers (1975).

32. *Singapore Parliamentary Debates,* 16 March 1976, col. 331.

33. *The Straits Times,* 22 January 1980, p. 1.

34. Goh Chok Tong, First Deputy Prime Minister, "The Security of the Sea Lanes in the Asia-Pacific Region," Singapore Government Press Release 2 May 1985, p. 2.

35. C.V. Devan Nair, ed., *Socialism That Works—The Singapore Way* (Singapore: Federal Publications, 1976), p. 84.

36. Augustine H.H. Tan, "Singapore's Economy," pp. 42–43 and 49.

37. United Nations, Industrial Survey Mission, *A Proposed Industrialization Program for the State of Singapore* (New York: United Nations Department of Economic and Social Affairs, 1963), p. 12.

38. The study is by Chia Siow Yu, referred to in Noeleen Heyzer, "International Production and Social Change: An Analysis of the State, Employment, and Trade Unions in Singapore," in Peter S.J. Chen, ed., *Singapore Development Policies and Trends* (Singapore: Oxford University Press, 1983), p. 109.

39. Reference to these data is found in Ronald Findlay, "Trade and Development: Theory and Asian Experience," *Asian Development Review* 2:2 (1984): 35–36.

40. Mario I. Blejes and Mohsin S. Khan, "Private Investment in Developing Countries," *Finance and Development* 21:2 (June 1984): 28.

41. This paragraph was drawn from a study by Federic C. Deyo, *Dependent Development and Industrial Order: An Asian Case Study* (New York: Praeger Publishers, 1981), pp. 63–74.

42. *The Asian Wall Street Journal,* August 8, 1983, p. 4.

43. *Far Eastern Economic Review,* 28 September 1985, p. 104.

44. See Peter S.J. Chen, "Singapore's Development Strategies: A Model for Rapid Growth," in Chen, *Singapore Development Policies,* pp. 3–26. See also Linda Y.C. Lim, "Singapore's Success: The Myth of the Free Market Economy," *Asian Survey* 23:6 (June 1983): 752–64.

45. "Singapore," *Asia 1984 Yearbook* (Hong Kong: Far Eastern Economic Review, 1983), p. 253.

46. *The Straits Times,* 22 December 1976, p. 1.

47. Ibid., 16 August 1980, p. 6.

48. Statement by Dr. Koh Lip Lin, M.P., *Singapore Parliamentary Debates,* 24 March 1980, col. 1306.

49. *The Straits Times,* 10 September 1984, p. 1.

50. *China Post,* February 10, 1982, p. 3. See also *The New York Times,* May 20, 1982, p. 11.

51. The foreign scholar was Francis L.K. Hsu of the University of San Francisco. See *RIHED Bulletin* (Singapore) 9:3 (July–September 1982): 18.

52. Aline K. Wong, "Notes on Social Transformation in Singapore," Paper prepared for a Conference on Singapore and the United States into the 1990s at The Fletcher School of Law and Diplomacy, Medford, Mass., November 1985, p. 2.

53. I am indebted to Wu Teh-yao for this summary of the role of the Chinese family. See his *The Cultural Heritage of Singapore* (University of Singapore, Department of Political Science: Occasional Paper Series, No. 25, December 1975), p. 14.

54. V.G. Kulkarni, "The Non-Chinese Syndrome," *Far Eastern Economic Review,* 22 March 1984, p. 25.

55. Wong, "Social Transformation in Singapore," pp. 8–9.

56. V.G. Kulkarni, and Rodney Tasker, "Don't Talk Down to Us," *Far Eastern Economic Review*, 11 July 1985, p. 34.

Index